Media Education

Jitendra Singh

Mahaveer & Sons
New Delhi - 110002

First Published 2006

ISBN 81-8377-008-8

Published by :
MAHAVEER & SONS
4346/4C, Ansari Road,
Darya Ganj, New Delhi-110002
Ph. 23287638, Mob. 9811008339

Editorial :
1/10302, West Gorakh Park,
Street No. 1, Shahdara, Delhi-110032

PRINTED IN INDIA

Published by Sh. Mukul Sharma for Mahaveer & Sons, 4346/4C, Ansari Road, Darya Ganj, New Delhi-110002, Printed at Rajdhani Printers, Delhi.

Preface

This book 'Media Education' undertakes to study theories of Communication in a broad perspective that includes corresponding theoretical positions available in Indian Education, philosophical and religious traditions. Media strategies in the western world have acquired a degree of sophistication that is not available in India. The realization by Indian thinkers that communication is the key to the social development is comparatively a late understanding. This is the task of many pupil's of media communication journalism every day, every hour from every corner of the world they can reach. The journalism these days has acquired a wide dimension and the journalists have more and more job added to their list of duties in this age of computers and satellites.

It is hoped that this book will fulfill the demands of a wider section of press persons and students of Communication. The editors are painfully aware of the shortcomings, and shall welcome any criticism and suggestions from the readers for improvement in further editions.

—Editor

Contents

1

T.V. Programmes for Women

The Indian Constitution has pledged the country to the creation of a new social order based on equality, freedom, justice and the dignity of the individual. To that end it is dedicated to the elimination of poverty, ignorance ill health and gender inequality. The Constitution further empowers the state to make special provisions for women and children. The colossal investement in an expensive electronic medium such as television has been officially justified as a part of the effort to redeem these pledges which have, at best, remained pious hopes for so many.

The argument as to whether television can subserve this purpose has now conclusively passed into the realm of rhetoric. The reality of today is that a vast investment is being made in this medium in the name of the poor and the vulnerable segments of Indian society. The need of the hour is to ensure that the medium begins to truly subserve that cause.

Many distinguished speakers have already highlighted the anomaly between television's stated objectives and the actuality. The very fact that special efforts such as this seminar have to be made to draw attention to televion's utilization for the development of women and children is itself a reflection of that anomaly. For, given the context that women and children make two–thirds of the total population a medium that has been encouraged for the laudable aims mentioned earlier should be *automatically* catering predominantly to the requirements of those segments who form the majority and are widely recognized as the most vulnerable sections of the Indian society. It is only through serving the interests of women and children that TV would be able to fulfil its role as a development tool. Therefore, women and children cannot be thought of as special segments to which the medium must cater through occasional or even regular programmes. Rather, its overall philosophy and approach have to be determined in a way that accords these two categories the overriding importance that their numbers and needs deserve. Their betterment is central to the social transformation TV seeks.

Yet, even the most casual viewer knows that at the present this is far from the case. In this presentation, I will not take up the issue of children which has been already addressed at a special session, nor indeed do I intend to talk only about television programmes for women as has been indicated in the programme schedule. Special programmes for women are just one essential but small part of the total effort for attitudional change about roles, rights, responsibilities and opportunities for both sexes that the medium must address itself to in order to project the constitutitional goals of equality, justice and individual dignity, and indeed for it to be a viable instrument of development.

Nearly ten years ago, the Committee on the Status of Women observed in its eye-opening report on the condition of Indian women :

> "The content of communication at any given time reflects the pattern of values of the society. The way subjects dealing with women are treated indicate

to a great extent the prevailing attitude of that society towards its women. In any case women who are half the population are often half the audience. The success or failure of development plans in education, family planning, community development, health anhd nutrition depends upon the involvement and participation of women. (This) investigation shows that compared to men and women are underprivileged in many ways and suffer from serious disabilities. Since education is a costly and long term process it is essential to harness the mass media. However, incidental studies on the impact of the mass media indicate that women's exposure to the mass media is often marginal and unsatisfactory. It appears that the mass media has not been as effective instrument to inform and prepare women to play their new roles in society. The committee's investigations reveal a general lack of awareness about the rights, problems, opportuni-ties and responsibilities among both men and women. Since government controls a significant section of the mass media it should set the pace".

In the decade since that review, a decade internationally acclaimed as the Women's Decade within which, coincidentally, television came of age in this country, it might well have been hoped that this powerful communication tool, totally in the government's control, would have a prime responsibility to redressal the women's situation; the need for redressal of women's condition had been felt at the nation's very birth but has remained so unfulfilled more than three decades later. Shaping the strategy for the nation's Sixth Five Year Plan at a time that was midpoint in the Women's decade, the policy makers had noted : "Despite development measure and the constitutional legal guarantees women have lagged behind men in all sectors".

Yesterday, Dr Joshi analysed the reality of development and raised fundamental questions about development processes and their intended and unitended and unintended effects on the lives of the people for whose benefit these measures are supposed to be initiated. But perhaps the most devastating evidence of the distortions of development, it is now recognized, comes from the female experience. It is evident that women have had unequal access to the fruits of development and have often borne the brunt of its unintended backlash. An examination of the female "lag" throws up searing statistics which show that for the Indian female the discrimination and disadvantages of her condition have added up an unequal struggle for survival itself. India is one of the few countries in the world where the female species has had a declining sex ratio over the century-only marginally reversed in the last decade. This has been the result of higher female mortality at practically all ages including from birth to the age of 9, but with an unconscionably high rate maternal mortality, pointing to a pervasive neglect of the female child and female needs.

There is extensive research documenting that the differentials in suvival are paralleled by differentials in all important aspects of life itself-poorer nutrition, lesser health care despite higher levels of morbidity, lower education and skill formation. The problem of universal education has been long identified as one mainly of women, schduled castes and tribes : notwithstanding progress in female education, literacy has reached only 1 in 4 women as against 1 in 2 men and in absolute there are 100 million more illiterate women and girls today than there were in the fifties. The outlook for the next generation of women remains bleak with two–thirds of the children outside schools today being girls and the female drop-out rate at all educational levels consistently remaining much higher, the displacement of women from traditional occupations without adequate alternatives available has skewed work opportunities for the vast majority leading to greater female exploitation of different types. The planning process has finally come to recognise that the enormous economic contribution of women both within the family and to society has remained largely submerged from view and therefore denied the essential support services that could assist women to be more productive in fulfilling their multiple roles. But the government owned television far from "setting the pace" has notably failed to see and reflect this reality, much less carry out a concerted campaign to redress deep-rooted wrongs being compounded by new insensitivities.

This is grievous enough that a medium ostensibly invested in to help remedy the imabalances and inequalities of society has been largely oblivious to the grim reality of the lives of the vast majority of women. Even more heartbreaking than the low priority television seems to have attached to the subject of women's status and betterment, is the complete impunity with which it has allowed itself to be used to the detriment of women. A number of critiques made by citizens wishing to galvanise this powerful media to a meaningful role have pointed out this aspect. A seminar on Doordarshan's role in Women's Equality and Development conducted last year by the Centre for Women's Development Studies and the Committee for the Portrayal of Women in the Media made two major points : (1) a very wide distance exised between the national policy objectives vis-a-vis women's equality and development and Doordarshan's present role and programming and (2) the general tenor od Doordarshan's programme counter to its stray efforts to be purposive on women's behalf.

As Prof. Yashpal pointed out yesterday the totality of effect is the question. An occasional serious programme put out to raise debate or stir the conscience may be convenient to quote as an illustration of efforts be I & B administrators and Doordarshan programmers but is lost in the flood of puerile negative imagery constantly from Doordarshan as a consequently of its complete domination by the commercial formula film to which now has been added the influence of the advertisement world. The time alloted for socially relevant discussions or programmes is not only inadequate in itself but the message connot even be heard in the midst of so much populist material pandering to the lowest common denominator. In recent weeks, Doordarshan has undoubtedly launched a socially purposive family drame that is in the right direction, though yet somewhat amateurishly handled. Even while this serial takes up the right issues, its handling highlights the inadequate understanding of the problems on the part of those posing creative solutions.

In any case films and film-based material continue to constitute substantial chunks of Doordarshan's output and as the report on Doordarshan's Role in Women's Equality and Development highlighted, "These programme are loaded with derogatory images of women and are usually explicity of implicitly sexist. They play a significant role in reinforcing negative stereotypes". What are these stereotypes? Basically drawn from a middle class vision of women that sees her and glorifies her *solely* in the role of wife, mother and homemaker. Not only is this a travesty of the vest reality, but equally a gross injustice that denies-and therefore serves to kill rather than help blossom–the richness of a women's total dimension and her critical larger role within the community and the country. Thus, the medium instead of widening the women's horizon and taking her further up the road of partnership, is now carrying into remote areas a distorted perspective that pushes women into a narrow niche and makes it more difficult, indeed dangerous, for those not conforming to this unidimensional type of personality.

The film and film-based programmes promote a culture antethetical to women. Let me quote again from the earlier mentioned report :

> "Both the commercial films and the film song programmes contain long sequences with semi clad women dancing for me either in cabaret scenes or supposedly rural settings. There is also a trend of growing violence in commercial cinema. The observed rising incidence of violence towards women in real life cannot be delinked from the depiction of such sequences in many of the feature films which are so uncritically projected on Doordarshan... In fact, the commercial cinema today is the prime medium through negative and derogatory images of women in our society are both created and reinforced. The films consume over 20 per cent of total viewing time leaving little for more significant programmes that can contribute to social and cultural development-large sums of scarce public resources are used to subsidize the already overfinanced commercial film industry".

I might also draw your attention to a study recently done abroad which has established that films showing violence to women not only desensitised men but also the women waching such films. Exposure to such films coloured the viewers assessment of women as *deserving* and *not* being *victimised* by such violence.

But Doordarshan remains immune to the weight of such findings. In the last year since that seminar brought into focus the anguish regarding the lewdness, violence and vulgarity of the commercial cinema shown of TV and its corroding impact on public mortality, for which women particularly pay a price, the content of films materials has stepped up, not gone down. While it may be argued that there has been an attempt to eliminate scene of out-right violence and to more strictly scrutinize the content of such programmes in terms of their portrayal of women, this does not really serve the purpose. In any case, the nature of the commercial formula film is such that while the most obvious crass displays of vulgarity and violence may be weeded out, much that is offending remains within its very structure. Besides, the violence to women has several forms of which physical violence towards a women is only one despicable extreme and the physical display of the female form for titillation the other. Equally grave a problem is that of the pshchological violence to womanhood by the more insidious subversion of women's self-respect through a steady and subtle glorification of her consistent subordination, Self-effacement and sacrifice which has been termed the "Sita-Savitri syndrome". The other side of this coin is the male image similarly unsuitably fed on a diet of aggression and self-centredness as a model of the macho man-and to be macho in the traditional society is a plus point! While self-effacement and sacrifice are values that have instrinsic merit and rightfully occpy a respected place in the Indian traditional value system, it needs to be recognized that these virtues are expected only from one half of society and not from the other half that has to a great measure contributed to the delibitated and decimated plight of Indian womanhood in general. A governed-owned medium dedicated to the rectification of the situation cannot place itself in a position that helps to perpetuate such a situation. But it does.

The Indian commercial formula film is not the only damning part of Doordarshan's contrary wave to women's interests; its selection of foreign film serials has imported the range of Westernized patronizing attitudes and biases against women into our lives. Scarce foreign exchange and peak transmission time is now devoted to showing people that women always scatterbrained like

Dear Lucy. Such programming cannot be conducive to the development of wholesome attitudes.

So much for an analysis of what exists. What is it that we need to do to make Doordarshan deliver on its promise as a change agent? What are the necessary steps? It is not enought to suggest a set of programme ideas. Much more fundamental exercises are needed to halt the dangerous drift which makes Doordarshan a lethal weapon against women rather than a positive instrument for their benefit. Programme ideas taken up on an *ad hoc* basis will only lose their power in the welter of conflicting messages presently beamed and end up serving little more than the purpose of politicians and administrators wanting to claim achievements that don't actually add up to anything in the field.

There is, therefore, need to press the government to announce that it considers the improvement of women's condition, status and image a primary objective of Doordarshan. Towards this end, it must formulate clearcut guidelines regarding the positive portrayal of women on television which take note of women in all facets of their lives, but particularly as workers and significant contributors to family survival and the national economy so that respect for the women's individual worth, undersanding of her special problems and the need to promote the integration of women in terms of equality in all sectors of national life and the development process is built up. Further, there is need for these guidelines to emphasise that the women's dimension forms an integral part of all Doordarshan programmes as far as possible and does not remain confined to isolated attempts to focus on women's issues or within the women's programme (The women's programmes, however, do need to be retained, given for more time, importance and wider base, so that women receive special attention to bridge the gaps till they are themselves ready to receive all programmes of diverse interests, an men are). Further these guidelines must enunciate the need for a portrayal of men that highlights and applauds them as caring, sensitive and self-sacrificing individuals, particularly showing them as co-operating in and taking on household, child care and other family responsibilties. The implementation of these guideliness cannot be left to good intentions. Alongsides a careful evaluation and monitoring system needs to be set up. Doordarshan should be made accountable and its performance ought to be open to public scruitiny.

Further, in order to promote a positive ideology that is sensitive and constructive about women's needs and ensure that it permeates all programming and that there is a co-ordinated, consistent policy on the subject, there is need for all Doordarshan policy makers, programmers and producers to have an orientation that sensitives them to the dimensions of the women's question within a framework of general social issues. However, to further ensure that the Women's interest is protected, there is need to constitute Programme Advisory, Monotoring and Purchase Committee for all major programme slots, including films and imported programmes. These committees should be predominantly non-official and at least half the members should be women; further, at least half the members should be selected from a panel of names compiled from those women's organizations and other public bodies involved in social issues. Similarly, a special committee should carefully scrutinize all advertisements to ensure that they do not portray women in derogatory and stereotyped ways. The purchase of foreing programmes should be limited to those that educate or promote a shared understanding or problems, particularly with reference to the roles, lives and struggles of women in other Third World countries. The reality of the ordinary Indian women's life needs to be explored through more field-based documentaries that rectify the myopia of the media's middle cass vision of women, but which also, through a creative search for solutions, offer an energizing, mobilizing experience that can motivate viewers to seek improvements. There is a general need to make the programmes more participatory and to draw is women and men, who are knowledgeable about women's issues, to develop the programmes. Last in my listing here but actually first amongst priorities, is the question of organizing access for the rural and urban poor women who form the most disadvantaged section of Indian society to have access to television programme through schemes the promote community viewing taking into consideration the special needs and appropriate timing for the women of the community.

In sum, what is needed is not simply compartmentalized thinking on a few better programmes for women but a sea change in philosophy, organization and metholodology. How far television succeeds in serving the interests of women is in fact a touchstone of how far television is made a genuine development tool.

The Social Life

For children from the age of two on, talk become more and central to the increasingly diverse events and transactions of life. In this chapter I will examine some of the ways in which talk serves the important social goals of initiating and constructing such focused engagements as teaching, trading, and playing; its role in shaping and organizing children's group activities; and its contributions to friendships. In some transactions talk appears to be primarily instrumental in achieving some immediate end, such as persuading another to return a purloined object, getting help in completing a puzzle, or gaining admittance to an ongoing group activity. At other, less urgent, times talk may be an end in itself, joined just for or for its intrinsic interest. An observer might postulate that the "conversationlists" have an urge to affiliate, but the children may be simply exporing the discovery that engaging another person in talk is in some ways more peasureble and exciting than talking without a partner. But whatever the immediate motive or effect, social talk becomes a part of each child's developing style of interpersonal behaviour. Recurring patterns of verbal interaction, along with nonverbal communication, come to constitute the somewhat more lasting complexes of attitudes, expectations, and interdependencies between persons that we think of as relationships. Before we examine the important transactions in which talk plays as central role, I will describe some of the characteristics of "Just conversing".

Just Conversing

What is a conversation? It proves easier to say what a conversation is not then to define it by its attributes. We do not consider business transactions or any interchange having planned procedures or previouly stated goals, such as solving a problem, teaching a skill, or disciplining another person, as conversational. The term is usually reserved for informal, more or less spontaneous inter-changes in which a few or just two persons alternately introduce and jointly pursue topics in a leisurely manner without an explicitly prearranged agenda. A conversation can be embedded in some other type of interaction or can constitute a whole encounter. When do children begin to converse in this sense? Certainly conversations occur during the preschol period, both with adults and with other children. Conversations thrive in familiar settings and with familiar persons, especially between pairs, since handling the necessarily responsive contributions of conversation if difficult with more than one partner at a time.

Young children, at least when they are well and at ease, are usually pursuing some line of action or are in momentary transition from one project to another. Much of a child's talk arises from and accompanies has own activities, and if two or more children are in physical proximity, the talk functions rather like a radio device that permits each to monitor where the action is and to "home in" on if it it seems interesting. A three-year-olds typically either invites another to join or attend to his own activity, "Look what I'm making", or displays his involvement both verbally and nonverbally so that a monitoring partner is drawn in and action can become coordinated, at least for a brief period before some distraction or new project begins. Making one's action, intelligible to another is a problem of some magnitude to very young children; if one is to one is to join the other's action, it is critical to determine what the other is doing. Understanding what is going on proves to be essential for a slightly older child who wants to enter into the ongoing activities of a group of mutually involved children, as we shall seen in a subsequent section of this chapter. But even in the pairs of young friends we studied, the question, "What you do in?" was often addressed to one child by another and rarely failed to bring forth an action-defining formulation, such as "Making coffee". A little less frequently both children together would construct a joint line of action and pursue it together, beginning, perhaps, with a "let's" suggestion, or by jumping directly into a coordinated activity.

In her several studies of the way actions lines converge among pairs of children, Grace Wales Şhugar found that three-year-olds joined a partner's action line less often than they drew a partner into their own line of action : four-year-olds joined a partner's line more frequently and were also more likely than the younger children to jointly initiate coordinated action. (In contrast, in the children's interactions with an adult, the adult tended to join the child's action line.) In this flow of converging, dissolving, and again converging action, brief conversations begin to appear between familiar and friendly children. Although they may emerge out of shared action line, these episodes of "topical discourse" become, as Shugar says, dislodged from the immediate action. They are instances of just conversing. The topics may be selected from memories, may be plans for the near future, or may express opinions or emotions.

Neither of the above conversations exhibited a playful orientation, but many conversational episodes do; playful teasing, contributions that are meant and are taken to be funny, and topics from the realm of fantasy were common in most of the pairs we observed. Indeed, Anca Nemoianu has used the term "conversation-play" to characterize the talk during social interaction of three children she observed over a six-months period, maintaining that it is often difficult to distinguish the boundaries of and transitions between playful and nonplayful attitudes in the flow of activity. In many cases this is true, although role play, does employ distinctive verbal makers to identify protrayed characters. One variety of play interchange, however, is distinctly different from other kinds of talk and must be mentioned here, since it has been suggested as one of the precursors of conversational exchange among peers. That is socially constructed sound play, so called because the content comprises sounds or nonsense words. In such episodes turns are alternated promptly and rhythmically, but each child successively repeats and/or slightly modifies the form, rather than the content, of the previous turn. In similarly rhythmic, but referentially interpretable verbal play episodes, it is still the form more than the content, or meaning, that makes the episode cohesive, with each child building on the other's turn by repetition and some limited modification or expansion of the prior turns. In the same session in which Judy and Tom produced the conversational episode cited earlier, they also produced the following rhythmic and playful episode in which repetition and successive modification were the organizing principles.

Among preschool children such markedly playful episodes coexist with more "serious" interchanges and with those that consist of dramatic or fantasy play. Although episodes of sounds play become less frequent, these ritualized play patterns do continue to occur and seem to have a communicative function and special form of their own. As such, they are not a likely preparation for just conversing. Further, sound play and ritualized verbal play are rarely observed in interactions between caregiver and child when the child in beginning has conversational life, although just conversing on a topic, usually one introduced by the child himself, often occurs in the interstices of more task-oriented talk with the caregiver. Just conversing, then, is one social activity that increases in frequently and in diversity of topic over the preschool years to become an important type of sharing among children and a major constituent of the interactions of most close friends, both displaying and reinforcing solidarity and intimacy.

Breaking and Entering

A child brought into a new situation, such as a newcomer to an established nursery school class, tends to speak very little at first; he behaves unobtrusively and spends his time watching the habitues. His first overtures are likely to be tentative. (Even a pair of children who do not know each other usually begin their interaction cautiously, with "getting acquainted" moves such as asking for the other's name.) Saying the right thing in the right way is one important step in initiating the interactions that will lead to acceptance and in avoiding ones that will lead to ever-worsening relations. When several children are together, in a day care center, at a birthday party, play group, or school, groupings inevitably appear. Some clusters may form voluntarily during a free period : some are engineered by an adult for routine activities, such as making valentines, working on an assignment, or having a snack. In voluntarily formed groups, particularly, and in those where adult supervision or direction is minimal, the basis of the temporary cohesion is likely to be a shared activity to which the members are committed. Members form a "we" and are protective of their psychological and physical interactive space and possessive of the objects involved in their mutually defined activity. Entering such a group (and such a group can appear powerfully attractive to a solitary child or one who is in transition from one involvement to another) poses a serious problem, not only to the socially inept or relatively unpopular child, but even to the more socially skilled and popular child. Members of a group will often react quite firecely to the outsider's first bid for entry. In fact, in nursery school groups of both three-and four-year-old children who had been together in the classes for several months and months thus were acquainted with cach other, half of all first entry bids were rejected by the involved group. Typically rejection moves were "Go away" and "You can't" play", followed by such reinforced rejection as "We don't like you today" and "You're not our friend." Knowing that such a reaction is likely, the outsider, not suprisingly, generally approaches the group with some trepidation, watching and hesitating before first attempting to join. He also realizes that he must be ready to persist in his attempt when he is either ignored or rebuffed.

A number of factors influence the probability of gaining access to a group. One is the perennial sex problem. A girl's chances of joining a group of boys are fairly poor. The group's rationale for exclusion is often quite straightfoward. For example, a girl ran up to two boys on a swing and asked, "Can I get on?" Each boy forcibly replied, "No," and one boy went on to tell her, "We don't want you on here. We only want boys on here." Another factor is the stability and solidarity of the group itself. If it is composed of close friends, who are probably engaged in established and jointly evolved play activities, the outsider has little chance of being accepted. The intimate group has its own language of friendship and familiar interaction patterns. Catherine Emihovich observed three very close four-year-olds friends in a nursery school class of fourteen childrens for a period of four months. At the beginning of the semester the friends were the only children who called one another by name, and they regularly played a domestic scenario together, each taking the same pretend roles on each occasion. They resisted entry aids from other children, and after a few sessions the other children in the class ceased trying to join their pretend play activities, although one girl did become a friend of the girl in the established group and was subsequently admitted to play a role in the "family," which was expanded to accommodate her.

The popularity of the outsider and the popularity of the children in the temporary activity groupings in a classroom or on the playground also influence the length of time a child watches, or "hovers," on the periphery of a group before attempting to gain admittance; the number of entry bids he may have to make before finally being admitted; and the likelihood that he will eventually succeed. Popularity is strongly tied to the communcative and interpretative skills required for successful entry into and functioning in a group. In the later pre-school and early elementary school period children distinguish between acquaintances and strangers, and they also categorize other children as liked, or popular, or as unpopular, and thus generally less desirable as playmates. Popular children require less time and fewer entry bids to gain access to an activity group, especially when that group is composed of popular children. It is bit more difficult for them to enter groups composed of unpopular children. Unpopular children, as might be expeted, have a very hard time joining a group of popular children but manage a little better in noining other unpopular children (although still not as efficiently and successfully as popular children entering a more favoured group). One secret of the popular children's success lies in their ability, displayed both verbally and nonverbally, to understand the structuring of the group's activities, to recognize what is going on, and to produce well-timed entry bids that accommodate to the group's involvement, thus mimimizing any disturbance of the ongoing action. They have learned, in effect, the following guidelines. The Don't's; don't ask questions for information (if you can't tell what's going on, you shouldn't be bothering those who do); don't mention yourself or state your feelings about the group or its activity (they're not interested at the moment); don't disagree or criticize the proceedings (you have no right to do so, since you're an outsider). The Do's : be sure you understand the group's frame of reference, or focus (are they playing house?); understand the participation structure of the activity; slip into the ongoing activity by making some relevant comment or begin to act in concert with the others as if your actually were a knowledgeable member of the group; hold off on making suggestions or attempting to redirect until you are well into the group.

Because of the normally strong urge to be included, a child usually tries again after being rejected or simply ignored. Of course, a child can simply repeat his first attempt, a tactic more common among five-year-olds than seven-year-olds. But even preschoolers have some techniques for revising the bid, making it either more forceful or more ingratiating. Five-year-old girls tend to be a bit more flexible than boys in this respect, especially when their motive appears to be to gain entry to the group rather than to perform the activity itself or use the objects or props that the group commands. David Forbes and his colleagues, in their study of "third-party entry" among small groups of five-and seven-year-olds, have pointed out that these two of motives, which often can be distinguished by the entering child's subsequent behaviour in the group, influence the tactics used in attempting access. A second or third entry bid is likely to be met with more elaborated resistance that rationalizes the rejection, a preferred basis being the prerogatives of the groups. In defending the group against intruders, members emphasize their solidarity and their rights to control the group's resources. If the group is involved in pretend play, their make-believe roles are one basis for exclusion; for example, in repelling an intruder from some cimbing bars, one boy said, "You can't get in [three times]. It's only for police. It's only for policemen." When the intruder left, the two playmates affirmed their togetherness: "Good. We got the run of *our* policehouse." In such ways, members of a group display and reaffirm their mutual involvement, not only to outsiders but also to one another. After all, they share not only their physical proximity and a use space, but also the psychological sense of doing something teogether, something "we" have jointed created.

Inside a Group

The processes of mutual construction of an activity can be seen in the way temporary groupings of children negotiate just what it is they are doing, what procedural rules are in effect, how to delimit space, and how to allot materials, props, and the various responsibilities. In situations supervised or arranged by adults, the adult may impose a decision about some of these functions, as when a teacher organizes a group for collaborative work on a project to a parent suggests that playmates might like to have a tea party. But the organizational functions must be fulfilled and are undertaken by the children themselves whenever possible. Sometimes the process is democratic, sometimes one child emerges as the leader, whos suggestions and ideas are likely to be accepted, even solicited by the other members. In pretend play, many, if on all, of these organizational functions are verbalized, so I will focus on how they are accomplished in such play. In a later section of this chapter I will examine the communication within a group involved in teaching and other classroom tasks.

Several investigators have made very similar observations on the two types of communication required for pretend play in groups of two or more children. Dramatization is, of course, essential, the roles must be portrayed, and activities must be enacted. The other type of communication has been called explicit mention of pretend, framing statements, or negotiation. Such communications are essentially metacommunicative; they are about the play and they serve the organizational functions listed above. The proportions of dramatization and negotiation about play differe, depending on the group. On any particular occasion a move directed at defining or organizing the activity may be accepted at once or may lead to a length exchange sequence. The statements concerning various suspects of the group's activity need not occur in any prescribed order, although the assignment of person roles and the definition of the activity usually occur early in the interaction. The following are the major types of negotiable organizing statements, with an example of each (all bearing on the ubiquitous domestic theme):

Definition of situation : "Let's play house."

Assignment of roles : "I'll be the daddy and you be the mommy," —"And what will he be?" (indicating a third child)—He's the little boy."

Defining location : "This is the kitchen."

Specifying the action plan : "I'll fix super for the kid and you get the groceries."

Assigning props : "This is my pocketbook."

Correcting operating procedures and refining the script : "Daddies don't wear pocketbooks."—"My daddy wears pocketbooks."

Regoing others' performance : "No, you have to really yell at him" (said by a girl when a boy playing Daddy did not speak sternly enough to the naughty "little boy".

Invoking rules relating to the real (versus the pretend) context ; "You can't *really* go out there" (said by a girl when a boy actually started to open the door to the playroom on his retend trip to the grocery store).

Termination of and/ or transition from one organizing theme to another : "Okay, all finished supper."—"What do you want to play now?"

Commenting on the interpersonal climate in the group : "We're playing so we're friends now, right?"—"Right."

Talk is vital to the conduct of play. First, it defines and coordinates the participants' actions. Outsiders also, whether investigators or children hoveing on the periphery of the group, poised to attempt entry, must listen in order to know what is going on. Imagine, for example, three childrens who could be objectively described as carrying to an enclosure of cardboard boxes. They could be transporting weapons to a fort, carrying beams to construct a roof for a new house, or lugging skis to a slope. Only their talk will reveal the import of their behaviour. Second, the talk inside a group, in addition to organizing and dramatizing, serves the function of displaying and affirming membership, both to insiders and outsiders. The members often verbally mark their territory, reinforcing their consensus not only with references to *we* or *our house*, but also by repeating on another's verbal formulations. These same children also used requests for permission in different ways depending on whether they were inside or outside a pretend engagement at that moment. As an outsider, a child would ask, "Can I try it?" and then wait for the response from the insiders who were working with some tool that was part of their pretend scenario (usually permission was not granted). The insiders, however, who had joint rights to their props, would ask permission of one another for a turn a using the prop but would not wait for a response. They would just begin the turn, having established a pattern of taking and relinquishing turns at using what belonged to both within the framework of the shared play theme.

The demostic theme (illustrated in the above examples of negotiations) is the first to appear in young children's play and it is familiar to virtually all children. It can be endlessly varied and can be combined with other widely popular themes such as taking a vacation, surviving a disaster, and illness or injury followed by healing or recovery. If the children are well acquainted and imaginative, variations can become quite elaborate (the previous examples are relatively simple). The value children ascribe to such play and to good players and the fact that the play requires skilled negotiation and flexibility are two reasons that children who have friends are children who engage in more domestic fantasy play than relatively friendless children.

Being Friends

The temporary groupings examined above provide the opportunity for interactions in which compatibility and mutual preferences can develop. Children who have friends are those who can get along with others. In the preschool period getting along means, first and foremost, playing together, taking turns at directing and being directed in play, and being able to defuse or resolve the inevitable disagreements and conflicts of interest the arise. But if friendship grows out of playing together, avoiding serious fights, and sharing things and activities (which is the definition of friendship that a preschooler will give, if asked), friendship itself is a relationship, a connection that extends beyond the actual interaction. Among three-and four-year-olds, the term "friend" usually refers to what they conceive of as friendly behaviour, and it is often invoked for purposes of control, "I won't be your friend if you don't let me have a turn." But although young children may not yet consciously or explicity conceptualize such an abstract ideas as "relationship" or think about friends as loyal persons one trusts and admires, they exhibit attitudes toward one another that go beyond the momentary behaviours of compliance or cooperation. Friends want to be together, miss one another when they are apart, and share an inteangible bond of memories, secrets, and understanding. In the late preschool period friends engage in fantasy play that reflects their (possibly otherwise inexpressible) concerns about being lonely, their fears and worries : and they are able to reassure on another. Having had more opportunity and greater motivation to understand one another's habits, moods, and preferences, they are better able to resolve misunderstandings and quarrels (and friends do quarrel), and are generally more responsive to each other than are children who are not friends.

Friends are able to construct together elaborate conspiracies, as John Gottman and Jennifer Parkhurst discovered in their study of good friends in their own homes. They identified a type of verbal interchange they dubbed "shared deviance," which involved planning naughty or forbidden acts, one lengthy example of which was a plot to poison the mother of one of the children by hiding some pretend lethal beans in a dish she was cooking. Mother was not poisoned, but the friends further consolidated their intimacy with the elaborate scheming. In friendships favourite fantasy themes emerge and generally reach more imaginative and creative heights than in the fantasy play of less intimate children, most probably because the shared understandings and mutually constructed history of their play and life together permits the communicative work of play to move beyond the essential organizational negotiations into the exploration of both personal images and feelings and new experiences they want to share and extend.

Teaching

Teaching and learning are achieved in a number of different ways; planned, explicit verbal instruction on a teacher-selected topic or task, as is common in classroom situations, is only one means by which children or adults transfer knowledge or skill to a young child. Much learning occurs outside of the settings of formal instruction as a child selects a procedure that interests him, watches and listens or asks a question, then recreates the procedure himself in his own, often modifying his behaviour in response to another's reactions. Those reactions include teasing, prompting, challenging, denigrating his ability, and ignoring certain inappropriate behaviours ; these are all ways to shape a child's behavior and promote the learning of such disparate things as playing a jumprope game with the "right" counting-in and counting-out formulas, riding a bicycle, drying the dishes, or even reciting the alphabet. Very little is known about how children teach other children, or whether preschoolers intentionally set out to impact information or skill to a peer or "shape up" a peer's performance on a task. Children do imitate one another, and the preschool-age child is more likely to observe and imitate the behaviour of a slightly older child than one his own age or size of a younger one. Children certainly do learn from one another, and in cultural groups in which siblings and other children assume part of the responsibility for child care, their influence may be of considerable importance. In our own culture, research on children's teaching has focused on the use of peer tutors in classroom situations, primarily during the later elementary school years. In these situations "teaching" is likely to take on some characteristics of the explicit verbal instruction conducted by adult teachers. Before examining some of these more formal tutoring techniques, I will discuss some early forms of teaching and ask what three-year-olds know about this type of interpersonal engagement.

If we define teaching or instructing as one person's intentional attempt to convey information or skill he possesses (or believes he possesses) to a person who does not, then one can observe attempts at teaching by very young children. (Teaching and learning do not always go hand in hand, and I will not be primarily concerned with the success of these attempts.) One person sets himself forth as knowledgeable about an object or even or about how to do something, and the other attends to the explanation, instruction, or demonstration and tries to follow. Thus two reciprocal roles are established, one generally taken by an adult, the other by a child. Teaching episodes may be initiated either by the "teacher" or by the "pupil." The teacher may respond to a request or other indication of need, or the teacher, deciding that the pupil needs guidance in some ongoing activity, may initiate the teaching episode. Before examining the attempts at teaching that arise when two children take on the roles of teacher and pupil, I will briefly mention the far more familiar procedures of adult and child i an instructional engagement.

The caregivers of young children have an extensive repertoire of instructional techniques. Further, they generally have certain priorities and a changing agenda of topics for instruction. The mothers of the three two-year-olds, Judy, Jack, and Sarah, were all working on teaching, among many other things, numbers, colors, and animal names. These subjects were introduced, usually be the mothers, during play sessions and in a variety of other situations. The mothers all, for example, led the children to count things—eggs, forks, vegetables—and to name colors they were working together in the kitchen, catching up on their teaching agendas on the fly and taking any other opportunity to explain such occasional topics as why yeast bread rises or why ice melts. More structured lessons on the continuing agendas were engineered during play with puzzles or blocks. In these situations the children entered easily into the pupil role, exhibiting their familiarity with the well-established, routinized exchange patterns. A typical example, between Jack (30 months) and his mother, engaged with a number puzzle, shows that Jack understood the procedure to the point where he could anticipate the next question (Only the end of this long episode is presented.)

The detiful pupil repeated his correct responses, which the teacher had prasied : provided, unasked, the colour and then the number name of one of the last two pieces (knowing, presumably, that he would be asked if he failed to volunteer the information); and put each piece into the puzzle after it had been identified. (The colour red had been a particular issue during this session. During the next puzzle the pair worked with, Jack was unable to "show something else that's red" after his mother told him the colour of an apple shape.) The format of the pedagogical "play" session with its clear differentiation of roles, the mother's elicitations (some masquerading as comments, "Now we have two left"), and the firmly maintained "on-task" orientation throughout the session will all be quite familiar and predictable to Jack when he concounters similar procedures for teaching in kindergarten and elementary school.

Did Jack and the other children ever reverse these roles and try to instruct their mothers? This happened in only one tupe of situation during the hours of interaction we recorded. Each child attempted to instruct his mother in how to take part in play events the child had devised. In these events, in which the child was, indeed, the knowledgeable party, the child explained his scenario, demonstrated actions, and told the mother what she should or should not do. In terms of instructional techniques, the children did not ask questions to check on the mother's understanding, did not praise her when she did something correctly, and did not even acknowledge her responses unless she asked for freedback, as in, "Is this the right way?" As a matter of fact, the mothers did not seem to play the pupil role any better than their children performed as teachers. They wree over achievers, asking too many helpful questions and not refraining from making suggestions to make the activity more reasonable or intelligible or to bring it in line with their own agendas. Mother's tendencies to shape play in this way have been observed to persist at least until the child is five years old.

With little practice in the role of teacher, how does a child carry out this function when the pupil is another child? And how does a child perform as pupil vis-a-vis a peer, whom he may not see as a properly accredited teacher or even recognize as a teacher at all? Judy, Jack, and Sarah entered into only a few teaching episodes with their friends. The children did not have, after all, any long-range instructional agendas and had little expertise to impact. For the most part the episodes that did occur centered on how to do something. In the first instance of beaching we observed between Judy (29 months) and Tom (30 months), Tom asked Judy how to operate a little box that had two switches on it that activated a buzzer and some lights, which were shaped like buttons. In this instance Tom asked for help and Judy gave him (incorrect) instructions but took no further responsibility for showing him what to do. In the following instance, the roles of teacher and pupil were reversed, and Tom initiated the step-by-step instructions.

In this instance the teacher attended to the pupil's response to the verbal instructions, reacted to her ineffectual attempt by adding a demonstration, then let the pupil do it herself. He did not go on to acknowledge her accomplishment but gave a new instruction relevant to driving the car. Judy accepted her male partner's automotive expertise.

The directive form exemplified by Tom's directions, "you push," "you click it," and "you do it," is often used, of course, in giving how-to-do-it instruments, and this form can also be used in teaching more general precepts, as can the *you have* to form. An example of giving a more general rule for behaviour was the response by a four-year-old girl to her boy partner's announcement that when he grew up he was going to be a policemen.

Anne tried to tell Jack about a conventional rule to guide his behaviour and supported her position, citing general and specific authority, but whether Jack realized her attempt or not, we do not know.

From these fleeting instructional gestures to the beginnings of peer tutoring in the elementary, classroom, we would expect the concepts of the reciprocal teacher-pupil roles to develop along with the appropriate verbal and nonverbal techniques and increased understanding of pupils needs. Indeed, in studies of peer tutoring in which children have been taught to take the teacher role, part of the training involves focusing the tutee (usually a younger child) on the task, making the instructions clear and explicit, and giving prompt and helpful feedback on the tutee's efforts, all steps that are characteristic of mothers' (and other adult teachers') instructional procedures.

Catherine Cooper and her colleagues hve conducted a number of studies of both spontaneous teaching-learning engagements of children in relatively open classroom where children are encouraged to work together and of situations in which children have been assigned the teacher role in an adult-specified task. In one second-grade classroom spontaneous engagements were initiated either by the leaner or by the teacher. In both types the episodes for more often dealt with substantive issues, the spelling of a word or the answer to an arithmetic problem, than with procedural issues, such as, whether to cross out items on a page or circle them. Interestingly, the majority of episodes were initiated by the leaner, and some children were chosen as teacher more frequently than others. These findings indicate that at least by the second grade, children do feel that they can gain information from other children and that they have some sense as to which child is able to provide it. Learner initiations varied in their directness, from explicit questions, "I still need help on number 3" or "The women saw *what?*" to more indirect irequests for help, "I don't get this right here" or "This one is hard for me," said while pointing to a task item. When children voluntarily assumed the role of teacher, they did not usually set up the task but began with an instruction or spontaneously corrected the pupil's work, "See the *d? d, b"* (pointing to each letter). "You were wrong." In one adult-assigned task a child who had been taught to use objects to balance a scale acted as teacher to a child pupil who was unfamiliar with the task. In this case Cooper found that the ability to give specific directions, both verbally and by gestural indication was associated with successful teaching. In neither the teaching task nor in the classroom episodes did teachers consistently try to focus the pupils' attention, not did they often given directive feedback, but when they did, these teachniques were associated with successful interchanges.

By second grade some children do display an understanding of the recpirocal responsibilities of the teacher and pupil roles. They know that the teacher must obtain the attention of a distracted or unwilling pupil, should confirm or otherwise indicate acceptance of a pupil's correct response, and correct an incorrect response or try again to elicit a correct one. John Gumperz and Eleanor Herasimchuk made a detailed comparison of the instructional episodes on reading of a second-grade child teacher and a first-grade pupil and those of the adult teacher with the children. The child teacher, they found, had to assert her role more forcefully to obtain initial co-operation on the task.

Once engaged, the teacher and pupil collaborated in a way that contrasted markedly, with that of the adult teacher and pupils. The child teacher used more direct elicitations and fewer indirect ones and hints did the adult. The child teacher tended to model the correct response and to acknowledge the pupil's correct responses with repetitions.

In this characteristic sequence the pupil reproduced not only the teacher's words but also the timing and intonation, which was the typical reading intonation, with individual words produced with level or low-rising pitch. The two children's contributions were balanced both in rhythm and in the actual number of words and utterances produced by each partner. The interchanges of the adult teacher and pupils were more asymmetrical; the teacher talked much more than the pupils, and her messages differed from theirs in form, content, and intonation. While there is some evidence that children in the elementary grades can and do fulfill the reciprocal functions of the teacher and pupil roles and that the child teachers have acquired some techniques for focusing attention, maintaining an on-task orientation, and providing informative feedback, they must also adapt their practices to the child-child relationships that exist concurrently and, perhaps, more basically in their classroom or work group.

Trading

Of the many social tasks the child encounters in his daily life that are constructed in part or in whole by talking, only a few have been described in detail. Trading is one type of well-motivated talk interchange that most probably engage in, and Elliot Mishler has analyzed the bargaining of six-year-old boys, who can engage in this strategic and orderly activity with some skill. A lunch or snack packed by a well-meaning parent often provides the basic resources for trading, but marbles or other personal possessions may also be used, as long as the participants know the rules of the game. As in many other games that children play, the rules are probably learned peers or sibilings, and learning is most likely by observation and practice during the later-preschool and early elementary school years.

The basic conditions for trading are that each party has a tradable object and a motive for exchange. Talk has a central role in the interchange from its outset. As Mishler puts in, "The problem for particapants is to express the trading relevance of their own objects and motives, to assess the presence of similar relevances in others, and to elicit their expression from them." Tradable objects must differ in some way; if two children discover that they both have Snack Packs or the same kind of candy bar,no trading episode will result. The objects must be presented in such a way that their differences can be assessed for their trading value. In the two complementary roles, person *A* must not only exhibit his interest in a possible trade but must also present his object as desirable to person *B*. *B*, too, must entertain the idea of a trade and convey the value of his object. Both *A* and *B*, as the process unfolds, may enhance their bargaining positions by playing down their eagerness to have the other's object, perhaps by devaluing the object. Both parties must know that what they are doing is trading, rather than joking, perhaps, or offering the object as a gift or just arguing about whose possessions are better. An intelligible episode of trading comes into being in the exchange of sequenced moves.

The first move is a delicate one. The objects must be displayed, but the first person to make an explicit trading request is likely to be in the weaker position. The other party might refuse or try to strike a harder bargain if he sees the initiator as being eager for the trade. For example, an opening display, "I got a Suzy Q" (candy bar), as rebuffed by a pontential trading partner, "That's not a Suzy Q," and the initiator was forced to argue that is was, indeed, what he claimed. He than selected another potential trading partner and tried again : "I got something interesting. Suzy Q's" He went on the make a trading bid : "What will you give me for a Suzy Q?"

Teaching, trading, engineering play sessions, gaining access to a group, and consolidating friendships by the exchange of views, plans, memories, and attitudes are some of the uses of talk in the child's social life. There are, no doubt, many others that await our discovery and understanding.

2

Use of New Media

What makes for effectiveness in educational media projects such as those we have been reporting?

If wer were asked to name the most basic requirement, on the evidence of our case studies, we would say; let it begin with a problem. Let the project not begin with a piece of new technolgy which someone thinks could or should be in use. Above all, let it not begin as an excuse for adding technolgy which is primarily for other purposes. Rather, let it begin with an educational problem which is serous and widely recognized, which cannot readily be solved by conventional means, and to whose solution one or more of the media would seem to be able to make a significant conntribution. Let the planners start with the problem and select the media system to fit it. There will then be a fair chance for the project to receive wide support and acceptance—which is another basic requirement for success.

For example, when educational television comes into use in a country as an excuse for appropraiting money for the facilities of entertainment television, it may succeed, but it starts with a dreadful handicap. On the other hand, when a country (like Australia) feels the need to bring education to many thousands of children without schools, or when a country (like Algeria) has to bring in 10,000 unqualified teachers and knows it must upgrade them as quickly as possible in order to get on with the business of national growth and development, there is then a good chance that the media systems selected for these purposes will be used seriously, supported adequately, and accepted generally.

But this is not a sufficient answer, becuase even when a problem is perceived, the media may still not be used effectively to meet it. An when media facilities and installed for non-educational purposes, it m may still be possible to use them effectively to meet an educational problem. Therefore, in the next pages we are going to speak rather generally about how the media work, and then become quite specific and list some of the elements and conditions which seem to make for effective use.

The Distrubutive Powers of the Media

The mass media act as devices to multiply and disseminate very widely and quickly certain selected parts of the information available to a social system. Since the media are so much more efficient than face-to-face communication for this type of activity, and can have such a widespread impact, the selection of the material to be disseminated is a matter of importance to the whole society.

When some of the mass media are taken over for use in the educational system—and therby become 'educational media'—their selectivity, and their efficiency as multipliers and disseminatiors, take on special importance. Let us recall the great development in education that came after one of the earliest mass media, the book, began to be used in such a way as to share the knowledge of great teachers and scholars. In theory, a similar development might follow the broad introduction of the new media, notably radio, television and films, which offer a parallel but still essentially difference contribution to education. Whereas the older media, such as the textbook, could share the substance of teaching, these mew media, and notably television and radio, can share the *dynamics* of teaching.

To an educator this means that he is in position to redistribute the most vital resource he has at his diposal—the teaching that goes on in his class-rooms. It has been taken for granted that some schools would provide better instruction than others, that a few lucky students each year would get the best teacher in a particular grade or subject, and that some subjects could not be taught in many schools because they required special competences not there available. Now the educator is in position, these new media, to share some of his best teaching more widely. He can share demonstrations with schools that previously could not afford them. He can let all of his foreign-language. He can let al of his foreign-language student, not afford them. He can native speakers of the language. He can offer specialized teaching (music, art, science, advanced mathematics, and so forth) to schools where specialists are not available. Thus he can spead and equalize the learning opportunites within his system, while raising educational quality, and in some cases extending learning opportunities where schools are simply not available and may not be for years to come.

Nor is the educational leader concerned only with the teaching of students. If the quality of educatin is to advance and keep pace with new developments in knowledge, the teachers must be constant learners. But to reach the widely scattered teachers of any educatinal system with new knowlede, ideas, and teaching skills is an enormous logistical problem. Here agains, the new media offer new and effective tools for doing the job.

Most difficult of all for the educational leader is the task of bringing about basic changes and innovations in a widely scattered educational system which, in an ara of rapid change in the world, tends to become obsolete and ill-fitted to the changing conditins and needs of its environment. Well concieved educational changes of this sort can only succeed if there is effective communication, persuasin, enlightenment and confidence between the leadership at the centre and the teachers and administrators in the individual schools. The new media offer a means of strengthening this dialogue, and a means of shaking the whole web of traditional attitudes and practices, thus contributing to the modernization and advancement of any educational system.

Outside of the school, in adult and development programmes, the new media offer similar opportunities. They can share experts and teachers of adult programmes more widely and swiftly then experts can possibly be shared by travep. They can extend the opportunities for skilled assistance and advice, maintain contact with local programmes, and contribute toward the equalizing of adult learning and development programmes over wide areas. Their distributive powers are thus enormous.

The Need for Acceptance

These uses, of course, imply that new media will be integrated into the present educational system. Whereas the 'new media'—e.g., television—when used for other purposes may stand apart from the educational system, the 'new educational media'—e.g., educational television —cannot. They are sharing the system's own teaching. They are multiplying and distributing the system's own resorces. Their content is the system' content; their only educational life is what the system gives them. Therefore, their effectiveness is bound to rest to a considerble extent on their support and acceptance within the system, and on the smoothness of their interlocking with the other learning resources and experiences the system offers.

Obviously, integration will be easier if the media are accepted by the chief groups and individuals in the system able to do something about them. This means strong support from top authority, without which any major educational innovation has a difficult time. It means co-operation between the owners and the operators of the new media, if these are not the same. In many countreis, for example, the facilities are owned by the ministry of communication, and their use for schools is under the ministry of education; if they compete rather than co-operate the programme will inevitably suffer. Successful integration also means broad involvement within the system, especially participation by teachers in deciding how the media are to be used and what content they shall carry. The more the new media are perceived within a system *as our* teaching, meeting *our* needs the more likely they are to operate smoothly and efficiently. Thus, paradoxically, local content, because it is seen as "our own' rather than some–thing from the outside may be more effective than imported content that might objectively be judged superior.

The Importance of Reception

One of the reasons why a high degree of integration is so important si that the effectiveness of the new media is coming more and more to be seen as dependent upon the amount of learning activity that goes on at the receiving end. A student may be taught by a variety of teachers, but only he can learn. The responses that he rehearses, overtly or convertly, the relationships that he perceives and stores away, are what he learns. Therefore, it is not productive to think of the media as pouring content into viewers and listeners; a better way is to think of them as stimulating *learning activity* on the part of their viewers and listeners. This means that if the media are to be used efficiently it is necessary to make special efforts, both in planning the content and the context of media use, to stimulate learnings activity in the users.

We are lumpingtogether in-school and out-of-school media use in a way that may be confusing. But the media are the same, and the principles of their use are the same. A context of learning activity needs to be provided for at the point of reception whether it is in the class-room (where a teacher is in charge of teh context), or an out-of-school learning group (where a monitor is usually in charge), or a village (where a good example of planned context is the rural forum).

Ordinarily such a context requires some organization. We have mentioned the radio rural forums, the viewing centres, and the class-rooms. Each of these is a learning group with supervision. The quality of supervision is in many instances as important a factor as the quality or teaching on the media. When it is not possible to provide a professional supervisor, as in the class-room, then most countries try to provide special training and guidance to their monitors or supervisors. When it is not possible to bring supervisors in for training, as in the case of the mothers who supervise their children's home study in New Zealand and Australia, then the radio or television is used to assist the supervisor as well as the pupils. When it is not feasible to create a supervised learning *group* at the receiving end (as in the Japan broadcast-correspondence secondary school, or the Chaicago Television College), then there is still need for some personal contact between the individual pupil and a teacher, whether by correspondence, telephone or radio, or occasional visits. Even when the conditions would seem to be most favourable for a learning context, in the class-room with a professional teacher, still it is necessary, as many of these cases have shown, to work very hand to involve the teachers in the programme and to help them learn how to bring about the most helpful learning experiences round the media.

The point is that, except in the rarest of instances, the

new media cannot be counted on to do an adequate educational job by themselves, and hardly anywhere in the world are they being asked to do this. Planned guidance for puplis, practice opportunities, and the opportunity of two-way communication if possible must be built into the teaching system of which the media are a part.

In effect, then, by their very nature the new educational media enter into a kind of team teaching. It is not precisely th kind of teaching usually called 'team teching' in modern schools, where the term usually refers to the division of specialized responsibilities for a large group of pupils among a group of teachers and assistants. But the principle is the same. Each teacher has a special task which, supposedly, he can do best. In the case of the media, a teacher at the point of imput, a teacher at the point of reception, perhaps another teacher speaking through textual or exercise materials, combine their efforts, each doing his own part of the task of stimulating students' learning activity. When the media are used for adult education (let us take agriculture as a possible subject area) the teacher at the transmitting end may be an extension specialist, the superivisor at the receiving end may be a forum chairman, or village-level worker, and the materials may be prepared by a group at the agriculture research station. But the division of responsibilities is the same. Obvioulsy such a division and combination of responsibility requires a clear and common set of learning objectives, the will to work together, careful planning, and adequate training in the special skills required.

So far as the dynamics of their use is concerned, then, the effectivencess of the new educational is likely to depend basically on their integration in the educational system, and their incorporation—both content and use—into a planned programme of learning activity. But certain large matters of planning and policy are also involved.

The Need ask Basic Policy Questions

When so much is being invested in new facilities, when teaching is going to be lifted from the privacy of the class-room into public view, then a decision to introduce the new media in-evitably raises basic questions bout what is to be taught and why, how it is to be taught, and what effect it has. An educational system rarely has a better occasion to re-examine its content, methods and results. If an educational system plunges into an extensive new-media operation without such initial self-scrutiny; if it begins to produce materials which are to be disseminated on a broad scale without reviewing the goals toward which the materials are supposed to be leading people; if it fails to weigh alternative ways, to pursue these goals in order to choose the best; if it invests so much money, time and manpower in new practices without measuring some of their effects and feeding back this information to its planners and programmers—then it is missing a rare opportunity to improve itself in fundamental ways.

It must be remembered that the great effeciency of the media in distributing education means that they can make either good or had education more widespread. They can distibute only what is put into them.

When the Media are Most Useful

Under any such careful scrutiny, the new educational media are most likely to commend themselves for use in a context of change. They are not likely to save money or to make a great impact if they are merely addd on to do a little better what is already being done. Not that enrichment and supplemental uses are not justifinable; films and television, for example, have often proved useful in supplementing and deepening direct teaching, and on a lower level of cost and complexity the use of cut-out pictures and home-made learnings aids has often made exciting differences in class-rooms that have not been accustomed to any teaching aids (the UNRWA schools are examples). But the broadcast media, especially, are most likely to be used at their full power and efficiency when a system is trying to solve stubborn, basic problems or to bring about some fundamental change. That is to say, they are likely to be most attractive economically, and most useful educationally, when they are employed, for example, to help extend educational opportunites to those who lack them, to upgrade the level of instruction significantly, to improve and update large numbers of teachers, to introduce new subjects or a new curriculum—in other words, to do something distinctly and significantly new. This is why the new media are especially attractive to developing, countries, even though the scarcity or economic and technological resources and of trained persons makes it more difficult to introduce them there. But even a more developed schools system will do well to follow the strategy of concentrating the potential of its new media on the most urgent change points' in the system—that is, the places where educators agree that change and improvement are strongly needed but most difficult to achieve by ordinary means. Herein lies the basic difference between an 'enrichment' approach and more strtegic and advantageeous uses of the new educational media.

The Concept of Critical Mass

Both economically and educationally, the concept of a critical mass is an important one for teh effectieness of the mass media. They are likely to be economically feasible and advantageous only after a certain critical point of size has been reached when their distibutive effieciencies can justify their relatively high initial cost. Although a small amount of suppoementary aid from the new media may improve the effect of what a teacher of field officer is doing at present, the media are most likely to justify themselves only when used on a sufficient scale and intensity of programme and audience, and on a problem of sufficient importance, to ensure a not-worthy impact on the learnig of many people.

Our observation has been that the broadcast media, in particular, are more aften under-used than over-used, and are frequently spred too thin over too many audiences and learning objectives to achieve a significant impact on any one.

In many cases, too little is invested in their programming and in delivering a usable signal and keeping receivers operating. They are often used too tentatively—so few programmes concentrated on any one group of learners, so few receivers—that the unit costs are unbearably high, and therefore no one takes their value very seriously. They are frequently used to give minor help in a class-room when with greater concentration they could in fact provide major help. Unless they are given important enough tasks, used in sufficient mass, made full partners in solving real educational problems, supported strongly enough to make their impact felt with adequte technology over a considerable part of the system, they are unlikely to justify themselves, or to be taken very seriously, by the persons expected to use them.

Prospective users should understand the new media are not miracle drugs for ailing educational systems. Rather, they are potentially powerful system components that may be employed either efficiently or inefficiently. To use them efficiently requirer not only a willingness to integrate them into the system and give them tasks of importance, but also a large amount of careful planning, investment of sufficient capital, provision of adequate technology, the preparation of the best content a system can produce and the building of a stimulating context for its reception, the solving of a number of logistic problems, and above all the training and utilizationof highly qualified personnel in sufficient quantity.

More Specifically

We have tried above to identify, from our case studes and other evidence, some basic requirements and principles for the effective use of the new educational media. We turn now to a short list of more specific factors affecting success. This is not a check-list in the sense that each item necessarily needs to be checked as in the building of a successful project. But when the cases are viewed as a group these are the elements that seem to set apart the more successful ones from the less successful. Not every item appears in every successful case, but they appear with sufficient frequency to let us say with some assurance that if these elements are well represented in a project there is a hight probability of its success.

Beginning with a well-defined problem to be solveds, then, here are some of the main determinants in achieving an effective solution.

Preliminary Decisions

The probability of success is greater if a project : grows out of a *critical appraisal of needs and alternative solutions;* represents *an alternative of feasible size;* and is supported by the allocation of *adequate financial resources.* A critical *appraisal of needs and alternative solutions.* Schools and nations have a habit of mudding into the use of the new media. They go into the New practices, because they are 'supposed' to be a good thing, or because the country' 'should have television,' or because someone is willing to give them some equipment or a little free air time (until the schedule fills up). In other worlds they buy technology rather than the solution to a problem.

Sometimes this approach works, if a problem is identified after the fact and the available technology proves to be able to solve it. Just as often, though, the users find themselves with technology which they cannot really afford to use, and therefore they under-use it or use it poorly; or they find them-selves with priority problems and technology that simply do not match.

There is a great advantage in begining with the problem rather than with a commitment to any specific technology. It is to be recalled how UNRWA went about this. It identified its top-priority educational problem: 4,000 uncertificated teachers scatterd among distant refugee sites, with such a large attrition of trained teachers that the proportion of uncertificated ones rises each year despite the input from three teacher-training colleges. In -service training was the obvious solution. With the aid of a Unesco expert, UNRWA reviewed the alternatives, rejected television and radio for practical reasons, and decided upon a relatively inexpensive combination of correspondence study, field supervisors to conduct weekly seminars and to advise the teachers on their class-room performance, and summer workshops for more intensive periods of training. The system uses on media technology more sophisticated than film strips and a few recordings. These are used only in the workshops; for their class-rooms the teachers are taught to clip pictures and produce home-made learning aids. The plan realistically fits the need and the available resources.

Samoa, too, reviewed very intelligently the logical alternative ways to solve its dominant problem, namely, how to raise the level of instruction very quickly. Among the possbilites considered was the replacing of the entire. Samoan teacher corps with imported and well-trained teachers, or replacing perhaps one-third of the Samoan teachers with such imports, or greatly expanding the teacher-training programme and sending the trainees out of Samoa for the last six or eight years of their preparation. For what seemed to be good and sufficient reasons, they rejected each of these alternatives as being too slow, too expensive or simply impracticable, and decided upon an approach making heavy use of new technology, consolidating the schools and sharing the teching of a few expert instructors through television, together with special help to the class-room teachers in managing their part of the task. That decision was made after calculating the resources likely to be required for this new and unconventional system and after assessing its likely educational results.

On the other hand, we have seen countries where $18,000 video-tape recorders are still in packing cases after many months, because there is really no use for them; where shools use their expensive television sets less than one hour per week while in class-rooms they are crying for help that could be given in far geater abundance through radio; countries where a sophisticated audio-visual centre with a quarter of a million dollars' worth of equipment stands little used, whereas a better analysis of the problem might have led the country to use the same money to help teachers make their own simple pictures and learning aids for their projectorless class-rooms. Obviously, these countries began with the technology arther than with the problem.

An alternative of feasible size. By 'feasible' in this instance we mean big enough but not too big; big enough to do the necessary job at acceptable unit costs, but not so big that it outruns the available resources. A large number of the projects we have studied would show a fairly dramatic rduction in unit costs if they could be used to serve several times as many people, or if they could be used during more hours in the day to carry more service. Economically speaking, they are under-used. Some of the cases have more technology than they need for their audience and their problem, or, to put it another way, they do not have enough people to serve to use their technology at its most efficient level. In other cases, however, there are more people still unserved, more needs to meet, and an adequate technology for the purpose; but, usually for lack of resources, the technology is used to only a fraction of its capability, and people go unserved, needs go unmet. Educationally, it is far better to meet the needs and have wasted capability, than to make little, ineffective use of technology an still have wasted capability. To put it concretely, with its present equipment Samoa could serve many thousands more pupils at lower cost per student (if more students lives in Samoa), but given the problem to be solved and the particular resources available for solving it, it makes better sense to cover the Samoan schools with sixf channels, as is now being done, and have some unused potential, than to make only minor use of television and merely scratch the surface of the problem.

It is tempting to say that a country that can broadcast only a few hours school television a week might well consider whether it should be in television at all—whether radio or something else would better meet its needs. But this is not always true, for it may be that the country has a need which requires only a small number of hours and which television can meet better than any other medium. Teacher training, to take one example, might conceivably be greatly aided (and without excessive cost) by a small anount of television time bought from existing stations. Similarly, a small-scale pilot project serving, say, one per cent of the school population of a country may be justified if it tries out a technology and builds a reservoir of skills.

Unfortunately, however, it usually does not happen this way. A country does not analyse its problem and prescribe a few hours of television, or engage in a pilot project to prepare for a possible nation-wide expansion. More often, it happens that a country finds itself with limited access to an expensive technological capability, and not enough resources in money or manpower to make any significant use of it for education. Or it disperses the limited broadcast time and resources over too many problems and objectives with little effect, rather than concentrating them on one or two in the hope of obtaining substantial results.

Adequate financial resources. The world of the new media is littered with cases in which the financial requirements have been underestimated, leading to lopsided schemes and disappointment. There is no need to name examples here. Well-meaning and courageous men have ventured into media projects, not realizing the full resource requirements for success or else trusting that the finances would become available, and have been handicapped constantly by lack of equipment, undependable equipment, weak signal, scarcity of trained personnel, inability to extent the service where it is needed, and the absence of other essential materials they could not afford. Countries have sometimes accepted outside help to initiate a without adeqately considering how and whether they could eventually carry it on with their own resources.

These problems should be considered in the preliminary stages. How much will it cost to provide a technology that will operate efficiently enough so that the focus of attention can be on education rather then on machinery or money? How much will it cost to expand the pilot project if it works well? If resources are not likely to be available to carry these eventual costs, then the desision should be reconsidered.

Matters of Organization

The probability of success is also greater if a project has: *strong support from top authrity; unity of purpose among the authrities responsible* for different parts of the facilites and programme: and *broad involvement* within the-educational system in the new project.

Strong support from top authrity. Our observation has been that strong support from the top, otener pperhaps than any other element, makes the difference between an easy an successful introduction of a media project, and a difficult and doubtful project. Samoa could never have undertaken the degree of change it did, against bult-in opposition and delays, except for the determination of the governor that change would occur. With this support, things that would have been impossible became easy. The firm support of the superintendent and school board in the pioneer Hagerstown project is picked out by all observers as one of the key factors in making that project possible. The stong support of the Minister of Education, who before he cecame minister had been chairman of the chief planning committee for school radio, played a large part in Thailand's successful development of its school broadcasting service. On the other hand, Colombia's first attempt at school television ended abruptly when the government changed, and the new chief of state did not have the personal interest in the project shown by his predecessor. In more than one country, support from the top has dwindled, after a country got television, and the educational part of television has found itself neglected if not disinherited.

Support from the top down, however, can be illusory, if vested entirely in one man, whatever his rank and position, for the one man's departure from the scene can bring the project to an untimely end. Thus it is wise to develop support from a number of well-placed leaders, both inside an outside the educational system, in order to ensour continuity of support over a sufficiently long period to get the project well established.

Unity of purpose among the responsible authrities. One of the things that strong support from the top accomplshes is to minimize organizational difficulties further down the line. The classical difficulty is between information and education, one usually owning the facilities, the other responsible for the schools. More often than not, initiative for the educational use of the media starts with the media experts rather than with the educators. The rural radio forum in India was organized mainly under All India Radio. Telescuola was organized as a part of Radiotelevisione Italiana. These two projects seem to have managed to work out their organizational problems, but others have not been successful. Typically the ministry of education comes in late, with some reluctance and much suspicion of the new techniques. All too often, when the reverse in true and the educators are eager to use the new technology, education has a low priority with the operators of the stations. It costs extra to broadcast during the day-time. They are reluctant to turn over station time they might sell. And so on.

Of course, these problems are minimized where an educational system owns its facilities, or where support from the top helps to integrate the services. Where this is not the case, it is useful to bring in the ministry of education early, and above all to start with a problem, rather than simply a technology. The country-wide recognition of Australia's and New Zealand's responsibilities for educating their rural children made it much easier for co-operation to come about between radio and educational services, and Algeria's obvious problem must also have united the different services there.

The need for co-operation appears not only at the level of ministries, however, but also much lower. Togo, for example, reports come problems of local co-ordination between various rural development programmes, which sometimes seem to conflict or even to compete with the radio forum. In Honduras, the recuitment of leaders and viewing group was effective especially in the districts where the parish organizations were strongly favourable. In India, one of the great problems in expanding the forum was obtaining enough help and involvement from the district and block personnel. An instructive example of the care that has been taken in an obviously efficient operation to ensure co-operation is described in the Japanese case, where an elaborate structure of interlocking committees and organizations involves the correspondence schools of the country, the NHK school, the Ministry of Education, the NHK producers, the teachers who write the textual materials and the class-room teachers, in a ten-month exercise of planning and consultation of the next year's programmes.

Another place where it is necessary to seek co-operation is between the central source of programmes and the schools or groups that use them. Sometimes this is a begin problem. For example, MPATI had difficulty in serving so many schools because of their varied time schedules and curricula. Even in Thailand, with a single school system run by the ministry, there were difficulties in fitting broadcast times to school schedules. In very few countries, and even very few large school system, do the schools observe common schedules. The story is doubtless apocryphal that a certain ministry of education official once pulled out his watch and remarked that at that particular moment every grade 5 child in his country was having a lesson on the Eskinmo. Because common schedules like this are so unusual, the need to co-operate in deciding on programme schedules is an important one.

Sometimes, however, the problem is not so benign. In some countries there is a deep suspicion of the centre. Schools tend to think that a new programme is being forced on them. Therefore, if local support and co-operation are desired it is necessary to invole representatives of these schools in the planning and despel their suspicions.

Broad involvement Attitude research on new media project indicates without exception, that the more experience a teacher has had with one of the new educational media, the more likely he is to be favourable toward it. MPATI research showed that teachers who had never used television in the class-room were more likely than others to oppose its use. Chicago Junior College research showed that one a college teacher had taught on television he tended to be enthusiastic about the new medium as a teaching device; but a college teacher who had only taught in the class-room tended to be suspicious of instruction by television and resistant to it. Attitude studies in general have demonstrated the value of involving as many teachers as possible, as deeply as possible, in the plans and preparations for the use of class-room television. By wide involvement and by using almost wholly local materials, Hatgerstown was able to build a sense of localness about the programme. It was their programme, their teaching. No threat was involved; nothing was being imposed. The responsibility for making it an effective programme was their alone.

In as much as the chief source of resistance to new-media programmes is usually in the teacher corps, and the chief source of effectiveness—after the content of the programmes—is the context built up by the class-room teachers, this kind of involment is a very important result to achieve.

In Samoa, the changes were clearly imposed from the top, and they were threatening to many teachers and minor officials. Furthermore, most of the technicians, and the teachers in the glamorous new television sutdios, came from the outside, as did the chief advisers to the project. This presented problems of morale. Resistance from a few officials resulted in one show-down which had to be resolved by the governor getting rid of certain United States personnel who had preceded the television project. A wholly new strategy of educational method could hardly be developed successfully if a substantial number of persons within the programme were hostile to the new strategy. Therefore, the action that was taken in Samoa to involve teachers in the project was specially significant. In the summer before the television began, the class-room teaches were brought together with the studio teaches, the producers, supervisors, and other personnel concerned with the new project, to work together in planning the curriculum. Nothing better could have been done at that stage to involve the teacher, inform the, and dispel some of their suspicions. Furthermore, it was in the best sense an in-service training device. The same thing was repeated the next summer, and in the meantime a great deal of help was given the class-room teachers and they were offered every opportunity to register their comments and advice after every television programme. These actions have paid off by raising the teacher' morale and by the acceptance of the new methods.

Without mentioning more examples, let us merely say that wherever in these cases there has been a broad involvement of teaching personnel there has tended to be broad local co-operation.

Matters Planning and Preparation at the Centre

The probability of success is greater if a project is given: *a planned and phased introduction; technical adequacy; a well-trained technical and programmer staff, with continuty of key personnel; and high-quality media content, based on the national goals.*

A planned and phased introduction of the new medium or method. Relatively few countries, in our judgement, give enough time and effort to planning and preparing for the introduction of a new-media project. Once the decision is made to go ahead, the pressures and compulsions are to get into action fast, ready or not, and let time take care of the problems. Those involved are usually so caught up with the technology or finacing or building, or so busy traying to do a new thing while continuing all the old responsibilities, that one day they simply find themselves operating an educational project with new tools. Nowhere in the old adage, 'haste makes waste', more applicable than here.

In this connexion, we can recally with admiration the carefully phased introduction of television for literacy and fundamental education in the Ivory Coast. The first year, when the method was being tried, there was no television at all-merely visual aids with a teacher and a group of students. The second year, they used closed-circuit television. In the thrid year, they put the material on open-circuit television. In the third year, they put the material on open-circuit television, but ony for groups in the capital city of Abidjan. Only in the fourth year did they begin to extend the programme on open-circuit elsewhere in the country.

Thailand also showed admirable prodence in moving into radio. When the ministry got its own station. It began with a series of evening programmes that required no adjustment to school syllabus or schedule. When the transmitter power was increased so that they could hope to reach a large number of the rural schools, where help was most needed.

They looked into the needs and requirements of a school service. They measured the area where the station delivered a usable signal. They they interviewed in some detail the school officials, and many of the teachers within the cover-age area, to find out what services they needed most, what their schedules were and what class-room facilities they had. They made arrangement by which schools could by sets on a favourable plan, assembled subject-matter committiees to decide on the content of radio courses, arranged a workshop for teachers who would be using radio in their schools, tried to give some training and experience to a few potential studio teachers, and only then—four years after the station was available to them—did they launch a school radio service. Now they are learning something about television by doing two thrirty-minute programmes a week.

Niger, likewise, has planned carefully and moved slowly into school television, and Japan into a television-supported correspondence programme. These are exceptions. Generally countries hurry into the new media without looking hard or long at where they are going. This often results in a difficult first year, sometimes in an unfortunate first impression, and occasionally in a pattern of ineffectiveness from which they can never extricate themselves.

It is not always easy to look beyond the first year. When Arequipa inroduced its first radio programme for the Andean community, it doubtless did not foresee that the drive and enthusiasm of the founders would lead them to take on four new programmes and fairly explode into a level of operation for which they had not prepared. When India operated the trial forums at Poona, the difficulties of expanding to a national programme were not foreseen, and in fact the expansion itself was not envisaged.

We are not suggesting that there should be no sense of urgency about getting started—for the problems which would warrant the use of new media are almost always urgent ones. Nor are we suggesting that the future be clearly seen and all the necessary resources be assured for years aheads before a start is made, for few starts would then every be made. But it seems to be a usefull principle that whenever a pilot project is undertaken some planning for expansion in case of success should be a part of the preparation for the project. Without that, a successful pilot project may lose momentum, as the rural forum did during the three years before India was able to expand it. Indeed, planning for a possible long-range extension may fundamentally change the nature of the pilot itself. It may be placed in more strtegic spot for expansion; it may take on a different shape; continuance and expansion may even present such problems that the country may decide the pilot projects is not worth doing.

Technical adequacy. A country pioneering in the new media should be sure that the technolgy is functioning well enough for a maximum of effort to be devoted to teaching effectively with it.

The excellent and extensive television network of Italy made Telescuola's job immeasurably easier. The massive technical capability of Samoa allowed the educators there to concentrate on teaching, rather than to worry over whether a programme would go out or be received. The widespread radio equipment and know-how in Australia, the presence of radios in most homes and of two-way radios in many of the homes in the outback, made it relatively easly to introduce radio as an ally of correspondence study. In Japan the almost universal distribution of receiving sets, the very large NHK netweork, and the abundance of electronic skills, removed all technical uncertainties from the decision to use radio and television for out-of-school pupils. The programmes could be delivered; the question was only, what kinds or programmes?

In situations like the above, the technical part of the operation is made to seem very easy. As in the Arequipa and Honduras projects, where technical facilities are not so satisfactory, where the signal is weak the sometimes unclear, it is not so easy. In Thailand there have been great problems delivering a signal to distant schools because of interence from new commerical stations. In one country we noticed that the radio transmitter was so old that the circuit diagrams had been lost, and a considerable job of rewiring was required for any except the smallest repair jobs. In another country the television equipment, although relatively new, was so poorly maintained that operators could never be sure that it would be functioning on a given day. We have already mentioned the troubles in one African country where there were power failures that would blot out the transmitter at one time and many receivers at another time, so that there was no predictability about any programme schedule. The problem of receiver maintenance is a serious one in every developing country. In some countries, ailing receiving sets and projectors have to be sent to the capital city where they may remain for several months before being returned. In others, the problem has been solving by a travelling maintenance service, as in Samoa or Maharashtra State in India.

It is never easy to solve these technological problems, but wherever, it is not done the potential effectiveness of a programme is being undermined, and the productive attention of a staff and teacher is being diverted from the main business at hand. Broadcast and film technolgy is no longer new. Good equipment and training in the skills required for its use are readily available. The least that a country moving into a project like-television or radio should demand is that the transmission facilities be reliable, that the sudio equipment be adquate to the task at hand, that enough sets be made available to reach the audience the programmes are meant to serve, and that there be some reliable arrangement for maintaining those sets. In the case of a film project, there should be a satisfactory way to obtain, store, and circulate films as needed. If these technical requirements cannot be met satisfactorily, then a country should seriously face the question of whether it is yet ready for this technology. Again we are not suggesting that, in developing countries especially, nothing be done on the educational side until the technical kinds are ironed out, but rather that a well-conceived and well-balanced project plan will provide for adequate means and time to take care of these technical matters so that the educational programme, once begun, is not shackled by technical difficulties.

A well-trained technical and programme staff, and continuity. In the case of educational television especially, technical training is a problem for any developing country where the medium is new and where there is no electronics industry. Yet in general it is less a problem than training in programme-making and production. For one thing, technical training is much the same throughout the world. The skills that will let a man operate a transmitter or repair a circuit in France will make it possible for him to do the same in Togo. And therefore there are many places were training can be given, many places from which trainers can be borrowed and many handbooks of wide applicability.

Programme graining, however, tends to vary in different place because of its substantive elements. The skills of camera angles, lighting, fading scenes in and out, and so forth, are pretty much the same throughout the world. But beyond these lie the problems of adapting a programme about a certain subject to a certain audience, and this has local elements than can be generalized only to a degree. Therefore, to train its programme staff a country needs not only the general kind of training that applies to the use of tèlevision everywhere, and which can be give anywhere that good intructional television is in use, but also some training or experience with a local audience and local subject-matter—and this can only be given at home.

The need has been solved various ways. A very large number of oversas training fellowships have been offered by the aid-giving countries. A number of experienced persons have been sent to give training in countries where the media are new. The general opinion is that, once equiment is a available in the country, more training and perhaps more realistic training can be given for the same amount of money, and with less disruption to the programme, by sending experts to that country than by sending trainees to other countries.

For the most part, the developing countries have improvised their training programmes on what was availabe to them. Thailand, for example, got its first educational radio training from a programme director who was experienced in broad-casting. On two occasions it borrowed experinced producers from the Australian radio. The stayed some months, giving training. It was able to send serveral people abroad, to the British Broadcasting Company among others, for short periods of study and practice. And gradually it has been able to raise the level of experteness in its staff.

Every case in our study, except those in the countries most advanced in the media, has had problems with training a staff. This obviously should be one of the first matters of central planning, after the mission and the general method have been decided upon. There should be a plan to train the needed personnel, and at least a substantial nucleus of them should be trained before the project starts.

Especially in television and radio, but to a certain extent in all the media there is also a need to train supervisory users of the media, who may be teachers or monitors or forum chairmen or extension agents. We shall talk about their training a little later, but let us record here that they too should be considered in planning the necessary training for the project, and they too must have some training before the project starts.

To derive full value from a trainings programme, one must have substantial continuity in staffo. Two customs espacially—the practice of frequently shifting government employees to other responsibilities, and the practice of bringing in expatriate help for short terms—have caused many problems for educational media project.

Neither this memorandum nor any project is likely to be able to do anything about a government's custom of transferring its officials, or the custom of hiring expatriates on short term contracts, if expatriates are needed. Yet what can be done, shoul be. Governments themselves should be aware of the effect on an innovative project of changing leaders in mid-stream. If expatriates are needed, every effort should be made to keep them longer than two years, which is a common basic contract. More than one administrator has remarked carefully about the two-year contract that it takes one year for a newcomer to learn to teach in a new culture, and another year for him to get ready to leave. It is hardly necessary to point out that if a training programme can be built into a project from the first it will supply a resource of able people for replacements at lowerlevels, and will ultimately increase the competence and experience at all levels and make it unnecessary to bring in short-term help.

We have talked at length about training, because a prerequisite to a full development of intructional media, and especially educational television and radio, is clearly an improved and greatly expanded programme of training. The product needed most by these media is still scarce even in the industialized and developed world—a truly professional instructional broadcaster. This kind of person need not necesarily have worked professionally in both fields, but he must have the professional skills and understanding of both fields. In addition, there is great need for educators who have learned to organize a school and to train a teacher corps in the kind of activities that constitute the school's part of a new-media teaching/learning system. These persons, too, are scarce. Viewed globally, therefore, the progress of these new media is being held up by a scarcity or training in the new educational strategy. Without such training, and a greatly increased supply of such trained persons, instructional television and radio will not soon arrive at the point where they can consistently produce programmes that will stand up from both an educational and a broadcasting point of view, and the school that enter instructional broadcasting will have to repeat many of the trials and many of the errors of the pioneers in the field.

High-quality media content, based on the national goals. There is no substitute for quality in radio and television programmes of in films or textual materials. Mediocrity can assume giant proportions on a mass medium. The complaints that we have heard round the world testify that a high standard of quality is not always attained. Television in particular makes unusual qualitative demands, especially because of its voracious appetite. A producer may be allowed to work for six month up to 100 television programmes. A teacher can sometimes work four years on a textbook, but during the same period he would have to prepare some hundreds of television programmes. Furthermore, educational television is often in public competition with other forms of television. It is compared not so often with class-room teaching where poor training is hid from view but with the more polished standards of entertainment or public affairs television, or with some ideal standard of what educational television ought to be. It is seen by a teacher's colleguaes, by his superiors, often by the parents of his students. Therefore, any teacher courageous and able enough to teach on televison deserves ample time and help to prepare, in short, a fair chance to do his very best. And the students also deserve nothing less.

Any country entering educational television will be well advised, despite the pressures to hurry, to recruit its very best teachers for the purpose and to give them all of the time and assistance necessary to do a first-rate, job. Only thus can the use of television be justified and the standards of teaching be lifted throughut the system.

We mentioned earlier in the chapter that when a

country begins to use the new media in their widespread and public way it has an unequalled chance to review its curricula and programmes against the national goals: what it should be teaching, and what kinds of graduates it should be producing. This is the kind of review that few countries seem to find the time for, amidst all the other demands of entering the media, and it seems a pity that this should be so. For only if they can step back long enought to look at what they have been doing and what now want to do, will they make the best of their new opportunity.

Matters of Relationship Between Centre

Logistics for delivering instructional materials. There is not much to be said about this, except that it sometimes paralyses a programme. Where the mail is reliable and transportation is easy, there is less trouble than elsewhere, but even under such favourable circumstances, a shipping and delivery system must be organized. Reports come in from many places about failures: materials for villages sidetracked in the corner of a development office; materials for study groups too often not delivered; reports from forums held up on an office desk before reaching the programme people, and so forth. The point is that these logistical arrangements are becomings increasingly important as the emphasis of media programmes shifts more and more to what happens at the point of reception, for this means that more guides, more study materials, more supplementary materials must be delivered.

Feed-back from users. As public as the media may seem to an audience, they constitute a lonely experience to a person using them, and particularly to a teacher who is used to talking to a class-room filled with reacting children. Every new teacher on television or radio speaks about this: he cannot tell whether his pupils are understanding, he cannot tell whether he is allowing long enough pauses for responses, he cannot tell whether his humour is going over. Therefore, most educational media projects put considerable effort into getting feed-back from the audience to the teacher. Where there has been no time or resource to do this, one field some of the least effective programmes.

Different countries and systems do it in different ways. Italy has six children in the studio to react to the teaching and to set the pace for the teacher. Most schools systems ask for regular reports from thef class-room teachers about the media programmes: Samoa has very good evaluation forms, which are illustrated in the case study. The rural farums encourage reports from the forum secretary or monitor back to the radio station, which then repeats and answers a certain number of the questions and comments. Togo in particular emphasizes the importance and delicacy of this dialogue between the forums and the government. Thailand receives not only written reports from teachers, but also reports from school visitors and occasional workshops—to keep the teacher from feeling 'like a blind marksman', they say. Japan commission certain schools to survey their correspondence students on the usefulness of the broadcasts.

None of these, however, is a complete substitute for a teacher's opportunity to observe reactions to his teaching in a full-size live class-room. Therefore, some countries tape a certain number of programmes so that studio teaches can visit class-rooms to observe their own teaching. Samoa tapes all its programmes, in order to give its studio teaches maximum opportunity to spend time in a receiving class-room. Japan even finds opportunities for its teachers to visit correspondence students in order to find out first-hand what they think of the programmes.

Contact with teachers and moniters: From an African country come reports that *animateours in* remote places often feel neglected because they have not been visited since the progrmme began. From a Latin American country comes an expression of gratitude for the special help that television has given the isolated, less trained teacher—but a reminder that even with television it is still necesary to supply that kind of teacher with advice an directions.

This relationship has become vastly more important than it used to be, because in media have vastly expanded the school. In an effective radio or television system, especially, there can really no longer be an isloated schoo, for there is one teacher in a studio and one teacher in a class-room who are co-operating in teaching the same children, even though the two teachers may be fifty miles curriculum, on a centrally determinded system, its teachers being on a team with central teacher. And therefore it is necessary to keep in close touch will all the schools, to solicit their ideas and advice, and to help them make good use of the central services.

In Thailand, the supervisors have had to work hard to keep good studio-class-room relationships. In Colombia, the Peace Corps utilization volunteers have done the job, and Colombians are now being appointed to take it over as the Peace Corps phases out. MPATI devotes a large section of its operating budget to relations with its member schools, throught visits, mail and workshops. And these requirements do not apply solely to schools, for in India perhaps the central finding of the rural forum is the importance of strong and competent field support.

Maters Connected with Providing an Effective Context for Learning at the Receving End

A study or discussion group at point of reception, adequately equipped and supplied. The evidence on this point is very impressive. Australia and New Zealand found that there was a great deal to be gained educationally by making it possible for their correspondence students to listen and study together. UNRAW decided that. Even with a good correspondence programme, a weekly field seminar was a necessary component of the learning system. From the begining, Italy recognized the superiority of teaching both secondary and adult television students in supervised groups, rather than alone. Ivory Coast found that it needed supervised groups in order to teach fundamental education by television. Peru and Honduras found that they needed a netwok of learning and viewing-and-listening centres. The Colombia research demonstrated that, even in the case of such sophisticated learners as teachers more learning resulted when the teachers viewed a class together and discussed it. Both India and Togo discovered that the listening-discussion forum made an essential contribution to the effectiveness of their village radio. And in the places where television or radio are fed effectively into school class-rooms, special efforts are almost invariably made to see that the class at the receiving end is indeed an active learning group, prepared to make use of the broadcast. There can be no doubt of the conclusion from these cases: whereas a motivated student will learn from the media by himself, he will learn subtantially more in a well-operated study group at the point of reception.

The equipping and supplying of this receiving group is a matter of some importance and often of some difficulty. Samoa found it necessary to consolidate and rebuild schools in order to have an efficient place to make use of televison. A survey of teachers in a Latin American country illustrates the difficulties that can arise when schools are not so well equipped for televison: there are not enough seats for the pupils while they are viewing (this was reported by more than one teacher out of three); electrical failures frequently blot out parts of the broadcast schedule (more than one out of three); it is impossible to make the viewing room dark enough (one out of three); there is only one televison set in the school, and changing class-rooms to use it causes great confusion (more than one out of three). An African country reports that it costs in the neightbourhood of $1,300 to install a television set because it is necessary also to bring in electricity. Oddly, enough, more problems of this kind are reported from school users than from adult users of the media, but it must be remembered that many adult groups use school receivers outside of school hours.

Maintaining receivers and other field equipment. In developing countries this is one of the nagging problems. In countries where electronics are highly developed and broadcasting is widely distributed (Europe, North America, Japan, Australia and New Zealand, and so forth) it is only a minor problem; repair facilities are highly developed. However, any developing country has to make special arrangements to keep its receivers playing. One African country, as we have noted, after broadcasting to schools for several years, found that only 25 per cent of its sets were in working order to receive the programmes. Thailands has mentioned the great difficulty and importance of providing repair service without having to sent the receiver to Bangkok for expert attention. Togo lists the problem of replacing batteries and repair sets in the interior of the country as one of the major problems it must solve in order to expand its forums as planned. In India, the problem of maintaining sets has been a crucial one throughout the history of the radio forum. Solutions to the problem have taken different forms. The slowed one is to send the equipment back to the capital city for repair. In some countries an attempt has been made to build up local repair competence, serving a town or a group of village. The most typical pattern, however, is that of Samoa and of parts of India, where competent technicians answer repair calls in a jeep or small truck. They do repair work that can be done on the spot; when they have to take a receiver back to headquarters to work on it, they are often able to leave a replacement set.

It is important to remember that maintenance problems are compounded when a variety of 'brands' of receiving sets or other equipment are used, for then more spare parts must be kept on hand, and the maintenance crew must learn the intricacies of repairing a variety of models.

Competent supervision of learning activity at the point of reception. This is another point that came out most impresively from a very large number of cases. Colombia found that systematic questioning on the main points of a broadcast would greatly incrase the learning, and that teachers could easily be taught to conduct this kind of systematic practice. Even where the reception group is a school class and the supervisor is a professional teacher, most systems try to help the techer develop adequate techniques for weaving a broadcast into a class hour, and for directing the discussion, review, and other learning activities that would reinforce the substance of the broadcast. In Colombian this has been the task of the Peace Corps utilization volunteer and his Colombian counterparts. In Samoa, supervision, workshops, in-service broadcasts, and teacher-guidance materials are all used to help the class-room teacher play his part.

Where the receiving group is not a school class, ideally the supervisor should still be as professional and as well trained for his job as possible. It is quite significant that Italy has turned from the use of reltively untrained monitors for its Telescuola secondary-school groups to the use of relatively inexperiend teachers or advanced students of education. This is a symbol of the change that has taken place during the last half-dozen years in the patterns of media use in developing countries. It used to be thought that most of the teaching was done by the televison, radio, or films anyway, and that practically and kind of chariman would be satisfactory for the group. Both experience and research cast grave doubts on this assumption. The better the supervision and direction, the more the group learned. And therefore a great deal more attention has been turned lately to the problems of now to select a monitor (or animateur, in the French-speaking countries) and how to train him.

A leader—an educated man-someone who has had some experience with teaching or at least with presiding over groups—these are the qualities most often sought in selecting a monitor. Of course, where the leaders are uneducated, where the best-educated man has had only two or three years of schooling, some improvising may be necessary. Some special training for the monitors is desirable. Most countries using monitors arrange training courses for them ranging from a few days to a few weeks. It is a cruel problem because the more definitely a man belongs in the leadr class, the less likely he is to be able to afford the time for a long taining course. In some parts of India, rural forum officers are brought together for a day or two. In Togo, likewise, the forum *antimateur* is sent to a central place for two to three days of taining. When an *animateur* is appointed from a community in the interior of the Ivory Coast he is sent to Abidijan for two weeks' course. This is about as much training as the new countries have found it possible to give to their monitors, but they report that is makes a great difference. In view of the brevity of this training, the original selection of the man and the help he is given after his taining seem doubly important.

Direct contact betwen pupil and teacher, if study groups cannot be brought together. The importance of motivation for learning at home has been imphasized by the experience of all of the countries oand organizations among our cases that try to bring schooling into the home. It is interesting that Chicago, dealing with a sophisticated group of college students, who would be expected to be in control of their own students, who would be expected to be in control of their own study patterns and practices, should still find it necessary to provide a great many opportunities for two-way communication between student and teacher—telephone consultation, papers sent in for comments, even a few meetings on campus. Japan likewise found that it helped greatly with its employed corresondence students to bring groups of them together for ten to twenty days a year. Australia has done interesting things to personalize the pupil/teacher relationship in its correspondence courses, by means of personal letters with each lesson, exchange of pictures, broadcasts especially designed to encourage and motivate correspondence students, and in some cases the two-way Flying Doctor radio—all these in addition to the supervision of study groups at home. New Zealand has tried to keep the pupil/teacher ratio in its correspondence courses about what it is in the class-room so that there will be plently of opportunity for getting acquainted by letter. It has school assemblies by radio, school colours, a school magazine. Just as a great deal more emphasis is now being put on the study group at the reception point, so also is there more and more attention paid to the problem of how to make the home student feel a part of the group with a teacher and class-mates.

Summing up

In this chapter we have tried to provide a brief theoretical framework, followed by a list of requirements which seem in large proportion to be well met by the more successful cases, less well by the less successful ones.

A theory of educational use of the media must almost necessarily begin with the distributive powers of the media—their ability to multiply and disseminate with great efficiency some selected parts of the information available to the system in which they work. Used in an educational system they let educators distribute teaching resources in a more efficient way. Whereas the older media, such as the book, could distribute the substance of teaching, the new media, notably radio and televison, can share teaching itself. With their help, the educator can share some of his best teaching more widely, offer specialized teaching and special subjects where they would otherwise not be available, and in some cases extend the opportunities of schooling beyond the school.

To do this well, the media must be integrated into the educational system. They cannot stand apart from it; their content is the system's content; their teachers are the system's teachers. This implies broad involvement, acceptance, support. It implies also that a context of learning activity will be built around the media at the point of reception. Except in the rarest instances, the media cannot be counted upon to do an adequate educational job alone. It is not enough to try to your content into listeners or viewers; rather the goal is to stimulate learning activity. This means that special pains must be taken with the content to stimulate this kind of activity, and that planed activity must be built around the media, whether in a class-room, in an out-of-school learning group, or a village forum. This requires some organization, some supervision by a teacher or a monitor, and arrangements for a flow of information back from the receiving group to the transmiting teachers. In other words, the most effective use of the educational media, especially the broadcast media, falls into a pattern of team teaching, in which a studio teacher, a class-room teacher or group monitor, and perhaps another teachers speaking, a class-room teacher or group monitor, and perhaps another teacher speaking through textual, exercise, and outline materials combine their efforts, each in his own best way.

The introduction of new median offers an educational system an unequalled opportunity to review its goals, curriculum and methods of instruction. This is partly because the media are likely to be most efficient, both educationally and economically, when used in a context of change—to expand the educational system, to upgrade instruction significantly, to introduce new subjects or a new curriculum, to upgrade large numbers of teachers, or to reach beyond the present coverage of the school in other words, to do something distinctly new. This is why they are so attractive to developing countries, althought it is more difficult to introduce them in those countries.

Another reason why the time of introduction of educational media is a good time to review goals and means is that the media by their nature require a certain critical mass to be reached before they are used most efficiently, either in terms of economics or in terms of education. The programme services and quality must be of a substantial scale and intensity if they are to achieve any really significant educational result, and the number of learners served must be large enough to translate the relatively high over-all investment and running costs into low unit costs which can be borne by available education resources. And the media are most likely to be taken serviously and built into educational practices when used for a problem sufficiently important and on a scale sufficiently large that the goal, the impact, and the result can be readily seen.

Turnings to more specific matters, we said that if we had to name only one prerequisite of effectiveness of a new-educational-media project, we would say, let it begin with a problem. Let it not begin with a piece of new technology, but with a recognized and singnificant problem for which the most appropriate technology could be selected. Then we listed seventeen requirements or elements that seemed, in large proportion, to separate the more effective from the less effective projects.

3

Creativity in Education

History reveals that there are periods when one dominant idea characterizes many facets of intellectual life, for example, in 17th and 18th centuries mechanistic determinism flourished in physics and was markedly reflected in philosophy and economics. Man always finds himself in the midst of such periods. He passed through biological evolution and stepped into the era of cultural evolution. The path of cultural evolution led him to the greatest intellectual excellence and he was able to solve some technical problems but still he is faced with many serious social, educational and economic problems. The solutions largely depend upon the minds of men. whether they have been trained to think creatively or not rests with education.

Research in the field of creativity was seriously carried out from 1950 onwards and too long it was mainly the province of psychologists. But in recent years, educators also started doing systematic research on creativity to find out the new discoveries on the one hand, and add to the national development through the efficient use of multi-faceted talent on the other.

Researchers have shown that children are creative by nature for they have the innate ability to see new relationships and produce new combinations out of the existing things or their parts. They exhibit this tendency while in interaction with each other whether they are at work or play. This can blossom fully in them if their parents and teachers provide proper guidance and conducive environment to them. But it is distressing that in our schools proper attention is not paid to it. The teachers encourage students who are intelligent to them and who can give correct answer to the question. They hardly encourage students who are creative. Our school programmes also do not give due place to the educational experiences and proper environment which are essential to the development of creative potential. Many factors may be responsible for this handicap. Either, our teachers do not have adequate understanding of the creative process and the factors which foster or stifle creativity among children or they do not tolerate children who are non-conformists. Vernon has aptly remarked that "the present system is criticised for favouring conformists mentality—the pupil who is good at accepting the learning what his teachers tell him and thinking along conventional lines whereas it discourages spontaneous and independent thinking".

Van Dyk says that if we accept that the development of a child is a process by which the highest order of involvement with the world is attained, then creativity should be the educationist's primary concern because this kind of experience (involvement) is creative in nature. In view of this it becomes imperative for our educational planners that they recognise the value of creative talent and re-orient the system of education to cope with this valuable talent. Getzels and Jackson too admit that our educational structure is hampering the development of creativity. Other researchers have also expressed the same views. Anderson and others say "that the problem is that we have not-rained ourselves to cope with the creativity!! Torrance and others go further and distressingly point to the fact that the teachers are ill equipped to meet the needs of students with respect to creative. They do not know how to initiate, conduct, or evaluate creativity. They also feel uncomfortable with creativity students. The need arises when this valuable human characteristic is recognised at its own rights and exploited by the educators for the survival and also better development of society.

Creativity in Teaching and Learning

The purpose to educating the young is that they create a better world than we have created. They should create better works of art, science and literature; better livelihood; and a more just system of distribution of wealth. More important is that they also create a peaceful world blessed with more creative freedom through their creative behaviour. But it is painful to see that our education system does not reflect this in educational process. Not only our education system neglects but it too often suppresses the natural creativity of the young. Our teachers are interested in encouraging mostly convergent thinking ability in classroom and the children who is adept, is considered by them as intelligent one. Such students are encouraged by teachers as they follow the lines what their teachers dictate them. Such students are better known as conformists. Rarely such children are able to come out with original ideas of their own. There are other students who do not follow the conventional lines, teachers hardly care about them and label them as non-conformists. Mostly teachers get disturbed with their behaviour and do not pay due attention to the queries they raise. Their simple fault lies with their thinking in divergent ways and it is the divergent thinking abilities which are mainly responsible for making such students as non-conformists and unconventional.

This divergent thinking ability enables them to go

off in many different directions, generating new information from the given information and arriving at varied and unusual solutions to problems. Such children do not get satisfied with the routine type solutions to the problem like intelligent ones. They instead attempt to discover, invent, and come with original ideas of their own. No doubt, both the thinking abilities have their place in life but it is the divergent thinking abilities which are possibly the most useful one as these help in dealing with new and complex situations of life.

Most of the subjects that are taught in the schools could, in particular be taught in ways that stimulate and develop the creative problem solving skills of students. What do we need to provide in the schools is not the content that may lead to quite predictable and uniform outcomes by the students rather the outcome should be of unpredictable and diverse nature. If we wish to create creative education for the young then we shall, at first, recognise that one of our main priorities should be to identify an array of problems in each of the fields we teach, as far as possible, that may provide children opportunities to create multiple solutions to indentical problems. Next, we must help them to understand that most of the important problems they are likely to confront in their lives have several correct solutions, not simply one. *Second*, we must make it sure not only that the classroom tasks provide the children opportunities to formulate unique solutions to problems, but also, equally important, that students have opportunities to learn how to formulate questions and problems themselves. *Third*, creative education should aim at cultivating the students' sensibilities, the ability to sensitively experience the world so that the content upon which the student can reflect would be expanded.

Education is understood a powerful instrument which can help students to realize the creative talent optimally and fully. The need, thus, is to shift from a mere routine type of teaching to creative teaching and creative problem solving.

Creative Teaching

Creative teaching connotes two meanings, *one* on the one hand, it means teaching creatively which is possible when the teachers become more creative in aiding their learners. *Second* on the other hand, it means giving attention to creative problem-solving skills of students. In both the cases, the role of the student assumes great significance. He needs to be an active participant in the teaching learning process. He is personally responsible for his own learning. The role of the teacher should be only to stimulate, to guide, to provide a conducive climate, and the necessary equipment whileas the student has not to be a passive learner rather he should discover himself what he learns.

Education should become more individualised so that each child is able to learn at his own pace and progresses accordingly. The child should make an effort to achieve the goal. He should have immediate and adequate feedback so as to get his efforts reinforced. Mostly, the feedback should come through intrinsic rewards.

The child should not rely only on memorization and storing of information rather he needs to develop skills that can be employed for using the information in new and newer situations.

Instruction should be based on presentation of problems and seeking their solutions. The student should be as courageous as to counter any challenging problem but due precaution needs to be taken in the selection of problems. Only such a problem should be presented that is challenging but not discouraging one for the students. While representing their solutions to the problem the teacher should in no way make any personal criticism to the learners. One important point needs to be considered by the teachers that they attempt at understanding the intellectual capacity of each individual student fully so that they can use this information in a teaching-learning situation.

Teaching of Creativity

The question whether children can be taught to think creatively or left to chance, has been answered by many researchers. In fifties it was commonly thought that creativity, scientific discovery, the production of new ideas and the like had to be left to chance but Torrance in 1964 in one of his lectures in Ontario contradicted this view. He lamented that how any reasonable, well informed person can still hold this view. The amazing record of inventions, scientific discoveries and other creative achievements amassed through deliberate methods of creative problem-solving should convince even the most stubborn skeptic. Both laboratory and field experiments involving these deliberate methods of improving the level of creative behaviour have also been rather convincing. Further, in his classes and seminars he observed that students improved their ability to develop original and useful solutions to problems.

Other researchers are also of the view that creativity should not be left to chance instead it should be fostered through deliberate methods. The evidence is strong that five year old children lose much of their curiosity and excitement about learning, nine year old children become greatly concerned about conformity to the pressures of peer-groups and give up many of their creative activities, the middle and high school students show a new kind of concern for conformity to behavioural norms with the result that their thinking become more obvious, traditional, commonplace and safe. In view of this, it becomes prime responsibility of the teachers to search out methods and techniques that they employ in teaching-learning process to help students to think creativity. The teacher is expected to perform this job only when he has the knowledge of those factors which inhibit creative thinking among students. He should make every attempt to eliminate such obstacles in the teaching-learning situation:

(i) The pressure to conform is the major obstacle in eliciting creative responses. These pressures may come either through teacher-chosen goals and activities or conventional tests and rigid curri-culum;

(ii) Authoritarian attitudes as well as environment suppress the creative potential of young people as they put obstacles to the free, self-directive and self-responsible learning. Authoritarian education directs students to learn only what others have already discovered and organised, and lays emphasis on following directions, to do what one is told to do, and to solve only those problems which have fixed and predetermined answer;

(iii) Threat or ridicule of any kind injures the feeling of self-worth in students and put blocks in the release of these creative potential;

(iv) All types of external evaluation such as rewards or punishments or overemphasis on success arouses defensive attitude in students and thereby inhibit creative responses. Inflexible defense mechanisms and compulsive fears part of teachers also deter the productive tendency in students;

(v) An excessive guest for certainty also inhibit the creative responses. Teachers instill this habit in the students while making the demand for right answers only. These attitudes afterwards are expressed by students in all the facets of their lives and stop thinking creativity

(iv) Intolerance of the teachers to the playful attitude of students in connection with school work also stiffle creativeness. Any innovation requires freedom to toy with the ideas, and materials, deal irrelevant objects and fantasy hence the environment of school which stops students from these experiences inhibit creativity in them.

Creative Teacher

It is true that creativity cannot be taught by the traditional authoritarian methods and it is also true that creative teaching is the best and indispensable way for promoting creative behaviour in students wherein the teacher needs to invent such creative techniques during the process of teaching in the classroom which are unforeseeable and unexpected and puts the students in surprise. Such experiences would, in turn, besides sustaining their interest in learning, induce students to think of different directions in order to come up with a large number of solutions to the problems. What techniques the creative teacher is expected to use in classroom are briefly discussed below:

Provides for Self Initiated Learning

The creative teacher provides for self-initiated learning on part of students. The creative teachers create such situations in the classroom in which the students make an effort for self-learning. It helps the teacher in eliciting creative responses from his students. Self-activity encourages students to make wild guesses, to explore, and to experiment with varied and different types of ideas. It induces spontaneous, and independent thinking among students. Most important is that students are motivated to learning on their own. This type of learning helps them in becoming self-starters.

Sets up Permissive Learning Environment

Researchers have revealed that non-authoritarian learning environment faciliates creative learning as in the conditions of freedom which lead to creativeness. The kind of freedom which is requisite to creativity is psychological freedom in which students feel free to express themselves and in which external evaluation is absent. Freedom to engage in unimpeded symbolic expression promotes creative learning as it softens defensive and rigid attitudes and creates an openness to experience. Further, freedom to explore within the limits of one's own abilities places the responsibility for growth in one's own hands. On the contrary, every authoritarian act of the teacher not only discourages the decision making of students but also affects the learning of responsibility for their growth.

Stimulates Creative Thought Process among Students

The creative teacher stimulates students to imagine, to think tentative solutions to problems, to attempt to seek for new connections among existing objects, materials or thoughts, build on the ideas of others, and use previous information in new directions and situations. He is encouraged to express theories which may appear ridiculous, unbelievable; to present information into new and unexpected patterns. Most important thing is that the creative teacher encourages student to take intellectual risks and to speculate.

Stimulates Intellectual Fluency and Flexibility among Students

The creative teacher encourages students to store the information and use in this varied situations. He stimulates them to come out with a large number of ideas while attacking a problem. They learn to go to different and varied directions till they arrive at a novel solution to a problem. He encouraged them to make a shift from simple observation to experimentation and not to fix up preconceived results. They learn to move from one approach to another in dealing with the materials at hand. He asks students to seek for new functions of common objects and to redefine problems. He encourages them to look for new meanings in familiar materials and to use old information in new contexts.

Imbibes Self-discipline among Students

This is the most important prerequisite for creativeness. Unless students are self-disciplined it is not possible that they can release creative responses. Self discipline is a discipline which only the student can impose upon himself as it needs hardwork and drudgery which are required for any type of discovery or invention.

Promotes Sensitivity to Problems among Students

The creative teacher assists students to become sensitive persons. Anything which is obvious may be ambiguous for a creative learner. The creative teacher helps them to become more sensitive to all external stimuli, to the moods and feelings of other people, to all social, economic, political, educational and other issues. Not only that, he also becomes sensitive to such issues which are unknown to others.

Fosters Curiosity among Students

The creative teacher has the adequate knowledge how to make the best use of the question. As is known to all of us that every creative act begins with some questions, the questions should be operational and opened on the one hand and meaningful to students on the other and which do not have predetermined answers. Operational questions always lead to exploration which foster curiosity. Contrary to it there are questions which have pre-determined answers, hinder creativeness because in them the learner has no choice for wandering in search of varied solutions rather he gets restricted. Such questions hinder creative responses among students

Assists Students to become Active Participants

The creative teacher provides opportunities to students for manipulating materials, tools, ideas, and concepts. The active handling of objects facilitates creativeness among students as it helps the students in understanding various on-going process. *Second,* the creative teacher encourages students to consider any problem as a whole instead of piecemeal as the understanding of problem occurs with greatest insight, when it is observed from the viewpoint of structural patterns and total structure.

Encourages Self-evalutation on Part of Students

The creative teacher encourages students to evaluate their individual progress and achievement themselves. This means that the teacher accepts his student as an individual as of unconditional worth on the one hand and on the other, the student senses a climate of safety and learns that he can be what he is, since he seems to be regarded as of worth no matter what he does. In his way, the teacher builds up feeling of self-worth in his students. In its turn, the feeling of self-worth among students supplies the criteria for making choices of the means and materials which determine their pace of creation. The criteria for evaluating novelty is personal and individual's own powers to judge values serve as the final standard in determining the worth of newly created products.

The creative teacher not only believes in self-evaluation of novel products by the creators themselves but also refrains from making any judgement. He knows that by announcing outcomes or solutions he is inhibiting the exploratory efforts of the students, he postpones the finalizing of solutions. He does not close up the issues rather shows his willingness to re-open them and invite further solutions.

Assists Students to become Adventurous

The creative teacher cultivates the spirit of adventure in his students. He makes them adept to uncertainties and ambiguities of life and teaches how these can be faced as a challenge. How one can cope with frustations and failures. Researches have shown that more creative persons have the ability to come out of uncertainties and ambiguities than less creative persons. Furthermore, the more creative person has the ability to draw new meanings from such ambiguities.

To conclude, the creative teacher encourages creative thinking among students in at least five different ways;

1. Originality : He welcomes original ideas from his students and also assists them in releasing more and more ideas, out of them some may be original. To be original means to break away from the obvious, the routine and the conventional. He can determine the originality of the responses advanced by students through statistical rarity. Statistical infrequency is the criterion to determine originality of a response. For example, if the similar response to a given problem has been advanced by more than five per cent then no value (score) is assigned to it. Only those responses are treated original that have been advanced by one per cent to five per cent and the corresponding values range from 05 to 01 per cent.

2. Novelty : Novelty means that the product must be new. The newness can be determined subjectively as well as objectively. By subjectively we mean that there is something novel about the product for the creator whileas newness of the object can objectively be determined in terms of statistical rarity or judged by a forum of some kind. Both are important however, the more important is the subjective assessment of the product in terms of its newness.

3. Fluency : Fluency is the ability to generate a large number of ideas to solve the problem. Other things being equal, the more ideas the students can command, the more problems he can solve. If he is fluent in his ideas then he can bring more immediately a fertile mind to his studies and can put what he has learnt to a wider use.

Inquiry

This is the ability which makes one to become sensitive to problems by which he gets puzzled when others take it for granted. It gives ideas one to identify the best, most important or most effective from a number of alternatives.

Elaboration

To be able to elaborate is to make an idea viable. This ability requires from the student to learn on one's own initiative, and through self-initiated learning.

Openess

To be open means is to resist premature closure. Openness calls for divergent thinking and implies many solutions to problem and arriving at the most effective one. Openness also means playing with ideas, making wild guesses and arriving at a novel solution.

Creativity in Art

Art plays a vital role in the education of young children. The process of drawing or painting is a complex one in which the child brings together different elements of his environment to construct a new meaningful whole. By selecting, interpreting and reforming these elements he is not preparing a picture only rather he exhibits a part of himself as how he thinks, how he feels, and how he sees.

In our present system of education, much emphasis is laid on the learning of factual information. The passing of an examination, mostly depends upon the mastery or memorization of certain quantum of information on part of the student. The school seems to have restricted its function of producing only such people who are able to vomit selected bits of information when asked to do that. That student who is able to produce the right bits of information at a proper time is considered fit for promotion to the next grade, what is most distressing is that the skill in repeating certain bits of information may have very little relationship to the person who is able to contribute significantly to the society.

It is worth mentioning here that more and more people are now realising that the ability to learn differs from one individual to another and this ability not only involves intellectual capacity but also social, emotional, perceptual and psychological factors. Our education system emphasizes, only on one factor in human development i.e. it asks for simple memorization of certain facts which is measured by the intelligence tests. As all of us now know that intelligence does not involve all the thinking abilities that are necessary to the survival of mankind. The other abilities which involve questioning, seeking varied answers, finding form and order, and seeking new relationships do not find their due place in the present system of education.

One of the basic abilities that should be taught in schools is the ability to discover, to search for varied answers than to become a passive learner. The experiences central to an art activity involves this very ability. *Second*, the mental growth depends upon the relationship between an individual and his environment. In creative art activity there is an interaction between the self, the symbols, and the environment which provides the material for abstract intellectual processes. Such a relationship is considered as a basic component of a creative art activity. But what is emphasized mostly in our schools is to learn the letters and numerals. The students hardly are provided with the material by which their ability to abstract is developed. *Third,* the ability to see, feel, hear, smell and taste provides the means by which man can interact with his environment. If the child is given the training to use his all the senses during the process of teaching and learning there will be greater opportunity for him to learn. But what we observe in our schools, they hardly give due place to all the senses while educating children. To develop the sensitivity to problems is a basic ability involved in a creative art activity.

Fourth, students are not encouraged to be open, to give vent to their emotions in ways that are constructive. In a creative art activity we find that it provides a means to the children to express themselves in a very open way. Young children have as many frustrations as adults and they may very well not be able to deal with these in a rational way. Being able to express emotions in a socially acceptable way provides a framework for emotional growth.

Lastly, we require such an education system in which the development of the total being takes place, and each individual's thinking, feeling, and perceiving powers develop equally so that his creative abilities can unfold. This is to a great extent possible in the art activity.

Art Process and Creativeness

No area in the elementary school curriculum provides more opportunity for children to grow in creativity than art. Art is based on experience, and experiences are very personal, the end product can not be predetermined or dictated. It is a re-organisation of impression in a way that exhibits their unique significance for the creator. It is impossible to provide real learning situation without giving the individual an opportunity to use his imagination and inventive powers. Art activity offers such a situation to a child. Therefore, art provides the most important means to develop the individual as a creative thinker.

In spite of much researches, still there are people who think of drawing and painting as being somehow removed from reality, and children seem to them possessing some magical power. In reality they are not empowered with magical power; they have the innate capacities with which they can manipulate their environment. The need is to provide them the adequate opportunities to develop their intellectual capacities.

Research reveals that there are, at least, *five* factors of creativity involved in any art process. These factors have been found, are at work while creating any piece of art, painting or sculpture.

The *first* factor that has been identified in the creative process is sensitivity to problems to attitudes, and feelings of other people. This ability calls for eyes not only to see but to observe; and hands not only to touch but to feel. Basically this is a central experience in working with any art material where the sensitivity towards a line or form is encouraged and developed at all levels. A small child can be sensitive when he touches any material and feels something; the 11 year old child can be sensitive towards colours; and the 16 year old boy may be sensitive towards something which is more exciting.

The *Second* factor that has been identified in creative process is fluency. This ability calls for thinking rapidly and freely on a problem and coming out with a large number of possible solutions. This ability we find in the numerous scribbles from a small child or a number of suggestions from a high school boy for portraying a picture or constructing something new.

The *third* ability which is involved in the creative process is flexibility. This ability enables children to shift from one thought to another in order to adjust with new situation and arriving at unique solution to the problem. This ability is reflected in all the types of art activities, for example, the paint may spill or the chisel may slip but the artist makes himself adept to it and continues this struggle, changes his thoughts rapidly till he completes his task.

The *fourth* and the most important factor that has been identified in creative process is originality. This ability is judged by the product's unusualness and novelty. In every art activity we find, that if any mental factor is stressed more, it is originality wherein the copying of illustrations work from the teacher, book or other material is usually discouraged.

The *fifth* factor involved in the creative process is the ability to redefine or recorganise which means to rearrange ideas, to see new uses of things or relationships. This ability is very central in any art experience, for example, in transforming paper bags into puppets, we are redefining the material in a new way in order to give it a new meaning and this very constant process of re-organisation brings out new discoveries and inventions.

The factors discussed above need to be considered by the teacher in planning an art programme. Most of these factors (abilities) fall under the domain of divergent thinking which is opposite to the convergent thinking. In schools, usually the convergent thinking is stressed more where the output of thinking is one correct answer or one acceptable solution to a problem. But in art, the stress is laid on divergent thinking where any number of outcomes in painting or drawing are correct. Any work of art requires men of having self-reflecting thinking, curiosity, openness, adventurous spirit and believing in self-evaluation.

Reseach on creativity vis-a-vis art reveals that teaching for creativity is complex and may depend upon the teacher's personal meaningfulness as to how he encourages self-reflective thinking, and self-evaluation among his students and to what extent he can develop greater student teacher interaction. He should know that there are stages of development in art; that there are motivational and environmental forces that provide for learning to occur. What he does in the class and how he reacts towards the child makes a great difference in how the child views himself and his environment.

There are individual differences in children in regard to their personality characteristics as well as intellectual capacities. The teacher needs to know that there are some children who are sensitive and react to things around them more than others. They are able to create some pieces of art. When they start their work, they begin with thinking of 'something' and this 'something' has a meaning for them, that is, a confrontation with their ownselves and with their own experiences. On the other hand, there are other children who may not be thinking in this way. Either they may be lacking sensitivity or their minds may be blocked. They need to be motivated. It becomes the responsibility of the teacher to assist the child in reacting towards objects around him and his environment. It is believed that the required motivation and psychological climate may help the child in thinking, feeling, and perceiving objects around him.

The teacher may be more important for young children than older children as the latter can accumulate subject matter on their own for information. The children can read, ask questions to clear their doubts, discuss issues with peers, or go to the library for gathering information whileas few of these things are available to the small children hence they need the guidance of an adult. The role of the teacher, therefore, becomes more important. It is he who determines the activities, gives support for action, passes on praises or criticism and decides the length of time to be spent on any art activity.

Some researchers have raised a question as to whether children are not restricted in their creativeness when the teacher is using classroom motivation, that is, when the whole group is motivated by one experience. Two things need to be differentiated clearly here, *one* is related to the subject matter and *the other* to the mode of expression. As long as the child is free to use his own mode of expression, his creativeness remains free and the position of the teacher comes down to mere guidance and to encouraging reflective thinking.

It is worth mentioning here that there is no single approach to freeing children in their creativeness or in making them more sensitive towards themselves their environment. However, the teacher needs to consider at least, *three* factors while stimulating creative thinking among students. *First*, is his own personality, as to what extent he is creative, sensitive and flexible. *Second*, is his own ability to put himself into the place of others. *Third*, is his understanding and knowledge of the needs of those whom he is teaching. It is upto the teacher to decide for the approach he uses. At one time he finds it better to divide the students into groups. At another time he may ask each individual student to work on his own. This all depends on the nature of activity on the one hand and individual needs of students on the other. The needs of the children change continually and the teacher must be too flexible to adjust to these changing needs. Sometimes, the outcome of the group approach is quite ineffective or even frustating when the child feels that the group is interfering with his own individual mode of expression or simply he may not be ready for it.

The teacher needs to plan learning situations in the manner which will give each student an opportunity to grow in creativity. This task he can perform satisfactorily only when he has the adequate knowledge of stages of growth and development of children and of individual differences in them. In order to encourage creative thinking in his students, he needs to consider certain point in the process of planning the art programme. He must provide adequate and stimulating physical facilities to the students. It is the physical environment that plays an important role in developing creativity among students through art activities. In a physical sense, facilities are referred to as space and materials that should be provided to the students so as enable them to implore, experiment and create. The classrooms need to be such where the students can work without any disturbances and distractions. Materials available to the students should be appropriate to their maturity level on the one hand and provide the widest possible range of choices tolerable to them on the other. The classrooms should be orderly and attractive. The whole arrangement should be functional, colourful and pleasing. Such an atmosphere in the classroom undoubtedly enhances the possibility among students to work for creative endeavours.

Opportunities for children to act upon their environment with their present state of knowledge, even if their actions are neither efficient nor completely understood by the teacher, are of great significance in the educative process. The opportunity to explore the unknown or to manipulate or alter the known provides support for children's efforts to think independently. They need to take chances, to question, to see alternative avenues for action. One of the ways to provide for greater alternatives for the child is to expand his frame of reference, that is, what the child is doing now, how can this be modified, altered or restructured in ways that can be understood by the child. A teacher who asks for alternatives is actually providing the child an opportunity to look for other directions.

Next, the teacher needs to consider the emotional aspects of the environment so as to enable the learner to be free and to be open to accept the new challenges. It has been observed in research that the art work suffers if the teacher is dictatorial and oppressive and it progresses if he is able to create a conducive climate. The teacher should know that before children will or can share their inner-most thoughts and feelings through art forms, they must be free and comfortable in the group and feel that their feelings and ideas will be accepted by the group members as well as the teacher. The more the teacher can do is to provide for adequate sessions of conversation and discussion to the children that will encourage them to contribute towards creative thinking.

The most important task of the art teacher seems to construct such a curriculum which may be rich enough to provide opportunities to each learner develop in accordance with his own pace. On the one hand he ensures desired growth rather than to a routine pattern on the other. Growth proceeds most effectively when children are placed in situations which call upon them to speculate, analyse, synthesize, sharpen sensory impressions and go beyond the situation where the teacher has left it.

The art teacher should assist students to become sensitive learners as sensory awareness is especially important for creative thinking in the area of art. It has been seen that children often overlook and miss the familiar objects in the environment. Sensory awareness means using eyes not for simple recognition but piercing through the detailed visual relationships which make the whole impression; using the ears not for hearing only but for the detailed relationships of sound. The teacher can make his students aware by turning their attention towards various objects in the environment by asking them to observe and compare shapes, colours and patterns of light and shade; listening to different sounds and identifying them; touching many things and have the feel of them and enjoying and discussing different motions of the body, machines and other objects.

The teacher can also make his students sensitive towards the works of great artists which in turn leave a favourable effect on their own art work. By comparing their own explorations with the art work of great people they can grow in the understanding that art is an expression of that what the artist can imagine, perceive and feel and not just a photographic reproduction.

Creativity in Science

The theoretical as well as empirical discussions have brought to our knowledge different types of creativity. The *first* type of creativity in which the product of creation is an expression of the inner states of mind is expressed in the works of artists, painters, poets, novelists, etc. as discussed in the previous section. The *second* type of creativity in which the product is not related to the creator, or his inner states is expressed in the research works of scientists, engineers, chemists, biologists, etc. In this type of creativity, the creator acts only as a mediator, between externally defined needs and goals. The creator simply operates on some aspect of the environment in such a manner as to produce a new product but he adds little of himself to the product.

In scientific creativity, the environmental needs and goals are of prime importance. It is also akin to problem solving creativity. Scientific creativity involves situations concerning the solutions of mechanical and social problems. This is mostly the fact-finding endeavour, using abstract type of creativity to arrive at the scientific discoveries. Scientific creativity is also termed as objective creativity which is judged by the appropriateness, i.e. whether the product fulfills the demands of the situation.

In Koestler's view, in scientific thinking nothing like complementary and self-assertive emotions are involved. Scientists mostly have been observed as having very few interpersonal relationships and keep a distance from their personal emotions, instead they devote energies and thoughts to impersonal matters and objects. This does not mean that their thinking is totally devoid of all feelings but it is well balanced compound of passions into which both self asserting and participating tendencies enter into highly sublimated form, which provide new insights.

Different conditions have been found necessary for scientific creativity. Psychoanalysts attach great importance to regression in scientific creativity. Psychologists largely agree that psychological, sociological and economic factors are most vital for the development of scientific creativity. While assessing the environmental conditions and creative thinking abilities of scientists, Andrews could find only simple relationship between the two. However, on further investigation he noted that it is the man's laboratory environment which matters in his creative production.

Creativity as has largely been agreed upon can be developed and each person, at least can be trained to think creatively. The same holds true for any student whether he belongs to art or science provided the necessary conditions are provided to him. Terman believes that scientific creativity in students can be enhanced in a climate and by techniques which can, in part, be created on the basis of a knowledge of those characteristics which distingnish creative from non-creative future scientists.

It is not necessary that all future creative scientists have the same characteristics which distinguish past and present scientists from their peers. One thing seems important being the ideal climate. If an ideal climate is provided, chances increase for the future scientists to become more creative.

Of all the characteristics of a creative scientist the one which is most related to his public image is his imaginative and unorthodox thinking. Nothing is spared his curiosity. He has neither respect for the past nor for the present. He is future-oriented in his ideas and is quite willing to make bold leaps into uncharted territory, guided principally by insight. This characteristic may be because of his over whelming interest in reading in general and reading science fiction in particular.

The creative scientist, sometimes, goes for day-dreaming also but knowing well that reality is something else and attempts at bringing his dreams to reality. He is more interested in goals than the method used to achieve it and is likely to support his conclusions with vigour. This tendency not only makes his mental peace disturbed, but also to the teacher who wishes him to mould in conformity.

Creative scientists are said having a high tolerance for ambiguity. They actively seek for situations and problems chracterised by complexity and discomfort, not only for the challenge they present but also for aesthetic satisfaction in the elegant solution for which they hope. Mental effort, then is to the creative scientist what physical exercise is to an athlete—a chosen activity and a necessity.

Creativity scientists are particularly open to new experiences. There have been found two factors responsible for the development of this characteristic in them. Either, the families of these children moved more often than most, or, as children, they have been left alone for long periods of time during which they have to seek for their entertainment on their own. These circumstances, possibly help them in developing their wide interests and long interest spans and are not inclined to feel circumscribed by their environment.

A creative scientist works very hard and persistently. He is very independent, and democratic in nature. He studies each and every thing in detail. This characteristic he develops as a result of his home climate which is mostly characterized by imbibing self-discipline among children and learning to satisfy desires through delayed satisfaction. Thus attaining a goal after much persistence, the resolve and creative thinking of an individual get stimulated.

A creative scientist finds ways to reduce demands of the society on him so that he has time to think. He generally starts thinking slowly on a problem, looks at it through many angles and increases his pace as he proceeds. He works furiously when he reaches the climax stage of success of the problem. Until he reaches the solution of the problem he is fully involved with the problem over extended periods of time.

Creative scientists, on the average are emotionally cool, aloof, dominant and introspective. It has been observed that as children they like to be alonc though companionship was available to them. They are said to be too intimate with their families. They are more socially concerned than sociable. They prefer problems related to things more than problems that are related to people.

Creative scientists are more sensitive to approval and disapproval. In spite of having a good self image, they need social recognition and aspire for rewards in order to continue producing their creative works. Similarly, they tend to learn most from those who are demanding but fair.

In regard to scientific creativity, a teacher has a variety of relationships with his students. To one he is a friend, to another he is taskmaster. The teacher who fully understands the student's creative tendency towards introversion will offer him a friendly, supportive relationship and also respecting whatever psychological distance he prefers. In order to encourage creative thinking, a creative teacher is willing to consider any question, any topic, at any time raised by his students.

A teacher who attempts at fostering creative thinking in his students is described by them as perceptive, kind, appreciative, but sometimes critical also.

To enhance creativity in science students, a teacher should be too flexible and humane. He should be socially conscious, individual-concerned, human being first and the educator *second*. He should be knowing as to how enough of variety in course content could be brought about. He should know the proper use of audio-visual aids, conducting lectures of the outside speakers, arranging field trips, debates, seminars, quizes, discussions, etc. that help in the development of imagination and divergent thinking.

It would not be possible for a teacher to stimulate creative thinking among students unless a restructing of the overall curriculum takes place. The courses need to be revised in the manner that ask for raising student's interest in complexity to develop an inquiry mind. Puzzles, paradoxes and conundrums should also find their place in the curriculum. To cater to the creative scientist's desire for resolvable disorder, the content should correspond with complex concepts more often than is done today.

On the one hand, one value in required courses should be that they train students in the quality of persistence without which there can be no creativity. On the other hand, we must strike a balance, since to be creative, an individual must have un-programmed time. Our pattern of required classes, home assignments, and entertainments must be liberalized in order that the students have the necessary opportunity for reflective and creative thinking. An educational institution should ensure that every student, especially the creative one, is working hard, however, in some cases, the individual student can profit if allowed to go with his own chosen academically accepted projects. That is, schools must be rigid enough to force the lazy students to study and flexible enough to let the highly motivated one set his own pace. We need not, for instance, be strict with all students about class attendance and deadline, but we must ask for overall performance. One thing however, should be remembered that there are students who won't think unless they are forced to; others cannot exert their best efforts or develop to their full potential under excessive pressures to meet rigid classroom requirements. Only individual-oriented teachers are regarded to resolve this double-faceted issue.

Since many creative scientists are said to be introverts, others like to be with people and benefit from close association with their classmates and teachers. The job of the teacher remains to encourage non class activities such as attendance at professional meetings and lectures; publication programmes, visits to other institutions, libraries and museums wherein the students have an opportunity to interact with other students, teachers and people. Such contacts with imaginative and critical people help students develop their own imaginative thinking.

4

Visual Media

Today's educator is faced with an embarrassment of riches. He ha come to realize that in teaching and learning, more often than not, mere talking and listening or writing and reading do not convey their message sufficiently. The sensory presence of the objects and events to which language refers is indispensable if the words are to exert their impact and be grasped in their full meaning. This sensory presence concerns all perceptual modalities; but even if limited to visual images, the abundance and variety of "visual aids" must bewilder the teacher and the student.

Hardly any of the traditional procedures of picture-making have become useless, although their functions may have changes and become more limited. The prehistoric methods of drawing a likeness on a surface or shaping a figure in clay are still with us; they are still profoundly useful and will always remain so. At the same time, mechanical, photographic, and electronic techniques have given us new ways of creating, preserving, and distributing images. More or less clearly, we sense that some of the old and the new media serve certain purposes better than others. But our attempts to use them wisely still rely too much on trial and error.

So influential have been the technological innovations of our time that one is tempted to declare a fundamental difference between the media of today and the media to yesterday. And so pervasive is this influence that it may seem to shape our lives totally and thereby distinguish the mentality of twentieth-century man is principle from that of his forefathers. Such dichotomizing is more dazzling than useful. The basic capacities and reactions of the human mind remain what they always were; and, if one examines the visual media somewhat less passionately, one finds that they all rely on the same limited number of perceptual dimensions. Remote though the wall paintings of the ice age may be from the television screen, the eye looks at pictures in both instances; and with all differences between writing hieroglyphs on papyrus and setting type by computer, the psychology of reading has not changes substantially. By examining the media in the light of their dimensions, one can begin to clarify some of their similarities and differnces, and these comparisons of their character lead almost automatically to practical guidelines for the producer and user of visual material.

This seems all the more necessary since anybody who has set his heart, not to mention his money, on a particular medium tends to consider its capacities in isolation from what other media can do and perhaps do better. He will entrust his favourite contraption with as many functions as possible, whether it is suited for them or not. A glaring example of misuse is the kind of television programme that is based entirely or predominantly on talking and presents to the eyes of viewer the embarrassing presence of newscaster reciting the latest bulletins or of gropus of discussants uncomfortably perched on their seats. This goes on even though radio, ideally suited for the intelligent presentation of disembodied voices, is available to everybody.

The visual media differ from each other in certain fundamental ways. Some use two-dimensional surfaces, e. g., drawing, painting, photography, printing, and television. Others produce three-dimensional shapes, e. g., sculpture or the models of chemistry or biology. Some use immobile images, such as book illustrations, slides, maps, or writing and printing; others show things in motion, such as film or video. Some reproduce mechanically, some manually. These and other differences reflect profoundly on the best use to be made of the media.

Throughout this brief survey we shall have to keep in mind the active as well as passive use of the various media. Passive use serves the dispensing of knowledge. Pictures carry images of the world into the classroom. They offer the raw material for factual information. However, the pictures or models have been made by experts somewhere else. They arrive ready-made. Student and teacher act as consumers. Their acts are responses.

Active use of the media is furthered or hampered by technical and economical factors. Some material is readily available: a pad of cheap sketch paper, a box of crayons, a technique that can be mastered by a child without instruction. More forbidding is the equipment of the cameraman, the technical knowledge needed to make a simple film turn out as intended, the cost of material, development, and so on. However, even the more intricate and expensive media have become accesssible to common use beyond all expectation, and the educator needs to find out what equipment to put in the hands of his students for what purpose.

Before I go into specifics, one point should be stressed. There is no automatic correspondence between active and passive use of material and active and passive use of mind. Mere looking acan be a very active occupation, which strains all the cognitive powers of the mind. Learning material can be cunningly presented in such a way that it not only transmits data but raises questions and reveals problems. In such an intellectually active climate no apology is needed for the passive presentation of pictures, slides, films.

Drawing, carving, model-building, and flim-making favour an active concern with the subject matter. It takes a dull mind to make a drawing of the skeleton of a lizard without any curiosity about how and why all those little bones are put together in just that way, or to film the goings-on at a bus stop without asking who are the people who are waiting, where they are going, how they relate to each other. But it can be done. Mental interitia, if encouraged by the teacher, can use the gadgerty of picture-making as an easy substitute for the intelligent exploration of the things painted, collected, photographed. Under such conditions, "active" teaching puts the mind to sleep.

These considerations will concern us more langibly as we look at the properties of various visual media. The survey cannot be exhaustive, and perhaps all that is needed here is to define and illustrate some of the relevant dimensions and to suggest by a few examples what to look for in the use of instructional media.

Physical Presence vs. Recording

Man, as distinguished from animals, can represent the things of nature by making images. The urge to do so arises early and the advantages accruing from images are obvious. However, since there are irreplaceable virtues also in experiencing "the real thing," the educator must never assume without question that recorded mages are a suitable substitute for direct experience.

The "real thing" is tied its name and place. The local post office, the aquarium, the United Nations building must be traveled to in order to be seen, and a solar eclipse occurs rarely. This anchoring in time and place is not merely a limitation. Positively, it provides the observer with a context that may be indispensable for understanding. Post offices are strategically located in town, the acquarium is remote from the natural habitat of its prisoners, the United Nations have entrusted their headquarters to New York City; and it is essential for the understanding of aclipses to realize that they occur rarely. There are ways of pointing at these contexts of space and time when images are used unstead of the real thing. But we do well to keep in mind that we pay for the comfore of using substitutes by uprooting and isolating the objects and happenings we show.

Images store the visual appearances of physical things. Some such replicas can not only be seen but can also be explored by touch. Some can be heard. Even so, the replication is always partial. This has certain advantages. The limitations of what is shown make the mind concentrate on some of the aspects of a particular subject matter. An Audubon print lets the student look at the shape and plumage of a bird from a convenient distance, in clear sight, unhurrid, undisturbed by motion. If the picture is well made, it carves a valid likeness into the student's memory—an accomplishment not easily matched by the fleeting appearances of reality.

In the presence of a "real" situation we are fre to look at what is before us in an attitude of contemplation, unless it entices or assails us too strongly. But reality also invites active participation.

We feel impelled to explore what we see, to handle it, to walk around it and into it. If we notice something wrong, incomplete, unjust, we are challenged to remedy and situation. The image, on the other hand, lets and makes the viewer see what he would not see otherwise, but it also transforms the events of reality into objects of contemplation. It suggests the attitude of the detached observer, the philosopher, the pure scientist.

Visual aids are meant to alleviate the indirectness of much modern experience. The primitive hunter or farmer is in direct interaction with all that matters to him. The city dweller, on the other hand, rarely deals directly with the things that concern him. The businessman replaces products with paper; the student reads about distant things, sees their pictures.

Ironically enough, altough pictures are intended to remedy the blindness resulting from indirectness, they serve at the same time to replace real things by their images. The world becomes something to look at. The effect of the enormous amount of information poured upon the citizen by television and illustrated paper every day is notoriously ambiguous. It provides a direct look at violence, poverty, and injustice, but it confirms the status of these atrocities as things happening beyond reach. It risks confounding them with the figments of story films, which are exciting but, as every grown-up person knows, untrue. Hence the enormously important task of the teacher to counteract the sense of unreality that comes with all pictorial representation. He must keep alive the awareness that the world he shows is a challenge: something to be dealt with, acted upon, expored, imporoved.

The impressive popularity of photography and film among young people today may exemplify the problem. A generation suffering from a sense of remoteness and isolation seizes upon a medium that records the appearances of human existence with great immediacy. This closeness to the facts may express and activate a deep concern with social, political and natural events, as demonstrated by the work of our best photographers and film-makers. But the photographic medium can also provide the illusion of engagement, obtained simply by pressing a button. It allows the picture-taker to be present without having to participate. He can remain a detached observer with a good conscience because, after all, he is "reacting."

In the schoolroom the pictures must be prevented from fortifying the notion that the learning material is like a show to be consumed passively. Recorded or transmitted lecutres have the obvious value of supplying excellent teachers and facilities not otherwise available. But these opportunities must be used in the light of the educator's conviction that without response there is no true learning. And since the televised lecture, even more clearly than the "real" orator at teh academic lectern, is a person to whom one cannot talk back, it is again the task of the live teacher to transform the object of passive assimilation into an instrument of active learning.

The "real world," although a challenge to active participation, is at the same time much less easily manipulated than its image. The real world is given. The image is created. The subject matter of the image is selected from the array of exising things, and the various formal devices offered by the medium shape the image to suit the picture-maker's purpose. The power of determining what the image shall look like is greatest for drawing and painting, smallest for the photographic media. But even the photographic technique adapts itself to a variety of approaches. Recently this has become evident by certain basic differences that exist between the media of film and television. Offhand, it is not obvious that there should be such differences, if we ignore for the moment the social and perceptual factors that distinguish viewing at home or in the schoolfoom from attending a performance in a movie theater. Infact, the offerings of the two media largely overlap, e.g., when films are shown on television.

Yet, a very different relation to reality is suggested by the fact that television allows for direct transmission without recording. It is in the nature of such transmission that it eliminates much of the shaping, characteristic of film work. Direct transmission leaves the continuity of time unbroken. The switch from one viewpoint (camera) to another is possible but improvised. Good shots and bad shots, relevant and irrelevant sights reach the view somewhat indiscriminately. This lifelike messiness, so differentfrom the careful control at all stages of typical film work, can also be obtained with the film camera. In fact, some of the younger filmmakers, impressed by the style of television reportage, have adopted it. The new video-tape equipment favors this development. The reason for this preference is of interest here. It suggests that good visual material should strike the right ratio between carefully controlled form and the authenticity of good reporting. How much of the one and how much of the other is appropriate in each particular case must be considered by the maker and the user of visual material.

On the whote, it is advisable, of course, to see to it that visual aids make their point as clearly as possible. For instruction in chemistry one is not likely to use a film in which an experiment goes wrong or even lacks polish and efficient execution. Yet, the very perfection of a successful performance can cast a chill upon the viewer. He knows in advance that the demonstration will work. The suspenseful uncertainty as to whether an enterprise will be successful is one of the great thrills of the scientist's and the explorer's endeavor. A cooking lesson, transmitted live over television, gains rather than loses by small mishaps: ingredients missing tools pushed off the table, the cake sticking to the pan. The sense of adventure is a great asset in learning, and the realization that the teacher is not perfect proides legitimate encouragement. Recorded demonstrations tend to lack this incentive. We pay a price for the great virtues of prepared imagery. Here agains, a shrewd compromise between immaculate presentation and the lures of lifelikeness will often be in the interest of successful education.

Active and Passive

By its very nature the image excludes active exchange in the usual sense of debate, examination, or conversation. The viewer cannot respond, retorl ask questions—in the tangible manner of a discussion. Another factor that makes it difficult for the recipient to work up an effort of his own is that he knows it to be a "canned" performance; he knows that the effort needed to furmulate the lecture, conduct the experiment, address the audience is not being made right now but was exerted in the past. Right, now, nobody is exerting himself on the platform. This eliminates the incentive of responding to the teacher's effort with an effort of one's own. It is dificult to react genuinely to a mere wraith.

The educator should be aware of these drawbacks. But he should also realize that weighty counterarguments can be summoned in defense of the image. It is true that one cannot talk back, e.g., to a painting, but the silent response of some viewers is most powerful and active. This happens when two conditions are fulfilled. The image itself must be strong, relevant, interesting enough to deserve the response, and the mind of the viewer must be prepared for what the image has to offer.

These two conditions hold for the use of all visual material. An effective image must be able to arouse a sense of wonder, it must capture the mind by its novelty. To understand it should require a mental exertion. However, the material should also convey the reassuring impression that it is within the range of the viewer's capacities. Otherwise it will discourage him from the outset. It should offer a soluble problem, a challenge that looks as though it can be met. To decipher the map of one's hometown for the first time is such a challenge. To figure out how a cable car works is a discovery. To watch an astronaut walk under conditions of reduced gravity raises questions.

The image must not be too eager to explain. It is good practice to present the puzzle first, let the facts pose the questions, give the mind a chance to come up with an answer, and supply the solution in due time. Mere exposition of all the pertinent facts is not good teaching, because mere information does not educate. At the same time, the visual material must not be expected to do all the work of putting the student in the right frame of mind. Basically, the image is a tool, not a teacher. Since the older child and the adolescent are no longer as prone as teh preschool younger to be puzzled by the basic miracles of nature and technology and to demand explanation, it is the teacher's task to rekindle this native intelligence—to warn the student when he is taking things for granted that are not obvious. After all, the capacity to puzzle about the obvious stimulates the most productive thinking.

Ideally, the first move should not be up to the image. The visual material should not turn up for some purely extrinsic reason and demand attention, but the student should take the initiative to call for such material when he needs it in order to answer his questions. What does the skeleton of a dolphin look like? How do crystals multiply? What happens when a person lies down on his back in the middle of a busy street? The image is the answer to the request: Let's find out! There is now concrete experimental evidence to suggest than even animals learn much less from being passively exposed to an environment in which they are carried around than they do by actively exploring it under the guidance of their own initiative.

More technically, visual material varies as to the extent to which it can be actively manipulated. The photographs in a book illustrating, say, life in an African town can be consulted in any order, whereas it is quite laborious to pick out particular sections of a film without running through the whole in its established sequence. Furthermore, our view of an object depicted in a drawing or painting is limited to the particular aspect presented by the artist whereas the film camera can explore complex shapes, such as those of a building, from all sides. With the coming of hologrpahy it will be possible notonly to see photographed objects stereoscopically on the screen, but also to receive a different view by changing one's point of observation, just an in physical reality. This will make the exploration of projected image physically more active. If we wish to go beyond mere looking, we can employ three-dimensional models of biological or technological structures, which can be touched, turned around, and taken apart.

Always or Rarely

The mechanical mass production of images, which began with the graphic techniques in the fifteenth century, has made visual material readily available. The advantages of this progress are too obvious to warrant discussion. One need only mention the most recent facilities for the instant duplication of documents, drawings, or scientific articles—inventions we are not yet taking for granted andare still actively thankful for. What does require discussion is the cheapening of effect that results from mass reproduction under certain conditions.

A moment's reflection shows that it is not merely the frequent exposure such that creates the problem. To be sure, everbody knows how pictures on the wall tend to disappear. They are no longer looked at; they are not missed when they are taken away. On the other hand, there are images that require permanent presence: the altar statues in a church, the family photographs on the desk, the subway map in the station, the eye chart in the oculist's office, the trademarkon the product. Clearly, the problem is not permanence as such, but its relation to function. Consider a beautiful painting hanging in a room through which students pass every day on their way to the auditiorium. The painting not only disappears from sight, but it also loses value. The piece of scultpture in the living room vanishes from what psychologists call the life space of the inhabitants if it does not serve a continuing need. When Rembrandt's *Syndics* are used for the decoration of a cigar box or when the *Mona Lisa* or Van Gogh's *Sunflowers* are exploited in advertisements, magazines, and dime-store art, it is obviously the cheapening and falsification of function, not the multiplication of the object, that is to blame.

Shoddy reproduction techniques help to debase a valuable work of visual art in the eyes of the viewer. Such techniques put it in the company of pictures that deserve no better treatment. Here again it is up to the educator to take advantage of modern technology without letting its faulty use defeat his purpose. Bad prints that falsify colour and brightness values should be banned from instruction. Also, it is good practice to vary the pictorial equipment of the schoolroom, just as in the traditional Japanese home one honors one';s art treasures by showing them only at special occasions and for a limited time. Whatever is on display should be referred to as often as the occasion. A geographic map paling and peeling on the wall from years of neglect like an old window shade, acts as a symbol of disrespect for the insruments. of human knowledge.

Exposure to visual material should not be overdone. The showing of a film should be made an occasion to be looked forward to, not the tired routine of running perfunctory material through the projector. It is bad education to screen substandard documentaries offered free of charge by the public relations departments of industry, only because something is needed for scheduled assembly meetings. Just as a reading of peotry can be made a festive ocasion even though the poem is available in thousands of inexpensive copies, a useful or beutiful image will create a heightened experience even though it is available in millions of prints. Inversely, the visit to a rare original can be a tedious duty performed by an exhausted tourist. It is the attitude of the viewer, not the availability or the price of visual material, that makes the difference between gain and loss.

Movement and Immobility

Untill less than a century ago, movement could be produced only by live performance or by automata. Immobile pictures, known since prehistoric times, represented things in action as well as things at rest; and even though they could not show locomotion, good artists never had any trouble in conveying a sense of "life."

The main perceptual principle to be observed here is that a successful immobile image is rarely a slice of a temporal action. If one stops a film or enlarges single frames, one observes more often that not that the momentary phases of an action look absurdly paralzyed and unnatural. The same is true for many snapshots of sports scenes or animals in motion. A picture is not a segment of time; rather, it represents its subject outside of time. The sense of "life" is not guaranteed by the mere correctness of the representation but is conveyed by the visual nature of the shapes, their interrelations, and their orientation in pictorial space. A detailed treatment of these visual properties cannot be proided here.

Immobile images have the great virtue of permitting careful perusal without time limit. One particular aspect of the object or action is chosen to represent innumerable possible ones. The selection requires great skill, not only in order to do justice to the object "as such," but also to serve the particular purpose intended. The image may be meant to show the anatomy or the beauty or natural habitat of an animal; it may facus on the style, the aerodynamics, or the functional design of an airplane. In each case a different choice of aspect, distance, lighting, setting, etc., may be appropriate.

The recording of motion, as it has become available through film and television, serves first of all to make the vital distinction between motion and immobility. To the child this distinction coincides with that between the animate and the inanimate. Motion also introduces the essential element of causality into the picture. The interaction between things is presented as an actual occurrence, not just through its results. In a film one actually sees the thermometer rise when it is immeresed in warm water.

The conception and experience of nature as process is greatly enhanced by the presentation of change through movement. Change, however, must be understood in relation to what persists unchanged, and here it is the visible difference between a static setting and the action taking place within it that makes the particular dynamics of natural, technical or social processes visible. Also, apparent immobility can be shown to be due to the limitation of our visual sense, which registers change only within a definite range of speed and size. By now everbody is familiar with the spectacular enrichment of our world of visual experience obtained by accelerating or slowing down the speed of recording natural processes. Such adjustments of speed enable the viewer to study the characterstics of plant growth, muscular behaviour, splashes or explosions by direct inspection.

Movement is a prime means of increasing attention and facilitating identification. It is the most elementary and effective stimulus to the sense of sight. Even a small change in the visual environment will attract attention automatically. This means that in any demonstration the objects that move should be the ones on which the viewer is supposed to concentrate. Actors know from their experience on the stage that any slight action in the background will easily distract the audience from the principal happening.

The movement of a snake will detach the animal from the surrounding complex environment of underbrush, scattered leaves, branches, and rocks. Any change of place or shape creates a helpful distinction between figure and ground, the moving object being generally the figure, the immobile setting being the ground. Thus the principal object is effectively isolated from the rest of the scene, and the spatial relation between object and environment is revealed as being liable to change. The snake moving across the screen is not permanently connected with the objects surroundig it, as it is in a photograph or drawing in the textbook. It displays its independence from any particular location.

Identification is facilitated more specifically by the character of the movement. A butterfly, a goldfinch, a mosquito, an airplane are clearly distinguished by the shape and speed pattern of their flight path, even when the object is seen as a mere shapeless dot in the distance. This quality of behaviour also characterizes an object as energetic or weary, controlled or disturbed, quickmined or slow, liquid or viscous. The changing shape of clouds reveals them to the eye as being vaporous rather than solid.

Thus the visual dimension of motion in time enriches the learning experience if it is deliberately employed and controlled by the picture maker. The virtues of visual motion are well worth the greater effort it demands of the viewer. Being fleeting and changing, the mobile image requires quick apprehension and a good visual memory if teh viewer is to extract from it the lasting, invariant qualities of the subject matter.

It is necessary, finally to distinguish between the effects of two kinds of movement, namely, that of the object and that of the observer. If the object turns, bends, or changes place, it will display different shapes and different relations with its environment. By handling a small plyhedron the viewer can obtain an integrated image of the complex total form. The range of different partial aspects revealed by the turning supplies visual raw material for the mental acquisition of a form that cannot be covered fully by any one view. The mobile images of film and television can duplicate this sort of display by recording the object in rotation or locomotion. The effect will be particularly complete if the mobility of the image can be supplemented by stereoscopic vision.

Visual change is also obtained when the observer moves across, around or through an object or setting. Movements of the eyes, the head, the body are used for such exploration in visual space, and the film camera can imitate the displacements. However, the effect of the movingimage is strongly counteracted by the lack of the corresponding muscular sensations in the body of the viewer. Since his body tells him that he is sitting motionless in his chair, the displacements on the screen are perceived as motions of the image. This illusion of locomotion is fairly easily accounted for by the viewer, e.g., when he sees a scene taken from a moving airplane or by a camera traveling along the facade of a building. Much more serious is the change of the visual angle, carried about by the camera but not identified by the viewer. This interferes with spatial orientation, especially when the camera explores an interior by rotatioin. The three-dimensional room looks flattened out and the spatial relation between the walls is almost impossible to discern. A single screen offers no efficient substitute for looking around in a building or scanning the panorama of a mountainscape that surrounds the viewer from all sides.

Linear Sequence

All locomotion is linear in the sense that objects travel along a one-dimensional path. But there exists also two- or three-dimensional movement. The surface of an expanding inkblot changes two-dimensionally, that of an expanding ballon, three-dimensionally.

The movement of the glance is always a linear sequence. In order to see at all, the eye must constantly move or be moved, and if one records the path of the fixation movement, one obtains a linear trace. To look at a picture means, therefore, to scan its parts. In most cases, the order of teh scanning sequence is not prescribed by the picture and, in fact, does not matter. The resulting complete image is independent of the order in which its details were explored.

The process of perceptual integration is influenced, however, by the relative size of the image, i.e., by the visual angle resulting from the objective size of the physical object and the distance from the observer, if the picture occupies too much of the visual field, it is difficult to apprehend as a whole. The viewer will be induced to pick out details in isolation. This happens when students sit too close to the projection screen or a large wall map.

The compositional structure of the picture also influences perceptual integration. The more orderly the structure and the simpler the order, the more easily does the scanning lead to an image perceived as an organized whole. If the composition organizes around one central theme, it is more easily read than if there are two or more such centers. The distance between the centers also matter. If e.g., a marksman taking aim is seen at the right margin of a photograph and his target at the left, the picture may be read badly.

Naturally, the time needed to explore a picture adequately varies. A single shape on an empty ground is apprehended in a fraction of a second; a microscopic slide or a painting may require an hour. On the screen of film or television the scanning time available for perceiving any one phase of the action is inevitably short, and it is necessary therefore, to allot sufficient length to each scene, depending on its importance and difficulty.

Certain types of images prescribe the overall sequence in which they are to be seen. A Japanese picture scroll that has to be unrolled laterally establishes the direction in which the picture sequence should be viewed, but not the speed at which this has to be done. Film and television are also linear media since they impose a sequence of viewing.

Depending on whether the principal dimension of a medium is space or time, it serves certain purposes well, others less well. It also conveys a particular conceptioin of reality and promotes certain attitudes of the viewer over others. The immobile image on the wall or in the textbook shows each thing and, by implication, the world as a whole in permanent existence. It says: This is the way things *are!* Even actions are correspondingly transformed. A chart indicating the sales curve of a business surely depicts a process, but the emphasis is on the persistent being of the firm, as distinquished from the dramatic happening in the one would see if the rise and fall of fortune were presented in animation as a growing curve. Similarly, a painting showing Washington crossing the Delaware represents a milestone rather than the course of history.

To what extent an immobile picture is read as an active event rather than a mere state of affairs depends not only on the picture itself but also on the mental attitude of the viewer. It would be important to know whether children react more to the dynamic or the static elements of immobile pictures and whether these reactions are related to age, intelligence, experience, and so on. It is quite possible that a picture which tells an adult a dramatic story is read essentially as an inventory of things and characters by certain types of children—e.g., those who are constantly exposed to television—and that therefore pictorial material prepared for them must stress action more conspicuously or must even be replaced by films or television.

In the contemplation of immobile images it is the viewer who must introduce sequential action. He scans the picture, looks for essentials, traces relations. The process of understanding a picture runs along a linear track, even though the outcome of the effort is the integration of the immobile image in the simultaneity ofall its parts. Similarly, in order to understand the three-dimensional model of a molecule in chemistry or in order to "see" a piece of sculpture, one must continuously walk around the object or turn it back and forth. From the sequence of the sights emerges a nonsequential entity, the Being of the immobile object.

Film and television can initiate and control such a process of exploration, e.g., when the weatherman explains the maps with a pointer. It is he who imposes the sequence of apprehension upon the viewer. An essentially static situation can also be explored by action of the camera. The initiative is clearly with the explorer, the interpreter, the guide. In the lecture series *Civilization,* Sir Kenneth Clark often assumed the role of the museum guide or teacher of art history by directing the glance of the viewer to the relevant items.

This sort of procedure is at its best when it transforms a state of being into an event and animates itthereby. In one of the *Civilization* films, the camera traveled upward along the female figure of Bernini's marble group *Apollo and Daphne,* thus showing in dramataic sequence how the woman is gradually transformed into a tree. For another example, one may think of an anatomical model, sya, of the human body, which allows the removal of layer after layer, thereby creating a suspenseful sequence that leads from the epidermis to the sancturm of the inner organs. Another example is a film by Charles Eames which shows the changes of sight from the scale of the human range to that of the galaxies and inversely to that of the electrons. Here the stepwise leaps along the size and speed scales present the static architecture of the universe as an exciting journey to the infintely great and the infinitely small.

Such dynamization of static structure is a step toward the kind of effect obtained when film or television portrays actions, changes, events. The initiative is taken on by the movement and change of the subject matter itself, and the viewer plays the more receptive role of the witness. Things are presented as happenings and, in the larger sense, the world as a whole appears as a process, as Becoming rather than Being. The most typical example is the "story" narrated by the feature film. But the growth of the embryo, the conquest of a mountain, and the progress of a surgical operation are also subjects of this nature. The particular appeal of such a performance derives from the fact that the viewer is carried by the dynamics of the story rather than having to supply the impulse and leadership himself.

This means that the viewer himself is allowed to assume the role of the consumer. In any consumer society, which thrives on, the passivity of the customer, communication is based on the principle of supplied action. The work of the public media is concerned with "news vlue," i.g., with what changes rather than what is. The risk of this one-sided approach is that it tends to create an unnautural resistance to anything that fails to take the viewer on a trip of action, but requires action initiated by the viewer. The result can be a distorted image of the world, in which nothing counts or even exists except what changes, what "is going on." By the time a child becomes addicted to his daily television programme he leaves behind him the age at which he could explore an old clock with the endless patience of a scientist. Here, then, the educator faces a problem of attitude, largely created by a special use of the media but remediable, in part, with the help of the media themselves.

Written or printed language as a visual medium is neither linear nor nonlinear in itself. Posters, advertisements, inscriptions, charts and tables can use arrangements of words not intended to be read in sequential order, and the so-called concrete poetry distributes letters, wrods, or sentences on the page in the form of two-dimensional images to be perceived as nonsequential compositions like paintings. Dictionaiers, calenders, time schedules are to be consulted, not read. In all these instances it is important to design the arrangement of verbal materials in such a way that linear persual is discouraged and, instead, a different and freer order is suggested. To this end, sequences are broken up, items are separated by clear subdivision, dominant and subordinate elements are distinguished by size, color, and location, and cross-connections in space are established by visual means, such as similarity of appearance.

In the special case of consecutive reading, which develops gardually during the history of written language, the visual presentation of words is used in order to record the sequence of logical thinking. Here the writing provides linear channels, but since the medium in itself is immobile, action and sequence must be supplied by the reader, somewhat as in the Japanese picture scrolls. Reading, in other words, is a visual activity in which the initiative rests largely with the recipient. This demand, together with the indirectness of any verbal medium, calls for a mental discipline more stringent than that required for the intake of visual action. In this respect, the character of the verbal medium remains unchanged when writing is supplemented by printing.

It follows from the linear nature of speech that when written or spoken captions or comments are used to interpret pictures, they introduce a temporal sequence into the order by which the picture is apprehended. Obviously it makes a difference whether the verbal description proceeds mechanically, say, from the left to the right, indicating objects in the arrangement in which they appear during lineup, or whether the description starts with the most conspicuous element of the picture or—and this is by no means always the same thing—with the most revealing item, which holds the key to the whole story. Also the verbal description will pick out and make explicit certain relations between parts which the picture itself may not isolate or stress so clearly.

Simultaneity

All visual media have some aspect of spatial simulatneity. Even Morse code, the most linear of them all, requires that the dots and dashes be apprehended in bunches rather than one by one. In normal reading, not only every single letter must be perceived as a whole, but entire words and indeed phrases are grasped as units. The momentary images of film or television must be followed not only in their succession but also scanned spatially, to the extent to which a rapid change permits it. I have already referred to the task of apprehending a complex image, e.g., a painting of the sky ofa planetarium, as a whole by integrating the details scanned in succession.

Simultaneity becomes most explicit when several images are presented together. The projection of two or more slides at the same time has become so among educators that to limit oneself to one picture seems almost old-fashioned. The method is indeed attractive in that it permits explicit comparisons between scenes taken at different places. There are precedents in the history of painting: triptychs and altars, combining a variety of scenes, series of painting to be displayed in the same room ; photomontages, which combine shots of different origin. The first experiment with three film seenes propected on three sereens was contained in Abel Gance's Napoleon of 1925, and projections on the backdrop of the stage and on the walls around the audience were used in the political theatre, e.g., by Erwin Piscator, to supplement the principal action. During the last few years batteries of carousel projectors synchronized by programming tape have led to multiple-side shows as a matter of routine in teaching.

It is necessary to emphasize that such simultaneity of several visual wholes strains considerably the apprehensive capacity of the sense of sight and the mind. Therefore, unless there are clear relations between the units, the effect will be an amorphous bombardment, leaving the viewer with nothing better than a vague overall impression of what it is all about. In capacity to understand encourages a dedfeatist attitude of mere indulgence in sensory stimulation.

Therefore, the presentation as a wholemust be organized with sufficient lucidity. The organization concerns not only the subject matter of the pictures, but also their purely visual appearance. For a somple example, various aspects of the same object can be shown in multiple presentation: the back and front sides of a coin, different shots of the same building, and so on. The two sides of a coin are easily related by their common roundness, but the facade and the north wall of a church may display no such obvious visual kinship. Different views may be derived from the same object, and yet the eyes may be unable to relate them properly. How they belong together may not be evident. It is not enough to rely simply on what the viewer knows about the subject-matter. Images will not do their work unless the eyes are persuaded, and the eyes require a sufficient common denominator as a visual base for any comparison.

If, for example, several pictures are meant to show objects possessing the same property, say, various minerals of crystalline structure, this key property must be clearly emphasized by visual means; and if crystals are to be compared with sedimentary rocks, the geologist must have the eye of an artist to make the confrontation convincing. Confrontation is effective in showing contrasts. However, if the student is to compare two pictures—a city or landscape before and after the destruction of war—the views must be sufficiently similar to make the contrast dramatic. If everything is different, comparison does not come easily.

Simultneity requires even greater skill when two different media, notably, images and sound, are to be combined. Little needs to be said here about the benefits of recorded noise, which help in identifying animate and inanimate things, introduce them by their sounds even when they are not visibl, emphasize the rhythm of machines, and complement the mood of teh scene. Music prevents the ears from straying from the performance, defines the dynamic nature of a setting as quiet, gay, or foreboding, and promotes a general sense of action and liveliness. Music can be disturbingly hyperactive. It should not emulate the reckless appeals of television commercials by trying to "jazz up" the sobriety of an instructional picture. Music can legitimately enhance the action inherent in a film without resorting to false dramatics or romanic gloss. Quiet prusuits deserve quiet sounds.

By far the most delicate problem is posed by the combination a picture and speech. Pictures and spoken commentary, when properly used, complement each other quite naturally. In particular, photographs, films, and other realistic images can be helped by language because they show human beings, animals, plants, minerals in all their individuality. They make the viewer remain aware of the endless variety of actual existence and stay away from schematization. At the same time, however, learning aims at general concepts, the language helps to nail down the general in the particular. By naming a part of the picture an Irish setter, a colonial mansion, or a spinning machine, the commentary defines the species, class, and function of that particular image. Language also helps in singling out defined items from the continuum of the visual world. When we are told in so many words that next to the cottage there stand an oak and a birch, it is as though someone were cutting out each tree with scissors and setting it apart for special examination.

The combination of picture and speech can be achieved successfully in two fundamentally different ways: the first is epitomized by the slide lecture, in which a coherent speech presentation dominates while the illustrations accompany it as subordinate aids; in the second, a coherent visual performance plays the leading part and is merely supported by the commentary. The decisive difference between dominant and subordinate medium is not one of quantity, i.e., the subordinate medium does not have to be limited to occasional entrances while the dominant one holds the stage all the time. It is rather a matter of content.

The slide lecute, as just mentioned, may be a coherent train of thought, presenting verbally some principle, e.g., of visual perception or social behaviour, and illustrating it by as many examples on the screen as needed. However, a lecturer can also function as a mere commentator. He may present a dominant and coherent series of slides, let us say, the sketches for Picasso's painting Guernica, in chronological order. In such a case, the words should limit themselves to what can be seen in the screen image or directly deduced from it. The lecturer must make up his mind which attitude he wants to create in the viewer. If he wants him to be absorbed by the procession of pictures on the screen, he cannot hope for attention when, in the midst of the show, he takes off on some historical or theoretical consideration.

Experience seems to indicate that the dominance of speech is almost negligible for the purposes of film and television, unless the speaker himself constitutes the visual spectacle, made more rewarding perhaps by interesting demonstrations during the talk. The nature of the two media requires that the picture be dominant. In the aforementioned lecture series, *Civilization,* the presentation was successful when the lecturer underscored and explained in words the art objects he was showing, but the unity of image and speech came apart when he introduced historical or philosophical expositions, thus forcing the pictures into a background role, for which they could only be much too dominant.

The spoken commentary has always been the bane of traveloques, documentaries, and instructional films. It has been much ridiculed ("and as the sun descends in the west....") but hardly imporoved. The principal trouble is that when the picture, a nondiscursive medium, predominates, the spoken commentary cannot fit as long as it is discursive in thought and syntax. The filmmaker, like any other artist, convyes general statements through concrete sensory experience. The freshness, directness, and originality of the images aresabotaged when the spoken commentary reduces the objects, actions, and qualities to their conceptual names. This deadening of the picture by words is hard to avoid since the commentary has precisely the task of spelling out the message of the picture. It should not duplicate in dry or, worse, falsely poetic words what picture tells more attractively but, rather, amplify and explain, always within the range of the visible subject-matter.

The very form of logical discourse adapts it self badly to the free flow of film images. One should experiment more boldly with commentaries made up of questions, dialogue, exclamations—anything that breaks the flow of discursive reasoning. Instruction can be equally well served—perhaps better—by such freer linguistic expression. Granted that in order to produce a good sound track of this nature one needs an expert practitioner of theatrical speech, the kind of person not often employed by the makers of educational films.

Size and Distance

All images have two sizes: that of the physical carrier of the image itself and that of the objects represented by it. A picture of an elephant may be only an inch high; a plastic model showing the anatomy of a flower may be twenty times the size of the real flower. There are obviously good reasons for making an image small enough to fit the page of a book and large enough to show the needed detail, but the educator must be wary of the misleading effects of what is, after all, the "wrong" size.

The older student is not likely to be fooled by the giant size of an ant on the screen. However, in the teaching and learning of art history it is hard to protect oneself against the distorting effects of a miniature painting appearing as large as Michelangelo's David. On the screen all things, from the microscopic to the astronomical, are the same size. It is well known also that children have trouble realizing that maps differ in scale, so that Belgium, although it fills, the page of the atlas just as does Africs, is nevertheless much smaller.

Correct comparison is a particularly critical matter when intimately related objects are shown at different scale. Machines or organisms consist of parts in all sizes, from the tiniest detail to the whole mechanism or body. Any such part, in order to be shown, has to be adapted to the optimal visual angle of the viewer, who nevertheless has to be made to understand how all these contraptions fit together in their correct sizes. Here the teacher may have to resort to additional resources, preferably to the inspection of the original object itself.

Size has other, less tangible but educationally important, connotations. An insect enlarged to giant size is put in the company of prehistoric monsters. A highway viewed from a helicopter produces an image that makes the traffic artery look like an artery of the human body, through which blook corpuscles run their course. Such comparisons can be poetical and they can also be enlightening by pointing to unexpected similarities. But the difference of character obtained by a change of size must be intended and controlled. The peaceful order of the landscape seen from the air hides the nosiy struggle of human existence—an effect that may or may not serve the educational purpose.

The relativity of size inherent in all visual representation can make the student realize that man's view of the world, dependent on the accidental size of the human body, has no absolute validity, but there are as many realities as there are size levels, and only the synthesis of all of them provides us with an intelligent sense of the world, whose measure we are not.

The human size in relation to the size of an object affects our attitude toward it. A small artifact or living creature seems powerless, graceful, remote, miraculous in its functioning. A monumental status is equally remote from our own kind, but awe-inspiring, threatening, overpowering. The room-filling sizse of

Renaissance murals, abstract-expressionist paintings, or giant screen projections is designed to surround and overwhelm the viewer, whereastoday's small television screen remains something of a toy, never quite an arena for the sort of power that can assail us from the movie screen. The television set is a piece of furniture, like the blackboard or the desk, subject to our handling; therefore its images also seem to lack the strength to subdue us. This can make for more detached judgment. *Ceteris paribus,* it reduces the sense of real presence.

Both kinds of experience, the one that sucks us in and the other that keeps its distance, are educationally productive, as long as the teacher exploits the character of each medium with sensitive awarencess.

The Range of the Image

Every image is carved out of the continuity of time and space. It represents a selection, whose range must fit the purpose. By picking the correct range of a problem one goes a long way toward solving it. In photographic terms, the range of the image, determined by the distance of the camera from the subject and the focal lenth of teh lens, presupposes a judgment as to what "belongs." Depending on the correctness of the picture range, the viewer may or may not understand what he is supposed to see. The facial expression and posture of a disturbed child may be sufficient to suggest his state of mind, and therefore the sight of things and persons around him may be merely distracting for the veiwer. If, however, the attitude of the child has to be understood as a reaction to his direct environment, this environment must be shown, either in the same picture or before or afterwards.

A part extracted from its whole becomes a different thing, and therefore extirpation must be performed with caution. It was probably Andre Malraux who in his *Psychology of Art* initiated a whole new way of reproducing works of art when he showed the astonishing revelations obtained simply by enlarging details of paintings. The suprisingly modern-looking sketchiness of back-ground landscapes in a Venetian painting or in a Poussin discloses a variability of style easily overlooked under the impact of the picture as a whole. Yet, when the relatively small background landscape is looked at in the context of the whole work, it does not really possess the impressionist boldness it expresses in isolation. In other words, the practice of presenting parts as wholes offers revelation at the risk of falsification.

The sort of tunnel vision provided by any protrayal of reality has its pros and cons. The picture frame can clarify and intensify the subject, not only by limiting the quantity of what is shown, but also by cutting many of the relations the subject has to its surroundings. Such simplification may produce a one-sided impression. Just as the publicity folder of a resort hotel shows it surrounded by woods and topped by snowcapped mountains, but hides the other hotels and the highway nearby, so the limitation of the picture range may leave out relevant aspects of the subject. The film medium can remedy this restriction more easily because the borders of the image are not permanent as are those of a photograph or painting; they change as soon as the camera turns or trvels. From the continuum of the changing view the spectator can synthesize a more complete whole.

In the exploration of the visual world, time and space are inseparabale. Objectively, every human being, just as any other thing, goes through its existence in an uninterrupted continuum of time and space. Conscious experience, however, is not continuous. Anesthesia interrupts experience without leaving as much as a sense of time lost. Sleep hides large portions of our day, and in a less predictable manner an hour's or a lifetime's image is patched together from separate moments of more or less complete awareness. This possibility of creating a conherent whole from separate samples of time and space is also used by film and television. The art of film editing consists precisely in combining scense in such a way that the viewer receives a meaningful continuity while noticing, at the same time, the seams needed to tell him that objective time and space have been sampled rather than recorded compeletely.

The extent to which time and space can be skipped depends not only on the content of the happening, but also on the visual sophistication of the viewer. The director of a television reportage can switch cameras from the close-up of a single face to a long-range shot of a crowd from one visual angle to acountershot in the opposite direction only because his free handling of space is matched by the visual literacy of his audience. Evidently, this capacity to "skip" develops gardually childhood. Therefore, the material for the early years requires more continuity of time and space than is needed later.

To the educator, the elegance of economical editing means that topics can be presented with an intelligent grasp of essentials and a neglect of irrelevant and redundant detail. But the skipping of continuity may also favour superficial thinking. For example, our industrial age has trained the mind to skip the continuity between input and output. In the natural state, people obtain firewood by cutting trees they may have grown themselves. The urban child of today turns the switch on the radiator or electric stove to get heat energy. This reduces the chain of causality between input and output to the one instant connecting the turning of the switch with the delivery of heat, leaving outthe entire process of how electricity is generated and how it is paid for by the consumer. The shortcut from need to supply, characteristic of the child's experiences at home, in school, in stores, and in the street, is surely justified for the purposes of parctical behaviour, but it cripples a thoughful understanding of our way of life. Here, a film showing, e.g., how water gets from its original source to the faucet, refuses to imitate the shortcut of practical thinking and thereby contributes to insightful living.

Articulate Form

The optical mechanism of the eyes uses light energy to produce amazingly faithful images of the physical world; but, strictly speaking, it is not the recording of the object's visual appearance as such that provides information. It takes appropriate formal characteristics of shape and colour to make the object visible. What is it we need to know about an object? We want to be informed about some of its properties, and these properties are transmitted exclusively through articulate form.

If wc have to find out whether an object is round or angular, in motion or at rest, green or blue, only the precise form qualities of colour and shape can give us the answer. Most drawings and paintings are geared to this basic demand. They endow the object with defined shapes and colours and thereby make it visible. Photography and film cannot be expected to do this to the same extent. The person handling the camera can, by the choice of his subject and the clever use of lighting, do his best to shape the image as clearly as possible, but the result can be successful only within limits. Photographs abound in visually ambiguous or undefined detail. This heightens their realistic quality and can be advantageous artistically, but when precise information is needed, photographic images easily let us down. The adult observer is often unaware of these deficiencies because he is accustomed to supplying by inference what the picture is supposed to show but does not. The child, however, must rely on the concrete visible presence of the facts and qualities he is to gather from the picture.

If an illustration shows a Tyrolese playing the zither, the grown-up viewer, sufficiently informed about the insrument, may not notice that the photo fails to show the strings and to explain clearly what the man's fingers are doing. The child may possess no such knowledge and is let down by the picture.

Therefore, one fundamental rule for the use of visual material is this: Never take for granted that a picture which records a certain facts does actually convery the desired information! Especially when television transmits photographic material under unfavourable viewing conditions, the student, who is expected to see a beaver dam, may see instead nothing but an unsightly smudge.

The formal difference between handmade and photographic images can be exemplified by the use of the contour line in drawing and painting. Nature contains no contour lines, but the shape of most physical objects is perceived only when their borders are clearly visible and when they are characteristic of that shape. The round shape of an apple is characterized by its round borders. If I look at the apple through a keyhole so that only a part of it is seen I will not recognize its shape because its true borders are hidden and the outline of the keyhole does not correspond sufficiently to that of the apple. Similarly, if the apple lies on a tablecloth of the same colour, its outlines will be invisible by lack of contrast, and again I will not see the apple. The contour lines used by the draftsman, although unnatural," resemble the border of the object structurally and thereby make identification possible. It is an invention of the human hand and eye, designed to show clear distinctions between objects. Photographs contain no more contour lines than the objects they depict. Similarly, such informative qualities as the bulging surface of an egg or a sail, the textures of metal or rock, the spatial relations of overlap, surrounding, containing, matching, etc., must explicitly conveyed by formal means.

This is not to say that drawing and painting techniques gurantee the needed validity of shape and colour. The old-fashioned style of mechanically realistic copying, for example, makes things easy to recognize but "invisible" as to their various structural qualities. If the viewer's eye tries to "pin down" the shapes of a tree sketched in the manner of a nineteenth-century drawing teacher, the tree vanishes. Also, the draftsmen employed for the illustration of textbooks and similar educational material do not always concentrate on the rendition of the features that are crucial for learning. Being artists rather than educators, they easily give in to fashionable style, originality of invention, flings of caprice, pleasant enough to look at but often fatal to the educational purpose. Not that the illustrator should "leave out the art." On the contrary, in order to produce images best suited for learning by seeing, a good draftsman employs the means of artistic expression to depict the objects he is called upon to interpret. Outstanding examples of thsi selfless devotion to the nature of the object are the anatomical and technical drawings of Leonardo da Vinci.

Leonardo teaches us that to draw something means to interpret it and that one can interpret it only if one understands it. Therefore, students will profit greatly from drawing, painting , or photographing objects, provided the teacher guides and judges their work with the proper criteria. For example maticulous exactness in the rendering of detail may not be virtue when a student draws what he sees under the mocroscope. On the contrary, such mechanical faithfulness may obstruct the purpose and promote an attitude of thoughless copying and an incapacity to tell essentials from irrelevancies—a lack of intelligent abstraction. This leads us to our final and perhaps most important topic.

Abstraction as a Teacher

We have asked: What are the principal criteria a visual image has to meet in order to fufill its educational purpose? The notion of *authenticity* presented itself soon enough and we had no trouble realizing to what extent the mechanical faithfulness of the photographic media has increased the reliability of images, be they recordings of natural phenomena, reports of political or social events, or the reproduction of objectives or works of art. No handdrawn image can replace the authentic presence of a desert landscape, the Dead Sea Scrolls, ora medical syndrome shown in a good photograph or film.

At the same time, we realize that mere authenticity in the sense of unadaulterated reproduction of the original is not sufficient to qualify a photographic or man-made image for its educational purpose. We remember that learning means grasping relevant properties of a situation. To this end, the least realistic images are often the best.

Take as an example a series of drawings, developed by means of a computer which illustrate some geological hypotheses on how the Grand Canyon may have arrived at its present shape. Each drawing is limited to a single contour line, showing the profile of the canyon at a particular phase of its development. The drawings are most instructive. When combined in an animated sequence, they actually let us witness the dramatic geological event in live action. And yet, the picture could not be less realistic. It leaves out almost everything. the story of thousands of years is reduced to a few seconds. The huge canyon is scaled down to a few inches. The masses of rock and sand and the sky above them are totally absent. There is nothing but a greatly simplified outline, which represents a section—and this section is unobtainable in the real world. You cannot slice through the Grand Canyon. Even so, the lesson to be learned is presented with supreme clarity.

Of course, the simple diagram has to be supplemented by realistic pictures of the real landscape. Otherwise, the lesson will perhaps be learned but may relate, in the students's mind, to the wrong kind of reality or to no reality at all. However, it is remarkable how naturally this sort of completely unrealistic presentation is accepted even by a person of little education. In fact, it closely resembles the style of drawing spontaneously invented by young children all over the world. In those drawings also, the ground on which we walk appears as a mere horizontal line, and nothing could look more convincing and appropriate. In other words, a highly abstract and unnaturalistic style of representation is the earliest, most widespread, and universally understood style of visual imagery.

Abstraction, in the simplest meaning of the word, refers to the leaving out of properties. The least we require of such omissions is that they should not interferc with the desired information. For example, pictures in black and white abstract drastically from colourful reality. However, they suffice for surprisingly many purposes, even though the usefulness of a guidebook for bird watchers is severely limited if the illustrations are not in colour. Many art historians, repelled by the bad quality of most colour reproductions, prefer to illustrate their lectures with black-and-white slides. These are indeed sufficient for discussions of subject matter; but to evaluate pictorial composition by looking only at the shapes can be quite misleading since shapes and colours tend to interact. The shape and size of a certain area of the picture may be incomprehensible and indeed may look wrong unless one sees that it is coloured a strong red. A principal condition for the use of substractive abstraction, therefore, demands that omissions should not alter any characteristic of the whole that are pertinent to the desired information.

Perhaps it is permissible, under the heading abstraction, also to refer to certain other liberties taken with the realistic image. Normal vision is limited to the outer surface of objects and indeed to those portions of the objects can be reached by a strainght line from the eye or camera. We cannot see the back side of the moon; at the same time this back side can be a relevant part of the information we require. An image showing the whole object, e.g., the polyhedrons of the mathematician, is best represented pictorially by what looks like a transparent image but is better described as a complete projection of all the edges, including those hidden from ordinary eyesight. Charcteristically enough, when with the technique of computer graphics, the various aspects of a three-dimensional solid are to beshown on the face of a cathods-ray tube, a main difficulty consists in eliminating the edges hidden by the frontal surfaces because these are accidental substractions from the total shape.

Ordinary vision cannot penetrate beneath the outer skin of objects. This is a severe limitation since the inside may be what matters most. Image-making can overcome this deficiency to some extent. Architects and engineers use sections and so-called exploded views showing outside and inside of a building or machine together in their spatial interrelation. In the pictorial arts, it has been quite admissible to omit the roofs or frontal walls of buildings in order to show what is going on inside, and the Bushmen represent the inner organs of an animal as a legitimate part of its image.

Images can be made at any level of abstraction, from the simplest form to the most complex. The correct choice of the appropriate level depends on the nature of what is to be shown and on the intellectual maturity of the viewer. Of a geographical map, for example, only a few global features fcan be apprehended in the early school years, and the complications of the actual shapes, crowded with detail of crooked rivers and coastlines, are likely to distract from the grasp of the basic facts. Or, to use another example, once the arrangement of the endocrine glands within the human body has been understood as an abstract system, a more faithful and therefore more complicated picture of the anatomical facts can be introduced with profit. This principle holds for any sort of instruction at any level of development. It is an application of the commonsense rule that learning must proceed from the simple to the complex.

Our examples will have made clear what we mean when we say in conclusion that what anybody needs to learn about anything is never the thing "itself" but only an organized whole of selected abstract character traits. It is the task of the visual media to put these traits in evidence. A good example is the learning about numbers. If the student is to see with his own eyes how many legs a fly has, those six visual items must be presented with all the clarity that shape, brightness, and colour can muster. The same is true for the number of chromosomes, the number of jurors, the number of sport on a die. These quantities are an abstract trait of certain objects. Equally abstract are other traits of objects, such as their colours, their sizes, their movements, and they can be singled out for the purpose of learning.

A final step will remind us that the visual media serve not only to demonstrate the properties of physical objects. They also translate nonvisual facts into visual ones and thereby give them sensory concreteness. Curves showing the cost of living over time, barometric pressure or temperature changes display quantitative aspects of properties that are not visual in themselves. Similarly, flow charts, diagrams in books on logic or economics, and the like, suggest that there is no branch of human learning that cannot be helpfully displayed in some of its aspects by visual means.

The most appropriate level of abstraction for such a display may by the kind of highly realistic image that only photography can create or it may be as rarified as a geometrical outline figure. In each case the image helps to supply the human mind with the sensory vehilce that it needs for its travels.

5

Women and Children in the Era of Communication

The ongoing Communication Revolution has opened up new possibilities of acccelerating development, specially for the uplift of women and children. But if it remains uncontrolled and unguided, this revolution will have adverse effects on the life of women and children. This danger is till not very adequately perceived or appreciated by the promoters of the Communication Revolution.

It is necessary to focus our discussions directly on women and children in the context of modern communication and development. This is because when we reflect on the human condition in general, we miss the aspects affecting specifically women and children. Thus, we may go on discussing the general problems of development without ever touching on questions relating to women and children who constitute such a large section of our population. But when we take up the problems of women and children in the context of development, we cannot but discuss the human condition in totality, as the problems of women and children are rooted in their relationships with men in diverse roles and life-situtations. To put women and children in the centre of our discussion is, therefore, required as much by scientific enquiry into the social dimensions of development as by social objectives relating to women and children which are enshrined in the Constitution of India.

The focus on women and children implies identifying the structural constraints which inhibit their fullest growth and development. It also means appraising, even redefining, the very concept of 'development.' Development is broadly understood as growth of human capabilities for acquiring control over natural forces and processes with the aim of improving the material basis of human life. In the modern age man's power over nature is associated with the advance of scientific knowledge and technology, resulting in unparalled growth of material goods and services, specially in developed countries. But development in the wider sense means much more than the growth of material wealth through efficient utilization of man-and-women—power as a means of growth. It also encompasses the conception of utilising material wealth as a means of achieving *non-material* ends for enriching the quality of life. In other words, mankind is interested in growth not for its own sake; growth must become a means of *enriching* the lives of men, women and children. Mankind must, therefore, ensure that growth does not turn into an engine of social and economic *exploitation;* and that it serves as an aid to emancipation, specially of women and children from all forms of social andeconomic exploitation. The concept of development must therefore be redefined in terms of material progress at one end and social and economic *emancipation* at another end.

It does not require much logic or empirical evidence to prove that women and children have been and continue to be the vicitms of poverty and under-development on the one hand and socia-economic injustice and exploitation on the other. But they are also the victims of development itself—specially of *inequititons patterns* of economic growth and social change. Whether development emerges as an oppressive or a liberating force depends on the nature of the social framework within which development is achieved. It also depends on the nature of the new technology that is adopted for accelerating development. In an unequal, class-divided and male-dominated society, institutional and technological choices for promoting development tend to favour the dominant groups and the dominant gender. A critique of development in this context must be a critique of the *class* and the *gender* bias in development. Uncontrolled development processes act against the interests of weaker sections, specially of women and children, by eroding certain safeguards exisiting in the traditional economic and social systems. The pre-capitalist and pre-industrial civilizations had over the centuries evolved certain institutions and values which provided some degree of security and protection to the economically weaker classes of peasants, artisans and labourers and to biologically weaker sections like women and children. For example, the community controls on property and labour exercised checks on indiscriminate exploitation of the 'havenots' by the 'haves' they also imposed customary obligations on the 'haves' for sharing the fruits of the productive process with the 'havenots.' Such a sharing, however, did not challenge the domination of the 'haves' and 'havenots' nor did it alter the unequal access of 'haves' and 'havenots' to resources and to the fruits of production. These customary obligations, nevertheless, acted as mechanisms of redistribution and represented sources of economic and social security for women and children.

It must also be noted that under conditions of pre-market natural economy, the weaker sections had access to resources and goods freely provided by nature. There was access, for instance, to forests, to grazing grounds, to natural water flows, to community lands, etc. which contributed significantly towards releiving the burdens and softening the insecurities of weaker sections including women and children. Moreover, certain institutional guarantees and safeguards had evolved in pre-commercial civilizations protecting women and children from inhuman and brutal treatment at the hands of dominant groups who were their masters and employers. We have evidence from the history of developed countries how during their transition from a pre-industrial to the industrial society the labouring poor lost the securities of the old world without the gain of new ones.

Trevelyan's history of England during the Great Transition records that "there was more independence, variety and joy in life under the old system than under the new system at its worst; and the worst of the new economic dispensation came when it was first introduced." Further, when "the cow, the garden, the strips of corn land, the cottage industries and the good wages of the early Georgian period disappeared together, the poor had no means ofdemanding analogous benefits under any new system." Eric Hobsbawm also observes how "the iron and impersonal advance of the machine and the market... produced those multitudes of the declassed, the pauperised and the famished whose condition forze the blood of the most flinty economist." Again, "the Industrial Revolution ereated the ugliest world in which man has ever lived...or by uprooting men and women in unprecedented numbers and depriving them of the certainties of the ages, probably the unhappies world."

Any discerning observer and analyst of the Indian scene finds abundant evidence to show that modern development has been accelerating the distingeration of community institutions and customary controls which provided security and protection to the poor for ages. In particular, one finds that the transition from the natural to the market economy, from custom to contract, and from kind payment to cash nexus, has been eroding the age-old social relations which had been welding together groups and communities into a framwork of inter-dependence. The growth of transport and communication is operning up the isolated and self-sufficient communities to the influence of commercial forces and interest groups from outside. As a result, there has occurred the inevitable transformation of free natural goods into commodities. There has occurred also the dissolution or custom, of norms and values, of beliefs and faiths supporting and sanctifying the traditional system. All these traumatic changes have affected adversely the weaker seetions of peasants, artisans and labourers. But the adverse impact of this transition on the position of women and children is often the most traumatic and agonising. Women and children arc turned into commodities by the relentless forces of the money and market economy. Deprived of the protection and security of the traditional institutions, these vulnerable sections are yet untouched by the protective framework of a modern welfare stage. The phoenomenon of the uncontrolled exploitation of the labour power of women and child which we find fully recorded in textbooks of Western history can also be seen by any sensitive observer of the Indian scene in the urban and the rural areas. The new masters of property and new employers of women and children are far more covetous, acquisitive, and brutal than their traditional masters and employers.

The erosion of traditional social institutions also means the erosion of the traditional institutions of child care, protection and socialization. The outlook of treating women as saleable sex objects has spread on a large scale everywhere following the growth of monetisation and commercialization. In the Communist Manifesto Karl Marx took note of this tendency charactersising the newly emerging capitalist industrial economy and the social relations based on cash nexus. He observed that "the bourgeoisis has torn away from the family its sentimental veil and has reduced the family relation to a mere money relation.

During field work in the hilly region of Uttar Pradesh the author has noted how modern transport and communication and other developmental forces have resulted in increased production of food grams, milk fruits, vegetables and other varieties of goods and services. But it is not local communities, the weaker section and specially women and children who have acess to these newly produced goods. Access to these is not free any more as itis determined not by proximity to the sources of these free goods of nature. Access is now determined by access to mens of productions or by command over pruchasing power. Due to the transfer of control of means of production from the traditional to the new classes having money power and political influence, whatever limited benefits the people derived under the traditional system based on custom are being taken away from them. For instance, the govermmenta-lization as well a commercialization of forests has adversely affected the interests of weaker sections. Most conspicious in the transformation of free natural goods into commodities which has occurred on an extensive scale during the last decade and a half following the opening up of the hill economy.

It may be asked why the development which are formulated with the intention of benefitting the people and specially the weaker sections have the unintended consequence of snatching away from them even the limited benefits which they had under the traditional system, even under conditions of underdevelopment. It is important to note that the erosion of the traditional values and institutions has occurred without the parallel growth of new values and institutions providing support and protection to the weaker sections. The loss of teh old without the creation of the new creates an institutional void.

We learn from English history how in this social background the victims of modern development turned into *Luddites:* their discontent and wrath was turned against machinery which they mistakenly perceived as a destroyer of their livelihood and security. Such *Luddite* outbrusts by the weaker sections iincluding women and children are avery frequent occurrence even in contemporary developing societies. Such expressions of desructive rage are witnessed very frequently in different parts of India which are exposed to the impact of development programmes and projects.

In this background the conception of development will suffer from gaps if it does not subsume thc idea of protection of weaker sections and of women and children from the adverse consequences of development programmes. It must also subsume the idea of introducing such social controls on the property strcture, capital allocation and skill formation as are required to ensure participation of weaker sections and of women and children in growth programmes. The question of the Communication Revolution for the benefits of the women and children has to be viewed in this wider context of ensuring their protection from the adverse impact of development and of aiding and strengthening their access to development opportunities and to fruits of development. It must also be recognized that emancipation will not come to women and children as a gift from the privileged and dominant groups: nor will development programmes be automatically reorientedand restructured in favour of women and children on the basis of new insights and ideas. A powerful movement of women with the support of active allies from other social start is an indispensable condition for women's emancipation being in-built into development processes.

The ongoing Communication Revolution in India represents the extension of the scientific and technological revolution to the sphere of communication. We have not yet appraised the full implications of this communication revolution in terms of possibilities and dangers for women and children. We must first take into account the fact that every leap in the field of communication has represented for mankind a leap in the relationship between man and nature on the one hand and between man and man and man and woman on the other. The labour process, according to some social thinkers, played the most important role in the transformation from ape to man. Probing deeper into this phenomenon of the origin of man we discover that communication has played an equally crucial role in the transformation from ape to man and also in man's transition from lower to higher levels of economic and social development. The growth in the social chesion of human comunities and their capacity for more and more effective action a collectivity has depended on the two factor. First is the sophistication of the technology of speedy transmission of messages in terms of reducing time and distance. Second is the innovation of language and of more subtle and suggestive meaning systems, symbols and image, for inter-personal, inter-group and inter-community communication. Thus the development of communication systems has two separate but complementary and inter-related dimensions-one relating to the *medium* or technique of transmitting the message and the other relating to the message itself, its quality content and meaning. The first involves a technological challenge and the latter a *culturad* challenge. The communication revolution involves both a techonogical revolution and a *cultural revolution. It encompasses* a revolution in *hardware* as well as creativity of software. The first concerns the engineer and the technocrat working with material tools and the latter the creative artist and the writer working with the aid of images, sounds and words.

In designing its own version of the Communication Revolution in the contemporary world, a developing country like India has to give as much importance to the *artistic* and the *cultural* dimensions as to the *engineering* and the *technological dimensions.* This is because the extension of the modern communication to a developing country opens it up in a massive way to the techno-cultural influences and *stimulii* from the developed countries. This contact between the technologically under-developed and the developed countries has a positive role to play in stimulating developmental consciousness and indigenous creativity in the latter. Such a contact can potentially contribute to growth of national cultures within the framework of international co-operation. *But this contact also carries the dangerous potentialities of eroding national identity and of turning on under-developed country into a cultural colony of the developed country.*

The children of the developing countries, who have access to modern communication, are exposed during their most sensitive and impressionable period to cultural stimulii or to software from outside. How they are affected by this exposure depends on the quality of the software to which they are exposed. If they are exposed to programmes promoting scientific temper and spirit and the humanistic, democratic and egalitarian aspects of the Western tradition, the programmes will contribute to their wholesome development as modern citizens in the best sense of the term. But if they are exosed to low quality programmes preaching the doctrine of racial inequality and inferiority and concentration on the negative aspects of the social situation of developing countries, these programes will have a harmful impact on children, distorting their outlook and orientation and croding their rootedness in their own cultural milieu. A cosmopolitanism which erodes national pride and sense of national identity spreads like an infection in countries like India through uncontrolled communication with the developed West. *Cultural colomalism causing annihilation of national identity is much worse than erstwhile political colonialism: in most cases the former has persisted even though direct political colonialism has ended.*

The Macbride Commission has remarked that the concern for national identity has grown in a big way with the introduction of television in developing countries. This is so because television is exceedingly seductive and appealing; it is also a very hungry and expensive modium. If a country has not prepared itself for generaating its own software and for importing only relevant software from outside, it invites trouble for itself by introducing television hardware. It invites the danger of erosion of its cultural identity through non-discriminating acceptance of software from developed countries. It can also be overwhelmed by low quality software produced by commercial agencies within the country itself. Among developing countries India is one of the few countries having the cultural talent and technological knowhow to generate software relevant to its own needs and requirements. But these pofentialities still remain largely untapped. India has been moving ahead much faster in hardware and has been lagging for behind in software production. The Indian Communication Revolution is still predominantly an *engineer-led* revolution. It has yet to become a cultural worker-led revolution. This vast gap between hardware and software has created a void which results in inundation of the communication system by low-quality entertainment programmes produced by commercial agencies and by dry and didactic and sometimes crudely propagandist programmes by government controlled media. This lag in software planning means that we are missing the vast opportunities of ultilising the communication revolution for the purpose of development as defined earlier and for education of the people. It also means exposing the people to alien cultural influences.

The Communication Revolution exposes the developing countries to international demonstration effect; this means the dissemination of the values and outlook of consumerism from the rich to the poor countries. The full significance of this menace from consumerism in the wake of the communication revolution has not been adequately appreciated either by the ruling elite or the people. Attention must be drawn to the fact the perceptive social thinkers from the West itself have regarded the link-up between communication revolution and consumerism as the most conspicuous feature of the post-industrial society. Communication has been converted into a powerful means or promoting consumerist values. In this background, the main challenge before developing countries is that of creating their own non-consumerist version of the communication revolution.

We must realise that the communication revolution is already promoting islands of elite affluence in the midst of mass poverty in countries like India. The alliance between communication expansion, consumerism and elite affluence is a source of distrotion of all our planning processes. It subverts our plan perspectives and priorities for uplift of weaker sections and of women and children. Consumerism turns women into a naked sex object for glamourised advertising as required by a consumerist society. The child's orientation during childhood will determine his behaviour pattern as an adult and will, therefore, shape the character of the future society. In a consumerist culture the child also acquires a strongly consumerist orientation as it were from the mother's womb itself.

The women of the consumerist era is idealised neither as an enlightened mother nor as a self-fulfilled working person, deriving fulfilment from creativity both in the realm of the body and the spirit as the equal partner and companion of man in the proceses of living. A consumerist society puts the women on the pedestal as the glamourised sex object alone; her supreme purpose becomes providing titillation to the male-dominated world. Software producers in a consumerist society are motivated only to innovate infinite variety of forms and methods of voluptuous entertainment to men whose over stimulated and over-strained organism seeks lower forms of thrill, excitement and relaxation every moment of their life. Here lies a powerful, though invisible, alliance between managers of the communication system and the kings of the vast industrial empires. The former stimulate the appetite and greed for infinite variety of goods and services towards which then the latter channelise the enormous economic resources and the technical stills of a science-governed world.

Are our planners aware of the implications of every step taken by them for hardware expansion in tems of opening up of the country to the blighting winds of consumerism from developed countries? Are they aware of their responsibilities in terms of creating immunities for the people, for women and children, from the piosonous virus of consumerism? A poor country must have development in the sense of building up productive capacity for the economic uplift of its people. But development should not mean inviting the virus of consumerism from the rich countries. Communicators have a great responsibility in the context. Software producers must aim not at galmourising affluence and consumerism in the name of promoting development. They must aim at *deglamourising* affluence and denigrading consumerism which has become the most conspicuous feature of the post-industrial world.

It is necessary that the communication planners and policy-makers the full implications of the extension of the modern communication to the rural areas and to remote regions of the country. No doubt the rural masses and the poeple in remote regions need to be pulled out of their socio-cultural and economic isolation. They need to be drawn into the mainstream of India's development and social transformation. But putting an end to their isolation and their joining the mainstream should mean neither violent uprooting from their cultural moorings nor elimination of their cultural identity. Nor should joining the mainstream be equated with exposure to a kind cosmopolitanism which erodes national pride, to consumerism which destroys the balance between material and spiritual values and to vulgar eroticism which substitutes titillation for joy.

It must be noted that in tribal and peasant communities, less exposed, if not unexposed, to modernisation, women have enjoyed a certain degree of independence, dignity and respect derived from their being equal partners of men in the processes of work and the sharing of the fruits of work. They also have participated as equal partners of men in cultural like, in community singing and dencing associated with processes of labour in the fields and in farms or with rituals, ceremonies and festivals celebrated all round the year. Women also enjoy social independence as refledcted in widow remarriage, annulment of marriage as a sequel to maltreatment by the husband and right to remarriage with a suitable partner.

The impact of modernisation on tribals and artisans has often resulted in, what Srinivas has called. *Sanskritisation,* that is, adoption of the beliefs, practices and ways of life of the upper castes. Aping the super castes means being re-oriented to trating women not as equal partners of many in work and song and dance. On the contrary, search for higher status involves women's degradation brought about by loss of economic and social independence arising from withdrawal from work and from singing and dancing with men in community celebrations. It also means giving up the practice of widow remarriage and the women's right to leave a male partner who maltreats her. Such *Brahmanisation* of the way of life of the lower castes is a retrograde step associated with pscudo-modernisation.

Will the Communicatioin Revolution strengthen th forces of further enlightenment, emanicipation and uplift of women? Or will it contribute towards exposing women to vulgar modernism, that is, to distorted and disoriented forms of women's emancipation as in the case of ultra-modern urban upper-middle class females; or to newer forms of conservatism called fundamentalism, expressed in strengthening of male domination and oppression, as in the case of women of the lower classes subjected to loss of rights and freedoms earlier enjoyed by them? Will the Communication Revolution be an instrument of exposing the Indian people to the worst of both the worlds—the commercialism of the new era combined with the social evils of the old world? It has been reported that mass media have contributed to transforming dowry into a menace for young women who are asked to meet dowry demands in terms of goods and gadgets advertised and glamourised by the mass media. This has recently resulted in tortures, murders and suicides in large numbers in different parts of the contry.

Attention needs to be drawn to certain other fundamental aspects which have not received as much publicity and attention of social reformers, agitators and activists as has been given to the question of glamourization by the media of women as a sex object in a growingly marker-and-consumerism-oriented developing society like India. The exploitation of the women's image for commercial purposes has been noted and criticised very widely. This is an evil whch is easier to detect and against which growing social mobilization of women and other activist social groups is now witnessed, specially in metropolitan areas. But the emancipation of women poses the most formidable problems in such values and practices of social, economic and cultural oppression and domination of women which evade attention. This is because these values and practices are of the "normal" social life of millions and millions of Indian people in day-to-day interaction between husbands and wives, mothers and children, brothers and sisters, parents and daughters, wives and their in-laws, employers and their women employees and so on. In these outwardly very ordinary relations between women and men in various roles within the family and outside, men and women are constantly violating in practice what they profess in words. The attempt to love in a modern context by the values of a bygone age produces colossal tension and conflict. Women suffer from this inner tension far more than men. Centuries of conditioning has turned them into willing victims of subtle forms of oppression and cruelty, discrimination and inequality. Men are often unconscious of what they are doing to women and women are often unconscious of what is being done to them. Whether in matters relating to the distribution of food or other items of consumption, or of work or leisure, of property or income, of other rights and privileges, women are subjected to discrimination and oppression which assume innumerable forms. Far from bringing these to light, the media, specially the feature films, are all the time idealizing and rationalizing them. In fact, myths, legends, images and symbols are derived from the vast treasures of Indian mythology and folklore to mystify or rationalize patterns of man-woman relations which are injurious to women's personality and antagonistic to their emancipation and equality.

Modern communication can be a great forc for women's emancipation if it is utilized for promoting a critical consciousness on the women's question. But it can be a source of powerful support to the forces of *status quo,* to conservative and revivalist values and practices and to annihilation of women's personality and identity. Creating a new class of producers of women's programmes who are committed to tapping modern communication as a powerful force for women's emancipation is one of the most important government and creative persons outside.

6

Educational Media

The contributions to this volume were designed to be essays in speculation on the roles that may be played by the new educational media in American society of the next few decades. As editors of such a volume, there are several courses of action open to us. We can choose the coward's path and say nothing about the items in the collection. Or, we can attempt a summary or synthesis. Or, we may attempt to correct the errors of omission and commission made by the several contributors. We have chosen to do all the things and to add our own speculations as well.

Our aim is reasoned and reasonable social science fiction. Many of our "hunches" will appear to be unsupported; indeed, contrary to our academic predilections, this essay is presented without scholarly references, except for those to the other selections in this volume. Not all the predictions made here will necessarily come about. Our aim is to provoke thought, to raise questions, and to stir up interest in developments and problems of the uses of new media in education.

The book is organized into five parts. The first is this overview. The second deals with the concept of an educational medium and types of media. The third takes up the problem of the adoption of media in education. The fourth discusses media impact of education. The fifth is concerned with the impact of educational media and education on Western society.

The Concept of Educational Media

A striking variety of devices have been claimed as educational media at one time or another, including television, books, maps and globes, visual aids, language laboratories, teaching machines, chalk boards, and even pencils, papers, desks, lighting, or subject matter. In addition, the majority of those devices which we are fairly certain are "really educational media (such as television, book, or visual aids) may be found both within and outside of educational contexts. How, then, are we to decide what things are and are not educational media? What are the peculiar properties of this genus, and how do these properties relate to the problems of media impact?

For our purpose a medium may be defined as any form of device or equipment which is normally used to transmit information between persons. Thus radio, television, newspapers, billboards, letters, handbills, books, teaching machines, and all such devices are media by this definition. An educational medium is such a device used for educational purpose. Thus when television is used for education (rather than for entertainment or for other goals), it becomes an educational medium whether found in the home, tavern, or school. By convention, we are also apt to think of as educational those media which are found in a school context, whether they are used for education of for other purposes. Television and radio sets found in schools are usually assumed to be educational media, even through they may sometimes be used for entertainment.

This definition has several implications which are

worth spelling out. First of all, it is the use of which a device is put that makes it a medium. By themselves a stretch of smooth sand and a strike do not convey information. One may, however, draw in the sand with the strike, whereupon a medium is created. A similar case may be made for the chalk board. By itself, this device conveys no information. Indeed, it can be used for many non informational activities such as discipline (the writing of a lesson one hundred times), cleaning up, or light and sound control. Another way of making this point is to suggest that devices are never media in and of themselves. They become media only when associated with those peculiar processes of human behaviour which we have termed the transmission of information.

At a minimum, information transmission through media involves two types of human activity—encoding and decoding. Encoding consists of those activities engaged in by thc communicator of the message which place information upon the medium. Examples would be the processes of writing upon a chalk board, drawing a picture, or producing and acting in a television programme. Decoding are those activities engaged in by the user of the message who takes information from the medium. Examples are those of reading, listening, watching, cutting the pages of a book, and of forth. Most media are so arranged that the activities of decoding are made as easy as possible, and the role of the user is usually more passive than the role of the communicator.

Although certain simple media consist of but single device (for example, a megaphone), the majority of media are systems with at least several component parts. Even a chalk board, for instance, cannot be considered a medium until we have another device for writing upon it—chalk. When one turns to recent innovations in media, one is impressed with their complexity. A language laboratory consists not only of the microphones, booths, and desks of the immediate system, but also of the carefully prepared instructional tapes, circuitry, and methods of language instruction with which it is associated. By itself, a television set cannot constitute a medium. It becomes a medium when associated with a broad-casting system, writers, producers, actors, news gatherers, transmission lines, and all the accountrements of modern network production. Such media are not only complex in terms of "hardware," they also involve complex patterns of social behaviour, differential position, and roles.

Finally, since educational media differ from media in general in terms of educative use, we suggest the one can differentiate educative uses from other forms of use. In practice this is often difficult to do. Let us take merely those forms of behaviour carried on within an educational institution. Particularly in small communities, a consolidated school may serve not only educational ends but may also be used for baby sitting, recreation, a local meeting house, the focus of community pride, a major source of revenue and economic support, a creator of jobs, a locus of political power of controversy. Clearly, these latter forms of behaviour are not educative, although they bear relationships to educational activities. Media used, for instance, to transmit information for recreational purposes (a basketball scoreboard) are not educational in any strict sense.

Similarly, contemporary society is characterized by a diversity of educational settings. Formal (classroom) education proceeds in schools, churches, factories, summer camps, and in the armed forces. Informal education is found nearly everywhere, in homes, offices, stores, airline terminals, and on street corners. Education in any of these settings may involve media, but we would only term educational media if their primary use was educative. For instance, although the motion picture theatre may be used for education, its normal function is entertainment. Contrast this with an encyclopedia or privately owned teaching machine whose use is primarily educative.

These observations suggest a definition. For our purpose, education may be considered as those activities wherein the learning of one or more persons is being deliberately controlled by others. Education may be restrictive (socialization) or expansive (the encouragement of creativity). It may reflect a variety of strategies including practice, information transmittal, or discussions of thinking itself. It may be formalized and ritualized, or informal and sporadic. However, wherever education takes place, there are always two recognizable roles—those of teacher and student. Educational media are those used to support the processes of education, whereby teachers attempt to induce learning in students.

New Media and Technological Innovation

Media are devices, and the appearance of a new medium always constitutes a technological innovation. In this sense, the discovery of radio or television is as much as innovation as the discovery of steam, the motor governor, or atomic energy. Technological innovations affect society, changing the forms of a national society and affecting community life and organized forms of behaviour represented by our major institutions. Technological innovations affect social systems. Educational media, however, have particular types of effects.

Technological innovations often create new roles in social systems. New roles are established concerning the production and maintenance of the new devices. In some cases, whole new industries and professions are created. Consider the railroad. The appearance of this innovation created new corporations, jobs, industries, private fortunes, ways of life. Chinese and Irish immigrants were imported to lay tracks. Special laws were passed. New unions sprang up. Manufacturing, maintenance, and scrapping facilities were created that had not previously existed. In part, this same process may be expanded to apply to such innovations as the automobile, the airplane, the motion picture industry, and television. It is conceivable that the cybernetic revolution (the appearance of computers and robotic control) will obviate repetitive roles in other industries, but the computer and control industry itself shows a predictable tendency toward greater complexity and the appearance of new roles defined in terms of the innovation.

New roles are confined primarily to the invention, production, and maintenance of an innovated device. When one turns to device utilization, a different pattern emerges. The appearance of most technological innovations leads to a simplification of the life of the user. For instance, the automobile allows the user to spend less time and energy in transportation (at least under optimum conditions); the home appliance allows the housewife to complete her homemaking chores with less effort; the new duplicating machine simplifies and makes office routines less expensive. Thus the effect of most technological revolutions on the user is to reduce the drudgery of his life, to increase his leisure time or to allow him to do other things. Indeed, it is this simplication of life that leads most users to desire and adopt new devices.

However, this generalization does not apply to new media. Since media are defined as devices which transmit information, the use of a medium does not free time; it fills time. The use of television does not simplify life for the user; it complicates life. After watching the "idiot box," housewife is no further along on her housework, although she may be in a better mood and is almost certainly more informed than she was before. If media do not simplify life, if they do not increase leisure time and allow the user to do what he wants to do, why then are media adopted in innovations? The answer would appear to be to fill time. The media user chosen to watch television or listen to the radio rather than do "nothing" engage in sports, or seek additional employment. It is impossible to imagine much media use in a society where all persons were employed sixteen hours a day in labour. It is the appearance of leisure time that allows media use. And media fill the vacuum left when other forms of technological innovation free the user from life's drudgery. We shall return to this peculiar, time filling property of media in the final section of the chapter.

There is another peculiar property of media which also set them from other innovated devices. Because media provide information for the use, media tend to enlarge the horizons of the user, tend to make him a larger better informed, less satisfied person. Contrast the user of the newly invented machine tool with the user of the newly invented television set. The former is provided with a much faster and more accurate way of getting his job done. He can therefore produce more work (and get higher pay) one may have greater leisure time. But nothing has happened to his horizons. He does not necessarily know another thing about his neighbour than he did before. If he chooses, the may spend that additional money or leisure time in private pursuits, such as fishing or drinking beer or carpentering around his houses, and never learn any additional information other than that involved in operating the new device itself.

By way of contrast, the user of television has considerable difficulty avoiding contact with other ways of life. It is certainly possible for him to tune selectively, to program that fit his political persuasion or recreational interests, but it is difficult for him to avoid all contact with other parts of the country or the wider world. Thus Negro users become aware of the deprived conditions under which they are living, and Americans becomes aware of Europe underdeveloped portions of the world. So media have a direct impact on users—they enlarge horizons.

Types of Media

Media differ along various dimensions. Some of these are relevant to the understanding of media impact. Thus it is useful to examine media dimensions and to exemplify types of media at various points along them.

Literacy :

Some forms of media, such as books and teaching machines, require that the user be able to manipulate and understand symbols—in short, that he be literate. Other media forms, such as television and motion pictures, may be understood and appreciated by illiterate and literate users alike. Perhaps because of our familiarity with books and the centrality of reading and writing skills in educational practices, we normally think of educational media as requiring literacy. However, some media do not require literacy, and their intensive use may possibly interfere with the acquisition of literacy habits and skills. On the other hand, appropriate use may also be made of nonliterate media to inform nonreading users (such as residents of an underdeveloped region) or to stimulate interest in literacy those whose motivation would otherwise be low (such as those reared in slums).

Audio and visual :

Commonly available media make primary use of two sense modalities, seeing and hearing. Some media, such as disc and tape recordings, involve only audio information. Other media, such as books and visual aids, are solely visual. Finally, some media, such as television and motion pictures, make use of both modalities.

Various proposals have been advanced for the creation of media that would provide tactile, olfactory, or taste information, but nothing has come from these proposals.

There is a relationship between the literacy requirement of a medium and the probability of its being audio or visual. This relationship is easily seen in Figure 1. Note that many examples may be found of media that are visual and require literacy, that are visual and do not require literacy, and that are audio and do not require literacy. However, it is difficult to find even a single example of a medium that is audio and that requires literacy.

Static and dynamic :

A related phenomenon is the static or dynamic quality of the medium. This property may best be illustrated by considering the difference between motion picture film and filmstrip. The former portrays continuous sequence of events, a sequence of visual portraits whose presentation is so fast that the user has the illusion of continuous presentation. The filmstrip, in contrast, is stochastic. The presentations are discrete; they do not flow; the record is static. Other examples of both static and dynamic media may easily be found. Audio recordings are usually dynamic, although those associated with language laboratories may be static. Television is dynamic; books and chalkboards are static. The advantage of a static medium is that it allows intensive and analytic study. A complicated discussion of a mathematical equation may be gone over intensively until the user comprehends it. The advantage of the dynamic medium is that is facilitates intuitive and integrative understanding, particularly of those processes which vary over time. The motion picture of an athlete in action, for instance, is often far more useful to him and his coach than equivalent still pictures.

Programming :

Media differ in the degree to which they are controlled by both communicator and use of the medium. A television broadcast is highly controlled by the communicator. The user has little or nothing to say about what is transmitted to him; his option is confined solely to either paying attention or not paying attention to the programme that is broadcast. One may increase his control over the situation by providing alternate channels for him to watch; the greater the number of channels, the greater freedom the user has. (The increase in behavioural choices is probably the greatest single reason for urban living, where more television channels, and probably most other choices, exist). In another example, teaching machines are normally programmed more rigidly than are books.

It would normally be assumed that media control by the communicator and user were inversely related; the greater the communicator control the lesser the control and vice versa. Actually, this oversimplifies greatly. Given that media are assembled for information transmittal, it is actually quite unlikely that media would appear that were totally uncontrolled by communicating agencies. The only example which comes to mind is the public library, where "the widest" possible range of books is provided to users to be put to whatever purpose they choose. But even the library is occasionally under attack by citizens who object to the choice of books purchased or the public display of what is considered pornography.

Thus a lecturer who hands out chapters of his new book, one per lesson, is denying control to the user. Provision of a textbook at least allows the users to choose the order of their readings. Provision of a book shelf or set of supplementary readings allows even more use flexibility. With decreasing control by the communicator we find fewer examples of media.

Sole versus Group use :

Some media, such as books, are designed in such a way that use by more than a single person at one time is difficult. Others, such as a filmstrip projector, may be used by small group. Still others as a commercial motion picture theatre, may be used in very large groups. As a rule, group-use media make fewer demands upon user than do individual-use media, although there are exceptions to this rule.

Cost and Spread :

Some media, such as newspapers are extremely cheap. Others, such as computerized teaching machines, are far more expensive. Actually, there are two media cost figures that should be distinguished. The first, cost per user, establishes the basic expense of installing a medium for a given population. The second, cost per medium unit, specifies the absolute amount needed for each unit installation. For instance, the cost of installing a television transmitter is considerable, but if a great many users of this service are anticipated, the cost per user for the medium may be small.

As a rule, the spread of a medium in any social group will vary both as a function of cost per user and depending on whether the medium is designed for solo or group-use. All things being equal, expensive media will be adopted only if they may be used simultaneously by many people while any medium is likely to be more widely adopted if its cost is reduced. Media that have a really wide spread are commonly called *mass media*, the best examples being television, radio, newspapers, nationally circulated magazines, and commercial motion pictures. In strinsic characteristics of mass media are those of strong communicator and little user control, low cost to the user, and wide spread of use among the user population.

It has often been pointed out that mass media tend to homogenize a user population. The unscrupulous user of a mass medium has enormous potential for arousing public emotions and the desire for activity. More subtly, mass media have the effect of standardizing accents and forms of discourse. It should not be assumed that all media have the same homogenizing effects, however. Expensive media, such as hi-fi sets and teaching machines, will be adopted by only those portions of the user population who choose to spend their money for the medium in question. User-controlled media, such as home tape recordings or movies, individualize by their very nature. If homogenization of the user population is to be avoided (and this is a debatable point), the effect of mass media may readily be countered by the popularization of non-mass media forms.

It is widely noted that mass media must compete with one another for user attention. We not only must choose between several competing television channels but also between whether to watch television, read the newspaper, or listen to the radio. Competition for attention is usually a characteristic of the school-used medium. On the contrary the uses (in this case, the student) is required to use a medium if he is to remain a student of the specified curriculum. This difference in user conditions suggests the standards for judging excellence of a new medium vary depending on whether it is intended for mass or educational use. Mass media must, above all, be popular; educational media, effective. Mass media must gain and hold attention, educational media normally assume attention. Thus mass media communicators (such as television producers) are often at a loss when asked to turn their talents to the educational realm.

Mechanical Techniques :

The last typological distinction we wish to make refers to technique by which a given effect is achieved.

This is most easily illustrated by comparison of the portable motion picture projector with the portable videotape recorder. From the viewpoint of the user pieces of equipment produce nearly identical results. Both show a video and audio signal, and both signals are dynamic. The motion picture projector places its image on a screen, while the videotape unit's signal may be displayed either on a screen or upon a cathode ray tube. Both signals are adaptable to small, classroom group viewing. Both units may be used to display "canned" signals; that is, pre-recorded films or tapes distributed from a central depository. Both may also "take pictures" of local scenes for later, local re-viewing. Neither signal is really of high quality, although watching the picture for an hour a day is within reason for the normal user population. Both types of systems are within the budgetary range of an average school.

The mechanical means used for reproduction are the major differences between these two media. In the case of motion pictures, a camera is used to place light images of film which must thereafter be developed. The videotape recorder uses a television "camera" and electronic tape; and, as with audio recordings, the signal may be replayed immediately or the tape wiped and refused for another recording. As of this writing, motion pictures are still somewhat cheaper in terms of capital investment; however, the videotape system offers considerably greater flexibility, and its introduction constitutes an "innovation" that may someday supplant motion pictures.

Similar innovations of mechanical techniques have occasionally had far-reaching consequences for media. The introduction of the rotary press sharply decreased the cost of volume printing and made possible the modern news paper. Continual improvements are constantly being made in such new media as tape records. Basic media innovations take place when the media form is first introduced, for instance, the appearance of television during the second quarter of this century. Innovations in mechanical techniques generally improve or cheapen the medium and lead to its wider adoption.

Media Adoption in Education

The first of our predictive tasks is to deal with media adoption in education. We see the adoption of media as half the effect new educational media make upon the institution of education. Media must be adopted to have any effect at all, and the very fact of adoption (or refusal to adopt) is of significance to educator and medium vendor alike. We see media adoption as the result of two sets of factors—characteristics of contemporary education, and characteristics of media themselves.

Characteristics of Contemporary Education

American education is probably familiar to the reader. Nevertheless, it is useful to review several of the "obvious" properties of education because they are true only for the United States (in contrast, let us say, with other urbanized countries), because they are only recently true, or because they differentiate education from other forms of institutions. However, this review will focus on those factors potentially affecting media adoption.

Size : Education is the largest single institution in the United States. There are at present more than one and a half million active teachers in this country, nearly twenty million full-time and more than twenty-five million part-time and adult students, and thousands of administrators who run the schools. Formal institutions of education include public, private, and parochial elementary and secondary schools; public and private junior colleges, and universities; trade and technical schools of all kinds of graduate and professional schools;

training institutions operated within industry and other institutions; and a host of adult and continuing education services. Altogether probably 30 per cent of all Americans will participate in one or another form of organized education during the coming year.

In addition to formalized education, informal education takes place in many different settings including campus, churches; recreational settings; the Army, and the industry. Americans are also involved in various educational activities overseas which are paid for in this country including the Peace Corps, State Department and foundation supported programme, the Fulbright programme, and United Nations activities.

Finally, education reaches into nearly every corner of society. Whole industries are set up to serve the needs of the educational establishment: textbook publishing houses, the construction industry, school supplies and maintenance, etc. Educational policy is an engrossing political topical which occasionally erupts into local, state, and national debate. Educational settings are intimately associated with basic and applied research, with recreation, with status and positional verification, with the establishment and maintenance of community cohesiveness. Educational institutions are major employers. Some problems in education have assumed such regional and national importance (such as desegregation) as to have forced major changes in our sense of morality and have led on occasion to demonstrations, riots, and violence. Legislators have recognized the importance of education to a healthy society by proposing that children begin school as young as four.

Educational positions and the classroom : Certain social positions are well-high ubiquitous in American education, and most educational activities are organized around standardized settings such as the classroom.

Taking as our model the public elementary or secondary school, there are three major types of persons found in education; students; teachers, and administrators. Students are normally juveniles who have little power in the school. Although they constitute the majority in any school, they are usually categorized and treated in groups. At the worst, this process is known as "lockstep" education, a phrase that connotes the treating of all students within an age-grade as identical.

The classroom group usually consists of a set of students and one teacher. Although experiments are now being conducted in team teaching and other instructional forms that would provide more variability in student-teacher relationships, the usual pattern is for each teacher to operate with a group of students in isolation from other teachers. In primary schools it is normal for a single group of students to stay with a teacher throughout the day, except for the brief appearance of a few subject-matter specialists such as the music teacher. In secondary schools and colleges student groups move from classroom to classroom, often breaking up and reassembling under different personnel. Teachers at these latter levels are assumed to be subject-matter specialists. Throughout the systems students are graded into age or achievement categories, and entrance into the next higher grade (or school) depends on the student fulfilling specific achievement criteria.

American public school administrators break into two groups: principals and their assistants, and superintendents and their assistants. The principal is the administrative head of the school, a former teacher, and nearly always male. The superintendent is the administrative head of a school district, a former principal, and nearly always male. Whereas for women the position of teacher is usually as high as they can go, male teachers can and often do aspire to leaving teaching for administrative positions.

Other professions are represented among school personnel, although their jobs are less central, and they have less power and attention. These include health personnel dietitians, custodians, office staff, and engineers responsible for the maintenance of equipment.

Decentralization : American education is also decentralized. Again taking only the public primary and secondary schools, control over education is everywhere immediately vested in the public school district as created by several states. The local legislative functions of a district are performed by a school board whose full-time executive officer is the superintendent. Various degrees of control exercised over school districts, boards, and superintendents by the several states, but in general that control is remote. Even more remote is the federal Office of Education whose functions are primarily those of record keeping and the encouragement of research.

This pattern of decentralization contrasts sharply with patterns found in certain other urban societies, such as France, Australia, or New Zealand. In these countries public education is largely directly state controlled through federal or state ministry. Uniform national or provincial curriculum plans are laid down, and adherence to minimum standards for education is demanded throughout the state. These standards are enforced by state-wide examination and an inspectorate who rate teachers and teaching performance on a regular basis. The results of centralization appear to be, on the positive side, the reduction of school variability in educational product, and, on the negative side, a possible stifling of initiative at the teacher school level.

Decentralization also appears at other levels in American education. American higher education is unique in offering students a wide variety of private as well as public colleges and universities. And although colleges offer degrees announced with more or less standardized titles, requirements for these degrees vary widely. Variations in quality are partially controlled by accreditation agencies created by the colleges and universities. Standing outside the system are a variety of proprietary schools, particularly those serving declassed occupations, often operating with only minimal state supervision.

Universality : American education is both universal and comprehensive. Universality implies that education is designed to serve everyone, this value being expressed in the statement that everyone is entitled to education, to the limit of his own ability and inclination, but at least through secondary school. This value is supported by laws that specify attendance for all children through some secondary schooling. Some amount of college education is now becoming the goal of more than 50 per cent of our youth. If the individual chooses to attend a private or parochical school, that is up to him. But public education is to be provided for all and is seen as a major avenue by which the children of the poor may better themselves.

Comprehensiveness : Education for all implies, in the United States, a second value—comprehensiveness. We attempt to provide an appropriate education for everyone and to allow much flexibility for an individual to change the direction of his education should he wish to do so. All pupils are encouraged to stay in the educational marathon as long as they have the stamina; and if they do not like the racetrack they have chosen to run in, they are encouraged to shift to another. This aim is accomplished by providing comprehensive schools at all levels of the system. Primary, secondary, and higher institutions presume to accommodate all kinds of pupils, from the sons and daughters of illerate immigrants to those of bluebloods. The comprehensive high school must provide not only a college preparatory curriculum but also terminal, trade school, and secretarial preparation.

The compressive college offers training in engineering, public school teaching, and social work in addition to the liberal arts subjects.

Comprehensiveness has its effects. Since schools must serve pupils with varying needs, specialization is weak. Schools are also forced toward increasing size in order to provide for the many tasks they attempt. Pupils may engage in various "false starts" before finding their true provisions, thus wasting the efforts of those who were previously involved in their education. A far larger proportion of American pupils enter college than in any other urban society, yet we also have a large dropout rate.

A contrasting system, seen in contemporary Great Britain, "streams" pupils by means of achievement tests various educational channels out of which it is difficult to move. College preparatory secondary schools are distinct institutions from trade schools. Engineering and preparation for college teaching are not taught at the university and a far lower proportion of English youth attend college. It should also be pointed out, however, that those pupil who do enter college are somewhat better prepared, specialize more rapidly, and are less likely to drop out of college than their American counter parts.

Diffuse goals : Partly because of its attempts to comprehensive and partly as a result of decentralization education serves a variety of purposes in our society, some of which are at cross-purposes with others. Thus American education presumes both to socialize and to train creativity. Pupils should not only be trained in the traditional, academic subjects but also in a variety of "practical skills such as typing, auto mechanics, driving, and home making. The entrance age for elementary schools has been reduced so that now kindergarten is nearly universal, public nursery schools are the coming thing. High schools and colleges present athletic spectaculars whose revenue provide major financial support for certain institutions.

People rather than product centered : Education produces people rather than tangible products. In this it is similar to other people-processing institutions such as Armed forces and hospitals. The advantage of a product centered institution is that success of the mission may be easily established. Are we making a reasonable profit this year? The success of people processing is more difficult to judge. First, the measurement of change in human beings is difficult. Educational output is usually measured in terms of achievement tests; but many critics have claimed, with justification, that the major values of a good education are not being tapped with this measure. In addition, the production of any people-effect is inevitably contaminated with the impact of other forces operating on the child, such as home, church, gang, and neighbourhood.

Labor intensive : Midtwentieth-century American education is also labour intensive; that is, the vast proportion of our expenditures are for salaries rather than for machines or raw materials. The majority of activities in the school still carried on by its staff; to date media have been used adjunctivel rather than to replace the traditional contact between teacher and student. Capital expenditures and equipment investment in education are still far less, proportionately, than in medicine or the armed forces. Indeed, we often make a fetish of labour intensiveness, claiming that to mechanize education would destroy a necessary personal relationship between teacher and pupil.

Little specialization : Although not a necessary concomitant of labour-intensive use, American education also shows little job specialization. Particularly at the primary level, teachers are interchangeable and may be shifted from grade to grade. Secondary teachers are often called upon to fill in fields which are not their specialities. Even administrative positions in the schools are generalized. It is normal for male teachers to move up to administrative positions after several years of teaching experience, and administrators at smaller schools often teach on a part-time basis. (However, specialization is characteristic at the university level where field boundaries are firm.)

Low status : Compared to other professions, the status of the teacher is not particularly high in the United States, nor are American teachers particularly well trained or paid. College students recruited into the teaching ranks are pre-dominantly female and from the lower levels of college student talent. Professors of education are looked down upon by associates from other departments, particularly by their liberal arts colleagues.

However, the relatively low status of education is not too far out of line with its character as an occupation. In many ways the job of teacher is more a craft than a profession. The teacher's job is a general one calling for many, poorly articulated skills; the teacher's performance is isolated; the teacher's success or failure is almost impossible to judge.

Although there are clear resemblances between teaching and other crafts, labour unions have been largely ineffective in organizing teachers. However, the teaching profession is not without its professional associations, which have performed prodigious feats in raising the status of teachers and placing more and more control over education in the hands of professional educators. Associations such as the National Educational Association tend to be dominated by school administrators and professors of education, with less influence emanating from the rank-and-file teacher.

Teaching has not attracted the gifted among college students; other fields with greater status and calling for greater talents have had more than their proportional share of the gifted. It does not seem likely that this distribution of talent will be changed, no matter how high the salaries of teachers are raised. Nor is it clear that great talent along intellectual lines is needed for teaching—at least on the primary and secondary levels.

Little Research : Finally, like other decentralized and labour-intensive industries, education in the United States spends remarkably little for research. Although other major industries today spend up to 10 per cent or more of their annual budgets on research and stress the necessity of research in order to survive, the majority of school systems carry on no research whatsoever.

Of course, public education is a noncompetitive industry. If School System develops a better procedure for processing pupils, it gains nothing over System B for doing so, although presumably it may gain more support from its constituency.

Most basic and applied research on education is carried on outside school systems by universities, foundations, state departments of education, and industries. Most innovations in education are discovered elsewhere and must be promoted in order to be accepted by the local school. School boards and administrators understandably are inclined to resist rather than to welcome changes in educational practices or equipment. Local conditions are salient to local control, and innovations emanating from ivory towers may often seem remote from local versions of "reality."

Factors Governing Adoption

Certain characteristics of interactional media are also instructional in aiding or slowing up adoption by school systems.

Cost : Cost is one of the more important factors affecting adoption of new media. Obviously, the cheaper the medium the more likely it is to be adopted. Capital expenditure costs and per pupil costs both govern adoption. Media that require a large outlay for each student, such as O.K. Moore's computerized typewriter that teaches the child to read before he can write, are unlikely to be adopted.

Cost per unit is the second financial element in adoption. Although many individual units are needed, cost per teaching machine is obviously far less than cost per educational television broadcasting station. Adoption of media requiring an enormous capital outlay will be confined to large school districts and will be engaged in only with much careful scrutiny by the school board and its supporting public. Adoption of smaller media units, even though their cost per student may be greater, is easier because adoption may be either experimental or piecemeal.

Flexibility : Media are more likely to be adopted that are useful for a variety of educational and other purposes. For instance, if a medium is only useful for the teaching of a single subject, it is less likely to be adopted that if it may be used with several subjects. It is also more likely to appear in schools if it serves both educational and noneducational objectives, for instance, if the medium is useful for both education and public entertainment.

It should be pointed out that media having a low cost per unit are not only more likely to be adopted, they are also more likely to be flexible in their use. Media having high unit cost must be used widely in order to justify the use; hence use is forced on teachers and students.

Teacher comprehension and control : Given the labour intensive character of American education, media are most likely to be adopted that are understood, approved, and controlled by teachers. A medium that is imposed on nonsympathetic teacher is likely to spend of its time in the closet gathering dust while the teacher continues to teach in ways that are familiar to her. On the other hand if a medium requires skill and understanding in its operation, it is more likely to be adopted if teachers are provided a training programme in the use of the new medium.

Fads and Pressure : To a certain extent, familiarity and approval are also necessary before the school administrator will advocate, and the school board approve, also sensitive to outside pressures. Some media are adoption of a new medium. However, both types of officials are adopted because school boards and administrators are persuaded that public demand for adoption is high, despite lack of sympathy on part of educators. Outside pressures arise from vested interest groups, from foundations or from the manufacturers. For example, the Ford Foundation has actively advocated the use of educational television. School administrators are bombarded by literature and salesmen from hundreds of manufacturers anxious to display the advantages of their latest media developments.

Support rather than displacement : Media are also more likely to be adopted if they support or slightly modify present educational practices rather than displace or change them. Any medium that makes an existing but difficult task easier for the teacher, that facilitates communication between teacher and pupil, or that increase efficiency of educational procedures is likely to be adopted. Media that imply a radical shift in educational roles or that require the creation or new positions or the retraining of personnel are less likely to be adopted.

Student response : Although one is less likely to consider students' opinion than those of teachers and administrators, "consumer reaction" is bound to be a factor in media adoption. A medium that was diagonally ineffective in fulfilling its advertised promises or was unpopular with students would not be as likely of adoption than an effective or popular medium.

Predictions

The adoption of a medium depends on the factors listed above plus others. The formula which properly mixes these into a precise prediction will probably never be written. Nevertheless, we will be bold (or foolish) enough to behave as if we were a sage computer. Looking our crystal ball, we see the following trends in media adoption.

Minimal adoption : It seems to us unlikely that adoptions of media will take radical changes. Education during the next decade is unlikely to cease being a labour-intensive activity, although there will probably be some increase in the proportion of budgets spent for media. Thus it is unlikely that the classroom teacher will be replaced by gadgets of any sort.

This prediction has several implications. First of all, given the pressures for media adoption, it seems likely that some media will receive token adoption. Token adoption has happened before. For example, 16mm motion picture projects are owned by most schools but are relatively little used in actual classroom instruction. Those media which are "forced" on the teacher are likely to be ignored, either out of ignorance or through preference.

Another implication of this prediction is that the adoption of newer media will not lead to significant savings (as claimed) in the overall cost of education. To save money with the use of media requires radical shifts in educational roles; for instance, the teaching of large groups of students using television as a replacement of many teachers. It seems to us more likely that media will be used for upgrading the general quality of education, and that educational costs will continue to rise.

Broadcast television : Our prediction is that airborne educational television (MPATI) is doomed to be abandoned. Although its impact on Midwestern education has been considerable, the system is so inflexible that we assumed its abandonment is inevitable. Since though somewhat less dramatic problems are presented in other forms of broadcast educational television. As pointed out by others, broadcast educational television is being used at present for more for general enlightenment than in support of formal education. Again flexibility seems to be the key issue. Given that an introductory course in Spanish is available only at 10 o'clock in the morning, the teacher must schedule at that time or make other arrangements for the teaching of the class.

The technological "breakthrough" which makes the abandonment of broadcast television possible is the video tape recorder. Given a portable television set in each classroom and a modest investment on recorders assembled at a central location in the school, teachers may be provided each hour with a choice of various taped programsmes from which to choose to supplement instruction. Tapes would be provided by the school district to all schools at cost comparable to or less than those of 16mm film. The conservative may decry replacement of the good teacher by the television set; but as we have already noted, there are far too few good teachers. If our prediction is borne out, we should see a whole new industry springing up that produces and distributes videotapes on a variety of subjects.

Motion Pictures : But why go to videotape? Why should not the same innovative uses be made of 16mm motion picture film or better yet equivalent use be made of the cheaper 8mm system? It seems to us likely that there will actually be considerable pressure brought upon the school for just these latter purposes, and that other industries will be set for the purpose of producing instructional films for extensive classroom use. However, film systems have some disadvantages which argue against their adoption in comparison with videotape. (1) Tape is ready for instant replay. Tape recordings may be used by the coach to help the student watch his own performance, whether the field be athletics, debating, or training in medical practice. At present, there is no marketed system of the instant development of motion picture film. (2) Tape may be played from a central location and distributed to individual video sets, thus relieving the teacher of the necessity of setting up and operating her own equipment. These disadvantages are not killing and might be obviated with new technological developments. At present, however, we would have to bet on videotape.

Teaching machines : The biggest difficulty with presently available teaching machines is their lack of sophistication. As pointed out by Stolurow, the ideal teaching machine is operated a computer that not only controls frame presentation but is also capable of diagnosing needs and lacks in the student. In short, an ideal teaching machine is the mechanical equivalent of a good teacher. Although approaches to this ideal are constantly being explored, it seems to us unlikely that a really sophisticated teaching device will be available.

Once available, a major problem with a truly adequate teaching machine will be its cost. Present annual expenditures per pupil in most public schools hover in the vicinity of $500. A computer-operated instructor is likely to require an initial investment of many thousand dollars; in short, to be as expensive as a broadcast television station. One way to reduce cost is to connect a variety of unit "teachers" to a central computer that operates all simultaneously. Such a system might provide individual instruction for each pupil one or more hours per day with each "teacher" unit used by several students during the class day. However, we lack much basic information about student behaviour that is needed before such a system is workable. Once such information is available it seems likely to us that adoption of teaching machines will proceed slowly, with private well-financed public schools setting the pace.

Books : Various observers have pointed out that mass distribution of paperback books constitutes a revolution, would assume continued expansion of this industry in education together with such auxiliary media as reprints, teaching texts printed in separable sections, and like. Although minimally programmed (which may have distinct advantage), books are portable and may be studied at the student's leisure. They are also available in the outside world (which is not true of teaching machines); the book-reading habit may be crucial to continuing education on the part of the student.

Some pessimists have suggested that as we developed vision and other forms of media which do not read literacy, book reading will disappear. This seems to us unlikely. Books have such obvious advantages as a communication medium that their use is bound to be stressed until a truly flexible and portable means for entertaining citizens is developed, perhaps a small television set with either a great many broadcast channels than are now available or a available library of videotapes that are also miniaturized. Thereafter we might entrain the notion that press toward literacy and the use of books would fall off, perhaps in the distant future, literacy may be a skill learned only by the professional—in the sense that mathematical symbols are learned today only by those who need know them.

Differential adoption : It is patently obvious but nevertheless worthwhile noting that various sectors of education will be more willing to adopt certain media than other sectors. We would suggest that homogenizing media (such as television) are most likely to be adopted in those school districts having difficulties recruiting and holding the teachers. Small school districts and schools serving neighbourhoods are good examples of this type of setting. In time, one might expect some schools to advertise or proud of their continued reliance upon "live" teachers. In contrast, because of the initially prohibitive cost we would expect teaching machines to be adopted first in those schools having the most money.

Media Impact on Education

Assuming that some of the new media will be adopted, what will be their impact on the schools? We turn now to the probable and not-so-probable results of media adoption in the educational institution in the near future. In order to explore this problem meaningfully, however, it is necessary that we first consider the goals and strategies of education, the roles of educators, and the uses to which media may be put. It will be recalled that our original definition stressed that communication devices were not educational media until used for educative purposes. This suggests that there are various patterns of uses of educational media and media characteristics change with use. Let us explore this insight.

Media and the Teacher

One of the first things to be observed is that the teacher may play a variety of roles with respect to a medium. Turning first to instructional roles, it is possible for a teacher to use a medium adjunctively, to supplement or aid her in presentation of material. Thus a teacher may write salient points upon the chalk board, may use visual aids, or rhythm sticks, or Cuisinaire rods, or a piano. Control of the subject matter rests in the hands of the teacher, who programmes use of the medium in question to supplement her distinctive style of presentation. A medium may be used to provide a close-up view of complex operations, a visual simplification of the problem, details beyond the lecture, or the "immediacy" of direct experience. (A variant of this type of relationship is found where rigid specifications of teachers media use are laid down through school regulations. Thus some teachers are subjected to rules for the "proper" use of visual aids and the like.)

A much more radical use is to replace the teacher by educational medium. For example, instead of the television with all students sitting in a darkened room watch a centrally broadcast programme. Under such use the teacher may or may not be present. If she is in the room, her function is reduced almost to that of custodian; or she may spend the time in private pursuits. This radical use of media to replace the teacher is only possible with a media as television or motion pictures which can fully engage the attention of students. In principle, of course, it is quite possible to replace the teacher with even single media. Consider the instructor who writes test question on the chalk board and then leaves the room. Provided that students are sufficiently motivated, they will carry on despite the absence of the teacher. It should be emphasised, however, that at their best even the most complex form of media available today are but limited in the varieties of stimuli they emit and, particularly, in their responsive to behaviour by the student. In addition, teachers perform variety of non instructive functions for the student, including those of consoling and acting as a role model. For these reasons, presently available media have but limited appeal as total replacements for the teacher.

Media-related roles for the teacher may also be defined in terms of additional, noninstructional capacities. "Master teachers" are often called to conduct classes by television or to help write, prepare, and act in education television productions. At a somewhat less exalted level teachers usually set up, operate, and repair education media. Teachers, along with educational administrators, parents, and school board members, are often involved in controversies over the usefulness and advisability of media adoptions. Finally, particularly in those cases when television or teaching machines have freed teachers from some of the drudgery of instruction, teachers may assign counselling or advising roles which are made possible through release of their time.

Educational Content

Another way of looking at functions of the medium is to discuss the various contents that are communicated to the student and which the student is presumed to learn in an educational context. Three such contents have been suggested in this chapter, the providing of skills and information, socializing, and mobilizing. The *first* of these is "classic" educational content, the "three R's," spelling, the facts of history or geography or chemistry, and the like. The *second* pertains to the task of civilizing students, the changing of a young "savage" into a responsible adult who can take his place in society. The *third* is the creation of motives appropriate to the positions which will be occupied by the student as he passes through later stages of his school career and into adult life. Other commentators have broken the providing of information down into subcategories such as subject matter and additional information about the world, while still others have identified group maintenance as an educational objective, the concept of mobilization.

So far the new media are conceived of as most appropriate to be used to teach subject matter. The only types of programmes yet prepared for teaching machines are subject matter programmes, and this is certainly the dominant use in educational television. Socializing is usually treated on a direct, person-to-person basis between the student and teacher, or sometimes between the student and school administrator, or student and counsellor. The major diffuse goals of group maintenance and mobilization are not organized for directly; indeed, it is often assumed that time spend pursuing these goals interferes with the presentation of subject matter. These last, then, are squeezed into the cracks of interpersonal relationship between student and teacher. One wonders whether they would be dealt with at all in a strictly mechanized school.

Educational Strategies

A third way to look at media functions is in terms of the strategies or educational forms which may be recognized as part of the instructional process. Each potential strategy may also be aided (or hindered) by the use of educational media.

Doing : At a minimal level, much educational activity involves doing by students. Examples of such strategies include drill and practice, group experiences, and ritual. The practicing of handwriting is a doing; so is group singing, performance of plays and pageants, playing football and reciting the Pledge of Allegiance. In each case, a student is learning through participation, and the teacher's role is minimal; he is but the leader or coach.

Two uses for media predominate in situations involving doing: social and self-feedback. Social feedback occurs when the student records information on the media which is then evaluated or scored by someone else, usually by the teacher. For example, the pupil who practices writing by using a pencil and notebook is communicating to the teacher about this ability to write and spell properly. Similar uses of media are found when the student uses tape recorder or language laboratory. Self-feedback occurs when the student uses a medium to examine his own performance with only minimal help from the teacher. For instance, the trainee may look at a kinescope recording of his performance or may learn directly from teaching machine responses.

Media may also be used in doing situations to supplement the coaching and leading roles of the teacher. Teachers who lead a singing lesson have greater success if they can play a musical instrument. Similar functions are performed by rhythm sticks or metronomic devices.

Dissemination : A second form of educational strategy involves the dissemination of information. In this strategy the teacher performs the role of lecturer, one who "gives the word" to students. In such circumstances, the role of the teacher is an active one while the students "soak it all in."

In this "classic" form of education, the possible uses of media have already been discussed in an earlier section. Media may be used either to supplement presentations by the teacher or to replace the teacher entirely. Since the teacher is merely lecturing, she may be replaced not only by a potentially responsive teaching machine, but in this case also by a nonresponsive medium such as a television set.

Exchange : The strategy of exchange involves two-way interactions between the teacher and individual students. Typically the teacher asks question of one student after another and receives answers designed not only to reveal the knowledge of that student but also to impart knowledge to others in the classroom. Exchange is also presumed to provide motivation for students in that it keeps them on their toes.

Only a responsive medium like a teaching machine can actually replace the teacher in the exchange strategy. Since interaction between the student and machine is usually private while recitations are social, the use of teaching machines is not the same as teacher-student exchange. There are undoubtedly ways in which it is possible to build in social support in the process of exchange using new media. One can imagine devices such as those used in television quiz shows in which partial information is provided to students or through which feedback is provided to the teacher from more than a single student at one time. However, such media modifications have not yet been proposed for the school.

Discussions : In discussions the students are assigned the role of communicating with one another while the teacher supervises or directs. Discussion provides role-playing opportunities to students in addition to providing them access to information from sources not normally tapped in the more traditional strategies. Thus, socializing, mobilizing, and group maintenance are stressed—often at the cost of accuracy of information exchanged.

Media may also aid (or hinder) in the processes of discussion among students, as when students pass notes to one another. Interestingly enough, use of media to support discussion has rarely been explored, possibly because other prejudices suggest that pupils should be passive and should not communicate with one another. One might imagine, for instance, an "I don't know what you are talking about," or an "Aha, I get it now!" meter that would provide instant feedback to others. Such devices would revolutionize discussions of all sorts, including those found in education settings.

Intellectualization : Finally, a fifth strategy, intellectualization, focuses upon the processes of thought, upon the logic, upon the forms of problem solving itself. In connection with dissemination, intellectualization strategies try to appropriate thinking processes about subject matter. Typically, intellectualizing may be recognized by the appearance of such provoking questions as "Why?", "How" and "Explain that, please." Dissemination and exchange are interested in facts, not in dynamics. Intellectualization aims at the creation of subject matter, interest, and effective study habits. The role of teachers in intellectualization is different to identify. Various tactics are used to intrigue, cajole, or push the student into thinking clearly about the subject matter. Exchange and discussion are encouraged, but only so long as they appear to be promoting understanding. The teacher remains "in contrast at all times; although his communications may be minimum when the student is actively struggling with intellectualization.

It goes without saying that media may be used in the strategy to supplement teacher presentations and that they would not be used to replace the teacher (with the possible exception of a superior teaching machine). The ideal media use in intellectualization is to provide student experiences through stimulation. Thus students best learn about auto mechanics not by reading a book but by actually taking apart an automobile engine that is mounted properly for education purposes. Model skulls, dinosaurs skeletons, and planetariums arc now available to facilitate student experiences. In using such media for this purpose, a teacher is needed to stand softly by and to punctuate student learning with appropriate observations about the principles related to those specific experience he is having.

New Media Uses

Apart from educational roles, content, and strategy, some media are capable of generating new educational strategies. Some of these have been referred to previously. It is useful to review likely new functions in this context.

Decision making : Various new educational media, particularly those controlled by computers, may aid educators in their decision making. In addition to their potential use in controlling teaching machines, computers may also be used to control the physical environment, to make recommendations for budgetary expenditures, to make classroom assignment, and to keep and assess educational records. Computers have also been proposed to make educational and mental health diagnoses and may eventually be used to fit educational experiences (for instance, choices of teacher) to the needs of the student.

Monitoring : Media offer a variety of opportunities for keeping tabs or snooping. One such use has already appeared in some secondary schools; the unannounced surveillance of teaching by the school administrator over the public address system (shades of 1984!). Teaching may also have monitoring devices built into them. Educational television also has this potential, as do hidden microphones and tape recorders, of providing the supervisor or rater with information about the progress of student or teacher. (Like any innovation, monotoring may be used for moral or immoral purposes. Contemporary American teachers are considerably afraid of the latter; indeed, the fear of media use for snooping is so great that one of the authors has had difficulty obtaining permission to make videotape records of classroom interaction for research purposes. The initial reaction of many teachers was that the proposed study was a veiled form of the scheme.)

Data storage and retrieval : Education requires various forms of information storage and retrieval. Some of the new media could greatly simplify these processes. School libraries are at present making use of microfilms, microcard devices which store formerly printed material in a fraction of their original space. The library of the future may also feature automatic retrieval of data with computerized search and recovery processes.

Media reproduction : Inexpensive and efficient education equipment has revolutionized record keeping in the modern school. Operated in conjuction with the writer, such media make possible the widespread use of standarized tests, the distribution of information, and maintenance of detailed records on students, other personnel, and the economics of school operation. Without such devices, many such services would either be impossible, or would require a much larger office staff. Newly available media of this kind include photographic devices which quickly and cheaply reproduce many copies of printed material, thus allowing the teacher to distribute materials to all her students.

Simulation : A completely new type of education strategy afforded by some of the new media is their use in connection with games and the simulation of complex relationships. Computers, particularly, may be used to provide experiences for the would-be businessman or military leader who would check his plan of operations against simulated economic situation or battleground. In the educational context, such uses of the computer may provide either instruction of fun for students. (In other countries similar uses predict the economic consequences of tax or predict the outcome of popular elections, and help us estimate the future behaviour of other nations.) At present most such games are difficult to play because of the nature to communicate with the computer in special language. In the future, playing such games may be simplified, computers learn to decipher and reproduce verbal orders and as outcomes are shown in visual displays.

Media Interchangeability

Much of our discussion in the previous sections may be summarized with a single observation; educational media should not be judged in terms of their physical properties alone but rather in terms of the uses to which they may be put. When used to supplement the teacher's lecture, for instance, many media are interchangeable for all practical purposes. But the same two or three media that are useful in the lecture may not be equally useful for another purpose, such as that of replacing the teacher in an intellectualizing session.

At present there is no all-purpose medium, and if there were one, it probably would be too expensive for most schools to afford. Depending on the uses intended, one or another educational medium may be preferred. Some media may be for several purposes, some for but a single purpose which they perform admirably.

Predictions

One again we shall go out on a limb and offer some guesses; this time about media impact on the institution of education. As before, these predictions are based on the factors previously reviewed, although explicit spelling out of our reasoning is left to the imagination of the reader.

Cost : Since we have previously predicted less-than-optimal use of new educational media (from an economic point of view), and since we have also predicted a gradual adoption of newer educational media, it follows that the cost of education will rise. In this prediction we are actually quite safe; along with most other things, the cost of education has shown a significant rise during the distant and recent past.

American education is undergoing several changes that are likely to increase its cost sharply. *First,* there is a continuing shortage of teachers combined with a trend toward better salaries. *Second,* the physical plants, particularly of secondary schools and colleges, must be expanded if only to accommodate the larger and larger proportions of youths who are attending each year. *Third,* the demand is increasing for technological and professional training to man in the expanded technical sectors of our economy. *Finally,* adoption of the new media, most of which is quite expensive, will force costs to rise.

It seems likely that some increase in the proportion of our national income spent on education is in the cards, these funds will probably come from the federal government. Local and state sources have shown themselves inadequate to handle the sharp increases in necessaries, and school districts vary widely in their ability to support secondary or higher education. Federal support is likely to come in many guises, many of which would tend to be characterized as "back door" routes. Federal finances are already available for urban redevelopment, such as building construction, educational research, the retraining of technologically unemployed, Peace Corps-type activities, and the war against poverty. Programme such as those that support education indirectly will be continued and increased. Direct support for the major needs of education particularly salary increases and new educational media will also probably come from federal funds.

Standardization : For various reasons, the adoption of new educational media should lead toward greater standardization of educational practices on regional and national levels. Broadcast television when applied to education leads inevitably to some standardization of classroom contents does the widespread distribution of films and videotapes as well as the use of nationally-advertised textbooks. Educational media also foster the use of standardized and rating systems for educational achievement (such as minimal standards to be met prior to college entrance), option not likely to be ignored.

Individualization : Some of the media can introduce flexibility and should generally lead to design a more adaptable curriculum that more nearly meets the needs of the individual students. Teaching machines, particularly, should allow for individualizing experiences, or even the tape recorder or motion picture projector promises to provide courses on some obscure subject for those students who want to take it, a course that a school would be otherwise unable to offer because it has no teachers in that field.

Thus we are presented with a paradox; on the one hand, new media should allow for a more flexible curriculum with more options available to the student and variations in methods and rate of teaching; on the other, methods of presentation and standards of achievement are likely to become widely adopted and perhaps overly rigid.

The abandonment of grades : Given these two paradoxical effects, it seems likely that education eventually will move to abandon arbitrary pupil grading. Imagine the student's being free to study what he wishes from a wide variety of subjects (some of which are requirements for entrance to certain types of higher education). His achievement in each subject chosen for study is certified by an appropriate evaluating medium. Instruction is carried on in each subject independently, and the student is instructed at his own level, perhaps together with other students who are, for that particular subject, his peers. Contact between student and teacher is either on a specialist basis or in terms of counseling, discussion, and role modeling. Best of all, the student's "report card" is instantly transferable to other schools at distant locations who will know just the right level to begin his education in each subject the following year. Thus the educational media may help us toward these goals.

Although the system envisaged above is within the conceivable capabilities of the new media, it is by no means entirely clear whether they will be used in this fashion. There are good and strong objections that can be raised to the erection of a network of computers from whose strands it is difficult for the individual to space. There will undoubtedly always be some elements of the total educational system of this country which will resist the all-out use of such machinery on moral and political grounds. It may very well be that the problems of negotiating in terconnections among computerized school systems is too much for our fragible political unity to sustain, hence that networks will be incomplete, stopping of school systems of states and not covering a part of the private sectors of the lower levels of the educational system (e.g., the parochial schools of the Catholic church or the secular private schools).

In short, computers will be used. Whether they are used to their fullest potential (both for good and bad) rests upon political decisions that will test the political climates of the future.

Varieties of adoption : For the present, it seems that differential adoption of educational media would lead to all sorts of disruptive effects in the educational system. For instance, we have already suggested that adopting educational television is more likely in poorer school districts and that teaching machines are likely to appear in well-supported suburban schools. If this is correct, we may shortly see a radical bifurcation of the education world into "haves" and "have not" institutions and perhaps the adoption of European separation between types of schools. Something of this sort is already taking place at the college and university levels where the range and quality is enormous, with some of the smaller school experiencing great difficulties in obtaining qualified faces. It seems possible that such differentiation may be situated at least in the early stages of adoption.

Another effect may be to slow down present trend toward school consolidation. Although it is debatable whether very large schools are beneficial to students, most high schools have found that they cannot provide the educational experiences assumed to belong to most secondary education. Thus throughout the rural United States, the past two decades have seen the abandonment of small high schools in favour of consolidated high schools and the transportation of children. (Parenthetically, abandonment of many local secondary schools has spurred the death of communities which they served since schools were often the major source of community cohesion and provide.) With appropriate use of new media, the reputed advantages of large schools appear to diminish. Small rural schools may now provide physics, chemistry, and modern algebra courses that are of the same quality as those taught in city schools, provided only that they are in the range of a broadcast television station. The larger school still has the band, the chorus, ballet training, and the famous basketball team, but these advantages may not appear important enough to justify dismantling the local high school. (Airborne television, MPATI, has apparently had just this effect—slowing down the rate of school consolidations in the areas it serves.)

School buildings and architecture : It seems inevitable that new media will have an impact on the architecture of school buildings. Indeed, some media (such as a system of teaching machines controlled by a centralized computer) require special buildings or at least some modification of school design (as pointed out by Lehmann). We may become involved in an architectural revolution quite as much as a media revolution, and it is most likely that these two innovative forms will influence each other.

For the present, however, except once again for "light-house" schools, school architecture will probably continue to reflect the traditions of American education, and media will have to be adopted to existing structures. This suggests that self-contained and compact media are more likely to receive immediate adoption than media requiring extensive building modifications. In the long run, school construction will have to reflect the needs of those media desired by the users.

Educational roles : As detailed previously, the new media provide a variety of new educational roles for both teacher and supportive personnel. It seems likely to us that this will lead to both an increased specialization within the teaching profession and the appearance of auxiliary positions in the school tables of organization.

At least the following additional roles for the teacher have been suggested in connection with media: planner, script writer, actor, consultant, machine sender, computer specialist, counsellor, role model. Some of these roles are likely to appear as duties ancillary to the more basic need of instruction. Others are likely to be picked up as specialities or as separate jobs in and of themselves. As many aenues for specialization appear in the teaching profession, the profession of teacher will appear to be less of a craft, that standards of teacher excellence (in various jobs) will be set and enforced, that there will be great competition for entry into the profession, that teachers will receive higher salaries, and that the teaching camps will not be terminal but will provide many avenues both horizontal and vertical mobility. At the same time, the status of the "generalist," the traditional classroom teacher is likely to continue at a low level.

At least some roles connected with media however, are unlikely to be performed by teachers or by anyone presently connected with schools. These are the machine tending jobs that require professional competence in electronics or related fields. Most universities now have a small group of electronics engineers responsible for the operation of educational television systems of FM radio stations on the campus. It seems likely that such positions will expand in importance and will likely that such position will expand in importance and will appear more and more in the secondary and primary schools.

Information retrieval : If we had to bet on a single media-related revolution in education, it would be the forthcoming improvement in data processing and retrieval. As media for instruction or entertainment, books have a great future in the next few decades. However, given the rapid piling up of information in most fields, books are becoming less and less useful as sources of information. We assume that the next two decades will see the rapid development of techniques for encoding, storing, researching information, and that research libraries may shortly be linked with one another by means of media that allow not only for information search but also for the production of desired materials for individual use. In fact, if methods for "home" reproduction get much cheaper, it will be less expensive for the student to order a copy of a desired work from his local library then it will be for him to buy the published volume. Should this occur, it would not only drastically modify the publishing industry but also force a completely different system of communication and status validation upon scholars. Once again, such media developments hold great potential for individualizing education to suit the needs of both teachers and students.

Centralization and planning : It seems inevitable to us that media adoption will tend to force American education toward greater organizational elaboration, creating pressures towards centralization and planning. Certain media, such as broadcast television, are too expensive to be used by any one school system, except the very largest. In any event, most media presently envisioned demand some organization for their full realization. For instance, videotape recorders and motion picture projectors are of greatest use when accompanied by sets of prepared tapes or films which may be used with them.

It seems to us that pressures toward centralization will be manifest at several levels. Local school districts are likely to consider more seriously consolidation with others or at least cooperation in federations for specific purposes. For example, consider the urban school district that would like to operate a broadcast television station but feels that it cannot support the station alone. Should it not then appeal for cooperation and financial support to surrounding, suburban school districts that will also benefit from the programmes to be broadcast?

Another type of centralization will take the form of planning or policing bodies. It seems certain that with wider spread of media schools will demand standardization of media and media-related practices, if only to protect their capital investments.

Finally, some type of centralization is implied by growing federal and state support of education. The time is not for off when Americans will no longer tolerate really bed local schools if only because students educated in these schools will have less and less of a place in our complicated economy. If standardization is in the wind, centralization and planning are also implied.

Media and the Evolution of Society

Our third task is to examine the impact of new educational media on society. Its difficulty is increased by the lack of separation between educational and noneducational uses of media. Thus, the impact of educational medium is difficult to separate from the impact of other social processes, particularly new developments in education itself.

Previous Impact of Media on Society

For the most part we have already covered in previous sections the impact of new educational media on contemporary education and vice versa. Before turning to the likely future impact of these developments on American society, it is worthwhile to examine briefly the impact of previous innovations in mass media of communication.

To begin with it is important to realize that those technological innovations that have affected society most significantly and most directly have not been media. Many societal forms have appeared to vary as a function of techniques of production. Thus anthropologists usually discriminate between hunting and gathering, food storage and exploitative agricultural societies in precommercial futures. Similarly, the rise of industrial civilization is usually tied to the use of steam generated by fossil fuels as a source of power.

Two previous media developments have, however, had significant effect upon the forms of society, the development of writing and the invention of printing. The first of these presented man with the opportunity to communicate thoughts to others at a distance and to supplement memory with relatively imperishable records. These facilities, in turn, made possible the development of commerce and commercially based civilization. It should be pointed out, however, that prior to mass distribution of printed materials, literacy was the property of the few. Slaves were not literate, nor need the lord learn to read and write. Priests, money lenders, and mercantile officers were literate, and often they guarded closely the "mysteries" of literacy.

The appearance of printing made communications media available to the majority for the time and provided an impetus for universal literacy. It also had the effect in Europe of turning over many old forms of society. Literate laymen were no longer satisfied with the interpretations of holy writ provided by the clergy, hence Protestantism. Literate citizens were no longer satisfied with the divine right of kings and later with economic bondage, hence the American, French, and Socialist revolutions. Science was made possible, and the rate of social change sped up. In a real sense, we are still in the toils of adjusting to the effects of printing, since a large proportion of the world's citizens are still, unfortunately, illiterate.

It is likely that we are presently experiencing a third, major media revolution, since the appearance of electronics has made possible not only the transmission of visual and audio signals but also the reaching of a mass audience simultaneously. However, this latest media revolution has been accompanied by other radical developments in sources of power, forms of transportation, and weaponry so that we cannot isolate the effects of the new media alone. In fact, changing technology is now proceeding at such a pace that adjustment to each new development is only just begun before a half-dozen new developments are upon us presenting their new and pressing problems. This rate of technological change has no precedent in history, and in this sense we are living in a historic times.

Predictions

Once again we take up the crystal ball and venture predictions, this time about the impact of educational media on American society. Some are but extensions of the predictions made for the institution of education. One counter to predictions made earlier where we feel different forces are aboard in society. Once again, each prediction is but minimally sketched.

New roles for citizens : One obvious effect of educational media is the creation of new citizens. As is pointed out by Knowles, the possibility of adult education through mass media are but to be stopped today, and individuals will soon be faced with increasing variety of educational opportunities that are active and worthwhile. This has at least two implications the first is that education will soon be so expertly packaged and painlessly administered that the educational media is compete with entertainment on equal terms. To give, an example, a large number of people today are learning history through historical novels and other paperback for pleasure. Their "education" is absorbed, pain lessly indeed, they do not even recognizes it as education. It is possible that with appropriate media use, we may do away surely with the experiences of "painful learning." Although it is still unclear whether intense professional environment can be created without "blood, toil, tears and sweet."

Another implication of mass education through shift in recreational patterns and a vast upgrading of level of education of our citizenry. As was pointed our earlier, other forms of technology tend to release fill time. Media also create a more sophisticated citizen group. It seems likely that increased exposure of educational media will created not only a more highly enlightened citizenry than heretofore, but also one that demand more and more varied forms of mass media, hopefully higher levels of sophistication.

The above changes pertain to the consumers of educational media. Changes must inevitably also come who produce and communicate through these for into with other technological revolutions in progress. It is clear that educational media will increase the professionalization of society. The invention and operation of media require a host of highly trained persons, and their jobs will remain essential to the operation of educational media—at least until the computers take over.

Media competition with schools : In time, the popularity of educational mass media may lead them to complete with, even to eliminate, some forms of schools. It, as we have suggested previously, educational achievement is to be judged by subject matter achievement rather than by arbitrary grade, there is no real reason why the student cannot study at home or wherever he has access to a teaching machine or portable television set or videotape player. If sufficient flexibility is built into a mass public educational system, it is possible that schools and colleges may become anachronistic for the purpose of simple information dissemination. We would assume. However, that the other functions of education, such as socialization or mobilization, would be harder to provide through media and would be recognized as major contribution of the classroom experience and an alert, understanding teacher.

Reduction of provincialism : One of the major effects of mass media today is the reducation of provincialism. Regional accents are dying out; regional customs are disappearing; more and more people are becoming aware of national and international problems and are less concerned only with the problems of their town or country. Educational media cannot but help to speed up this process. Indeed, we can expect that the reduction of provincialism will take place on an international level. (Today, radio stations and television are bridging national boundaries in Europe. Tomorrow we would hope to find the same phenomena occurring across the Atlantic and Pacific.)

In the long run, one of the consequences of loss of provincialism will be the amalgamation of languages. We are certainly not the last generation to live in the world largely separated by language barriers, but we are probably the last to be largely unilingual. Particularly with the spread of media that do not require literacy, such as radio, and television, we can expect the appearance of an international pidgin or lingua franca that is spoken and understood by all users of media. Changes in written languages will take more time, and for a time, persons of a given country speak to others in pidgin and write to themselves in the native tongue. We have already predicted that in the distant future, there will probably be a collapse of literacy. It is possible that the professionals of the future will speak pidgin fluently but know only the written or symbolic language pertaining to his own profession.

Individualization : Again, we would have to predict that the reduction of provincialism would be accompanied by an increased potentiality for individualization through the use of educational media. We are already seeing in the United States the specialization of certain communications channels; for instance, FM radio is used today for educational programmes, good music, and jazz. It is likely that we will find increasing use of functionally differentiated media; television stations specializing in news, sports or enlightenment; videotapes available on the market records and audio tapes are available today. The citizen in the future may find himself presented with an ending variety of educational experiences all available at prices he can afford to pay. This suggests that although no longer a provincial, our citizen of the future may have within reach a larger variety of skills, knowledge, and experience and that society will have to tolerate many interests and foibles in its citizens.

As-yet-undeveloped media : Finally, it is at least easy to speculate on new media developments that have not yet appeared but which may be in the offing. One condition is the all-purpose medium, the computerized teaching machine-television-motion picture set. Another development being tested today is the two way visual audio communicator. Although we would usually think of such a device in terms of science fiction. Bell Telephone has put into limited use a visual, long-distance telephone as this is being written.

Two related devices that will revolutionize both office procedures and social research are the dictating typewriter and the speaking reader. The former is a device that will accept spoken standard English and will prepare an accurate written transcript. The latter will scan a manuscript and read in aloud.

If one wants to go way out on the limb, we are probably not too many years away from broadcast power and efficient space travel. But for sheer impact on human society, we cannot think of any devices that could be more explosive in their effect than the antiagathic pill and telepathic transmitter. The former will be a some form of chemotherapy that will stay indefinitely the processes of aging. The latter will consist of a small device, perhaps the size of a hearing aid, that will transmit the thoughts and feelings of the wearer to others who are similarly equipped. Both devices will have radical effects on our form of society. The former will change our attitudes toward personal danger, particularly war, and will force a re-evaluation of the institutions of family and child rearing. The latter may act to reduce both personal and social inhumanity although it may reduce our access to privacy.

Beyond this point the crystal ball is too clouded. If there is one last message we would like to leave, it is this : Educational media have enormous potential for both use and misuse. Together with other technological revolutions in process, media are forcing us to new ways of life. If we accept the challenge, if we plan, if we anticipate the needs of people in connection with these media, we will build a better world for all. If we do not properly employ them, the world we build can be a grim, living or lifeless, hell.

7

Programme Development in Education

Having defined the framework of manpower planning and human resource development in the previous chapter, five examines the actual application of the planning network in education. To do this effectively, specific case examples are drawn from social studies in order to face up to the critical challenges which are prominent in these areas. This is the programme challenge, one of the series to be examined in the rest of the book. For this purpose, three factors determine the nature of events and activities in the network of development planning in education. Essentially these are: (i) the structures of framework of the network; (ii) the processes utilised by the structures; and (iii) the available finance for carrying out the processes, as they influence the smooth running of the entire network. Thus, in order to demonstrate the universal application of development (network) theory in educational planning, this chapter examines the problems and emerging issues as they affect the quality of educational programmes in contemporary society, especially in the social sciences. From here we shall move to the financing of programmes in the next chapter.

Scope of Development Planning

Planning has been described as a deliberate process of defining a particular course of action to follow in the future. Usually this is for the purpose of achieving organisational objectives. As Birley (1972) has described it, the whole process of planning in education involves a definite prerecognition of certain dreams which we like to realise in the future. Such dreams may even seem strange on a second thought but they influence the nature of our action because we want to have them achieved. Thus in development planning in education, we develop a set of policy and evolve necessary proposals which should lead to positive changes, which will ultimately result in goal achievement.

The most fundamental question in the process of development planning in education, therefore, is, why do we plan at all? In addition, what are the problems and obstacles militating against development planning in the field of education? Furthermore, what framework should be adopted to overcome problems of planning for growth and development? These and other related questions will guide our deliberations in this chapter.

Needs

Development planning, as the term implies, involves an urgent need to solve a problem. This concept has been applied in areas especially in need of urgent development, as in the developing countries of Africa, Asia and Latin America. The application of the concept is similar to what is obtainable in development administration, where administrators deliberately adopt management principles which are practically geared to the solution of problems of regional and spatial development in poor countries. As used in this book, however, development planning in education is applicable to both developing and advanced nations. This is the case because, even in the latter group of countries, areas of relative underdevelopment are still available, hence they can be addressed through this concept. For instance, the need for development planning is still felt in such places and areas as the Appalachian highlands of United States of America, the Welsh and Scottish country-side of Britain and the marginal lands of USSR. Thus the needs of these areas are identical to those of developing countries. Though not the same, they equally require development planning to solve some of their regional development problems. Even the advanced areas need to improve further hence development planning is equally applicable to them.

From this perspective it becomes obvious that development planning is adopted mainly where there is the need to solve serious problems in education, be in it is Nigeria, Asia, Europe or even America. The question which arises however, it do we wait until there is problem before we plan at all? Absolutely not.

Specifically, in education and other social services, and indeed industry and commerce, we do plan ahead to prevent problems. Thus in manpower planning and the entire scope of human resources development, we deliberately plan through forecast and projections to avoid the negative consequences attendant to shortages of high-level skills, since they are needed to promote the national development effort. In other words, we plan to make these skills available before we need them. Even in places where there are no obvious problem, which would be hard to come by, planning is also imperative to improve on present standards. In this case the issue of problem becomes a relative one hence there is always a problem to solve; if not society will be utopian. Usually such problems and obstacles are translated into educational purposes and objective which development planning deliberately seek to accomplish.

Since the introduction of formal education into

society, planning has also been pursued as a deliberate process for the design of future educational requirements to meet the need and demands of society, whenever they arise. Inevitably, some understanding of the past and present is mandatory to present a convincing or futuristic prediction of the nature and trend of forthcoming events. Thus, as shown by Cohn (1979), planning is imperative in education because of (i) the need to clearly ascertain the signals or parameters of demand and supply of educational programmes in the future; (ii) the need to reveal necessary market information to schools to ensure optimal allocation of resources, and (iii) the need to offer relevant strategies or techniques to schools to achieve chosen goals. In addition, studies by Cloud (1984), Peterson (1984), Christensen (1985) and Dilenshneider (1985) have identified other related necessities or objects of planning as (i) the need to cater for increases in enrollments. (ii) the need to meet up with the challenge of resource decline; (iii) the need to control the uncertainty imposed by the future, and (iv) the need to control crises within the organisation or school. Because the situation or problem conditions determine the style or orientation of planning, certain forms of analyses are necessary for a successful network of development plan. In this respect Cloud (supra) would like both external (environmental) and internal (workplace) analyses to be carried out before proceeding to define assumptions, strategies, mission, future commitments and action plans, especially in the context of the school.

On the specific concern of meeting the challenge of resources decline, Peterson calls for a change in planning orientation. Such change would necessitate the adoption of the seven R's namely: (i) redefinition of missions; (ii) rethinking of administrative, leadership and organisational models; (iii) reintegration of organisational processes; (iv) revitalizing members: (v) reparations or necessary amendments; (vi) recuperation and repatriation, and (vii) recommitment (Peterson, 1984, pp. 42-46). It is however realised that these steps cannot alone take care of the special, peculiar features of educational organisations, hence Dilenshneider recommends that we should plan ahead to avert crisis or harness this towards a useful purpose. In this regard, planning to control crises will involve (i) identifying the potential crises in the school; (ii) identifying the potential audience the crises would affect; (iii) determining who should communicate with these audiences, and (iv) defining the actions and responsibilities of audiences in case crises actually occur in the school system (Dilenshneider, 1985, pp. 35-38).

The above classification of the objects of planning shows the interrelationship of macro-structure (controlling devices) and micro educational facilities, such as schools. Thus, the first object in Cohn's classification is macro-centred hence society is guided by planning organs to articulate future needs. In the last two objects by Cohn, the concern shifts to the actual process variables which are mandatory for planning goals, estimates and projections to be actualized. This is the micro-level, whose main concern is the optimal utilisation of processes and techniques for appropriate results. While structures are defined by the controlling agencies and their orientations, the relevance of processes is the challenge of the school. As a result, the interaction of structural forces and process variables do pose some problems, which may be financial, motivational or otherwise. This chapter will explore how such difficulties come into play and how they may be properly channelled.

Micro-level Forces

Whether at the structural level or process stage, development planning has traditionally relied on three interrelated forces to ensure the success of processes at the micro-level. A classified by Taylor (1970), these imperatives are money (finance), motivation and manpower, the 3 m's of development planning. While finance and manpower are the major catalysts to the successful processing of school inputs, the motivation of society has guided the course of events more radically than the mere predominance of the first two forces. Although more common in political circles, the inspiration or philosophy of society has tremendously determined the nature of educational provisions in various places. For instance, the United States was forced to reassess the trend of the her education after the Russians launched into space in the late fifties. The space break-through became the motive force here. Similarly, economic recession in Nigeria has rekindled the achievement motive of Nigerians to adopt, adapt and adjust, by devising a more utilitarian form of education under the 6-3-3-4 system (Enaohwo, 1988).

Finally, Britain in order to de-emphasize class consciousness in her society, went head-long for comprehensive education in the sixties and the seventies. Apart from egalitarianism as a motive force, the British were also inspired by the need to guarantee basic utilitarian skills through the school system, instead of relying exclusively on informal paths to skill training and development. In the same vein, the equality of man has motivated Norway, Sweden and most of the Nordic countries to create open-access (comprehensive) schools which became the envy of Britain up to the seventies, as we have just revealed. Closely related to all these experiences is the Soviet Union and other communist countries where socialism has eliminated elitism considerably from the school system. The society therefore creates the schools it wants and the instrument for this purpose is motivation.

Planning Structures

It is necessary to reveal from the onset that finance and manpower are fast becoming status variables in the development process in education. This is so because individuals and various countries tend to feel they could rest on other oars once these resources are available. This should not be the case, hence the harnessing of these factors (in addition to motivation), through appropriate structural and process framework, is more crucial than their mere possession. In this regard, the availability of these attributes is useful if only they allow the structural levels of planning to operate efficiently. By this, output is produced as cheaply as possible by the micro-level or individual schools. This is what Jolly (1969) called the optimum educational output which includes the concept of quality as well as quantity.

In defining the quality and quantity of educational programmes, what should the planning structures ensure? This is the essence of development as applied to education. As a result, planning structures or controlling agencies are expected to guarantee growth in numbers to ensure that increased demands are attended to promptly. At the same time, improvements in minimum standards in terms of pupil achievement, teachers' work load, methods and techniques of teaching, supervision skills, accountability, appraisal and appropriate assessment procedures, must be explored. This is necessary so that expansion does not overtake qualitative improvement at the micro-level of operation.

In order to maintain quantity and quality changes over time, we need to define clearly what the planning structure should look like. But to maintain quality of provisions planning authorities should be guided by the seven-point criteria formulated by Bergquist and Armstrong (1986), which include attractiveness, congruence, distrinctiveness, effectiveness, functionality, growth potential and ability to benefit individuals and community. Although mainly qualitative in nature, these criteria are worth considering by appropriate planning agencies if they are working to cater to public needs. This brings us to the levels and authority of planning structures.

Planning Hierarchy

Generally, four levels of planning can easily be identified in the educational system. The placement of planning structures in the hierarchy determines the scope of authority, power and control. Thus, depending on the system of government in the particular society, the four structures of planning are as follows: (i) the micro-structure at the school level; (ii) the local or district structure or organ; (iii) the provincial or state structure and (iv) the central or federal structure of planning.

The School

The school structure is concerned mainly with limited planning models. Usually, these are often of short-term duration, and they are meant to attain the expectations of the super-hierarchy, that is the local or district structure. These are often tactical or action plans, or what may be referred to in some quarters as implementation plans. They are not concerned with policy formation or strategic planning. Despite their limitations, action planning at the school level, like other plans, must address three basic components. These are: (i) the situation or current state of affairs; (ii) the target or the desired state or goal; and (iii) the proposal or actions necessary to change the situation (Phillips, *et al.*, 1986). In addition, these three core requirements are not complete without effective evaluation, which is an essential element of planning in its own right.

Local Structure

The local planning structure, the second in the hierarchy, is always exemplified by the district or local school board. Such board is usually under the control of both administrators, professional planners and former teachers. The interest here is circumscribed in nature because it is localised to a considerable extent. Essentially, the scope of authority and power at this level is determined by the scope of centralization or decentralization in the particular system. In most centralized (developing) countries, such local units of planning are answerable to the state or third structure. In fact, sometimes, the local unit would be a branch of the third level, in which case the functions are focussed mainly on implementation too. On the other hand, in most developed countries, where there is a large measure decentralization, local school boards equally engage in some policy planning, recruitment, supervision and assembling of local education data and materials.

State Structure

The third in the hierarchy of planning structures is the state or provincial organ. Usually this is the state's education department or ministry of education. There is a lot of monopoly of power and authority by this agency because the law confers the control of policy on it. It is therefore the agency which has ultimate responsibilities for educational planning and development in the state. And the power of control here is immense, hence this varies from control of allocations, budgeting, educational reforms, establishment and recognition of educational institution, to setting of standards for the whole state.

Central Structure

Lastly, the central structure of planning takes various shapes in different countries. The powers here also vary from situations to situation. Thus, in confederal nations such as Canada, the centre contributes nothing essential to the process of educational planning, except research funding and promotion of education for international development. On the other hand, the situation in unitary states, such as France and most communist countries, is based on central suremacy. In this case, policies and programmes evolve from the centre for implementation by other organs of the planning hierarchy. Mid-way between these two systems is the situation existing in federal states, such as Nigeria, United States and Brazil, to mention a few. Mexico presents a similar situation (Bruera, 1987). In these countries, educational planning and development is placed on the concurrent legislative list in the constitutions. The States' planning organs address areas of state interests, while the federal government handles areas of national interest. However, the dichotomy of power play is so ambiguous that there are occasional clashes between the two levels of governments, especially in interpreting what is or is not national interest. For this purpose, Britain is in a peculiar situation because her local authorities play the roles of both district/local and state organs in development planning in education.

Planning Processes

Relevant processes adopted in development planning in education can be considered from two main perspective. First, we have the global or general processes which are utilised by any of the structural organs to chart the future course of educational development. Under this framework, strategic or long-range programming is pursued through systematic forward planning (SFP) which consists of six closely related stages. As developed by Enaohwo (1984), systematic forward planning revolves around six cyclical stages, as follows: (i) problem survey and deliberation; (ii) goal definition and delineation; (iii) programme planning and design; (iv) programme provision. Implementation and supervision; (v) programme study and evaluation, and finally (vi) programme regeneration and recycling. These stages of the planning process are similar to the linear model of academic planning proposed by Bergquist and Armstrong (1986). This lays emphasis on (i) needs, goal or problem assessment; (ii) identification of resources and constraints; (iii) the building of a series of alternatives to take care of different options of resource uses, testing, decision-making and environmental influence, and (iv) utilisation of relative strategies for the purpose of evaluation.

To illustrate actual application of SFP, a model social studies programme is provided later in this chapter. Such a programme, it should be emphasized, must be addressed by the three upper structures of the planning network, with provision for adequate inputs by the local/district structure in order to take care of local diversity and cultural background.

Process Strategies

The second set of processes utilised in planning structures are more specific in nature. Usually these processes are available to entangle the mystery of the future in present-day perception. Thus, we have process strategies which are meant to take care of enrollments, teacher numbers, pupil and staff turnovers, transition behaviours, resource (physical) outlay and utilisation, staff workload, and budgetary allocation. For the purpose of this chapter we shall cite relevant examples in chapters nine and ten on enrollment projections and manpower estimates to buttress or illustrate processes in the above areas. The actual applications of these and other strategies are provided in O.E.C.D. (1976), Loxley (1987), and Psacharopoulos (1987).

Enrollments

Three processes or methods are commonly adopted for enrollment projections. Lows (1987) has classified these as follows: (i) identification of school age number in a given population for the purpose of compulsory enrollment; (ii) determination of the school enrollment ratio. This ratio or fraction is applied to subsequent live birth data to project estimates of future enrollments, usually in voluntary attendance, and (iii) used of regression analysis through the projection of the line of best fit. In this method, years are plotted on the horizontal axis while enrollment is along the vertical axis.

For projections arising from these procedures to be useful, there is need to adjust for pupil wastage or turnover. This is obtained by a net increase in obtained results by the relevant percentage level of wastage. This has a booster effect on the ultimate projection of future enrollments for the school system, as illustrated or revealed in chapter nine.

Teacher Numbers

Estimation of teacher requirements is carried out through appropriate method of manpower planning. Under this process planners have resorted to an interplay of three methods, namely: (i) the employers opinion survey method; (ii) international comparison of manpower or teacher requirements, and (iii) the density ratio method, which is made up of the staff-normative technique and the rate of saturation technique. While the former is derived from the teacher-pupil ratio, the latter is based on the proportion or stable ratio of high-level manpower (HLMP) in the economy. Actual applications of the density ratio method, through the staff-normative technique are clearly illustrated by Williams (1987), Hinchliffe (1987) and Miller (1986). These have been clearly examined in chapter four although actual illustrations are given in chapter ten.

Problems

The major limitations confronting planning and processes of development in education are methodological and social in nature. First, on the social perspective, there is the acute problem of obtaining accurate data and feedback from people, because these touch on their private lives. Such vital statistics on date of birth, age, births, death, fecundity rates and migrational patterns, are difficult to authenticate, especially if the machinery for statistical data is poorly developed in the society, as is the case in the Third World. Despite this setback enrollment projection and manpower planning depend heavily on the accuracy of these data, to arrive at any useful estimates for the future.

Secondly, the setback inflicted by the methodological problem poses greater doubts on obtained results. In the first instance, projections are hardly reliable if based on one method or approach. Often planners are forced to adopt two or more approaches to improve the level of accuracy of results. Thus, in manpower planning processes, there is hardly any reliance on the opinion survey method because of the problems posed by guesswork by employers, who provide data on employment levels, workload and modes of labour utilisation. If adopted at all, this method is used alongside other more sophisticated methods such as the density—ratio, the Parnes' M.R.P. Approach or regression extrapolation. In a similar manner, it is difficult to utilise international comparison along because of obvious limitations. Countries and regions are so diverse that the transformation of the characteristics of a model, buoyant country into a poor nation is definitely an unwise course to follow. This is why comparisons should be handled with extreme caution because nations differ politically, geographically, culturally and economically.

Computer Use

Another methodological problem is the challenge posed by computation of data in educational planning. Basically we are dealing with data based on trends of human behaviour. As a result, one wonders occasionally if these could be subjected to accurate projections by statistical computation. Although the computer has eased this problem considerably, too many assumptions and adjustments are made on data that the originality of the materials could be lost altogether, by the time they are fed into the computer. For instance, in rate of returns analysis, adjustment must be made for (i) inflation; (ii) increase in income or perhaps decreased in earnings; (iii) unemployment; (iv) present value calculations; (v) death; (vi) ability; (vii) age, and (viii) foregone income. By the time all these are carried out, the impact of original data on ultimate results is reduced considerably. Moreover, we must realise that such adjustments are even based on unreliable premises or prevailing rates.

Finally, as Inbar (1986) has revealed, errors in the process of planning may also arise from misuse of information, method or procedure, depending on the expertise of the planning team or personnel. Occasionally, too, unknown variables could intervene and change the course of action in unpredictable ways, hence uncertainty makes error-free planning ridiculous. Other problems in the connection arise from errors of judgement, human biases, emotional dispositions and obvious contradiction which are imposed by conflicting methods of planning (*supra*, pp. 3-4).

Ideology

Another major problem of development is the issue of ideological orientation, especially in Third World countries where the search for a suitable system is still in progress. This brings us to the situation in social studies where ideology imposes a lot of influence on curricular programmes. This issues is addressed by thoroughly examining the elements or essential focus of an appropriate social studies programme which takes full cognizance of the ideological question. The choice of social studies is deliberate because it is this discipline which exposes children early enough to the ideological question in education and society.

Notable authorities in the field of educational planning strongly believe that the planning process in education is ideologically neutral (Coombs, 1970). In this respect it is opined that the planning of education, especially with reference to the curriculum, is value-free. To some extent this perception is applicable in the western world or the so-called free democracies. However, to a larger extent, this is hardly applicable in the developing setting where no suitable ideology has been found relevant in these areas.

For western nations, such ideology like capitalism has become a principal characteristic of the culture hence no deliberate a principal characteristic of the culture hence no deliberate approach he is necessary to infuse this into the younger generation. This cannot be said of the Third World, a group of people in dire need of development, and faced with the perennial problem of instability in government. Countries of the Third World are therefore in search of appropriate ideologies to govern the political and socio-economic lives of their people.

For this search to be a thorough one, it is often explored through social studies. Once a stable system is identified, be it identified, be it capitalism or socialism or welfarism, mixed economy or what have you, it could be transmitted as well through the educational system, especially through the disciplines which constitute social studies. It is therefore against this background that the planning of a relevant social studies programme for the Third World is focused. Social studies is the amalgam of the culture of any society and, since ideology is a living aspect of this culture, any prescribed programme will be deficient if it fails to address this issue. Because of this, any discussion of a suitable programme inevitably has the ideological stance as one of its cardinal objectives or goals. To think that a neutral position will provide the Third World any salvation is a forlorn hope, for this will only lead to the imposition of the established ideologies, which may or may not be suitable for these areas.

Planning Cycle

For the purpose of this discussion, therefore the orbit of concern will centre around the following: (a) the identification of a problem associated with the present social studies programme. This could be achieved through problem survey and deliberation; (b) setting objectives for the emergent social studies programme. These articulate the goals of the entire educational system for the social studies programme; (c) identification of alternatives for pursuing these objectives. This is through a thorough and coordinated programme of actual planning and design. In addition to these, there is the stage of programme provision, implementation and supervision, followed by programme study and evaluation, and finally programmed regeneration and recycling. The whole process is a cyclic one hence each stage gives effect to the next, until the whole process is completed and recycled or renewed. That was implied in the cyclical planning process examined earlier on in this chapter.

Scope of Social Studies

Before looking at these stages in detail, let us consider briefly what is referred to as social studies. Since the definitions of the field are legion, the concern is to find a suitable identification for the purpose of this analysis. This is carried out through a process of conceptualization. In this regard Wronski (1981) identified three forms of organization in social studies; namely: (i) social studies as separate academic disciplines, made up essentially of history, political science, geography, economics, anthropology, religion, psychology and sociology, (ii) social studies as interdisciplinary and multi-disciplinary studies, with a focus on concepts, paradigms and principles drawn from two or more disciplines. From this, a new academic discipline may emerge by fusing older ones, (iii) social studies as an integrated subject, drawing upon known principles from many fields. In this conceptualization, issues, questions, topics and social problems are resolved by relying on the relevant disciplines for facts, theories, principles methods, concepts and generalizations. In the last two conceptualizations, social studies is a subject in its own right, unlike the first approach where social studies is a broad field, taught in the school system through different subjects of the humanities and social sciences. It is needless to say therefore that it is through the interdisciplinary and integrated approaches that the needs of the Third World can be satisfied adequately. Apart from the savings in cost in training individual specialists in the separate disciplines, specialists emerging from these two approaches will be more adaptable to the solution of the multi-disciplinary problems in such areas. Specialists in the individual disciplines can hardly cope alone in tackling the diverse problems of the continent. In this context, it is necessary to evolve a conceptualization or definition which sees social studies as a deliberate approach to the organization of spatial experiences, through multi-disciplinary and integrated studies, for the purpose of resolving issues, questions and problems which confront developing societies in their quest for development. In Lawton (1981)'s words, this field "helps young individuals to develop fully into human adults by relating them to their society by means of appropriate knowledge and experience, from the social sciences and other disciplines"

The Need and Objectives

As indicated in the cyclical framework for the planning of an appropriate social studies programme, the first step is the definition of the problem. Such problems and issues constitute the needs of developing areas to which social studies should be addressed. From these experiences, the main problems are sociocultural, economic, political, technological and geographical, to mention a few. While the scientific and technological concerns are left to the sciences and applied sciences to resolve; the spatial problems must be the focus of social studies. These are the problems which confront man in the society. As a first step in the development of an appropriate programme, these problems are first defined and collated through inquiries, surveys and deliberations or discourse. From recent experiences these problems are mainly the threat of famine disease, political instability, lack of ideological orientation, shortfall in infrastructure, economic depression, shortages of skilled manpower and death of interregional cooperation, to cite a few. The new programmc must address these issues.

It is on the basis of identified needs of society that the purpose and objectives of social studies are based. Thus a worthwhile social studies programme would have two central purposes which are highly interrelated. These purposes are centred on the needs disposition of society and the awareness disposition, with respect to one's rights, freedom and responsibilities. Specifically, these purposes are further broken down into articulate objectives which are essentially to: (i) define the place of man in the spatial environment; (ii) identify the rights, obligations and responsibilities of the individual in order to lead a worthwhile life in the society; (iii) articulate, in clear terms, the needs and problems of individuals in the developing society; (iv) provide youths the necessary exposure to relevant academic, social and scientific knowledge for the solution of Third World problems, and finally, (v) enable people in these areas to rule themselves through effective and purposeful leadership and ideology. Through such orientation to the needs and right of society, a holistic approach to the organization of knowledge and skills is imperative for the society to stand up squarely to the challenges of development. In this context, it is submitted that a social studies programme that lacks either the needs disposition or the awareness disposition, is an aberration because it will exhibit a sheer ignorance of the situation in the Third World.

Cooperation

Another fundamental issue that should be pursued, through proper objectives, is the question of inter-regional cooperation and mutual coexistence among Third World citizens and other countries. In this area of concern, social studies provides pupils the orientation to prevent the forces of disunity in these societies. Thus, the evil forces of wars, the ugly hang-over of racism, fascism, and the obnoxious South African system of apartheid could be dismantled through appropriate ideological exposure in the field of social studies. In this regard, objectives are directed towards the elimination of the enduring shackles of such evil systems, in addition to the removal of the appurtenances of neocolonialism and imperialism. Such objectives therefore stress the need for a greater drive towards inter-regional cooperation through regional and continental groupings.

Writing on the need for countries to promote peace through social studies, Malkova (1981) opined that success is achieved only through the harmonization of programme materials across national barriers, the adoption of relevant text materials, exposure to museum, arts and artifacts of other lands, and a serious commitment to solidarity in regional groupings. No other area needs this form of orientation more than the Third World, if only to eliminate the series of national barriers which impede movement, understanding, growth and development in contemporary society. This is the time to move towards this direction, and the means to this end is basically integrated social studies.

A closer look at the discussion of objectives and problems reveals that there is a close relationship between these factors. This close relationship is what Dufty (1981) called the interdependence of goals and objectives. This level of interdependence shows that these objectives are not mutually exclusive, neither should they be considered as isolated. Similary national objectives and goals of social studies should be considered and given the same priority as internatinal goals and objectives. This is the only way to contribute effectively to the international peace forum, bilateral cooperation and mutual co-existence between member countries of the O.A.U. and other nations.

Relevant Social Studies Programme

As a planner charged with the responsibility of formulating an integrated social studies programme for the realization of set objectives, consideration is given to some pre-conditions or premises which should guide the production of satisfactory results. These are the essential characteristic of the programme. Thus, to start with, the following guidelines would influence what to include and what not to include in the programme. First there is need to ensure that the entire programme is based on the holistic perception of the entire field of social studies, that it to say, emphasis is focused adequately on all the essential concepts, principles and generalizations which are germane to the solution of the problems of the Third World. In this respect, any discipline which is relevant to the clarification of the points at issue is given a fair chance of contributing to the elimination of perceived needs. Secondly, there is also the important stage of providing essential skills and manpower through preparations in the field of social studies. This is an area where a lot of concern has already been expressed. This is so because it is generally suspected that products of the integrated or multi-disciplinary approach, to the teaching of social studies, cannot stand shoulder to should with their colleagues brought up in the traditional disciplines. To allay such fears, which may be genuine in some circles, care is therefore needed to ensure that the prerequisite skills and training, needed for the solution of prevailing problems, are adequately provided for in any new deal. Thus, expertise cannot be sacrificed for the sake of generalization or integration.

A third characteristic of any worhtwhile social programme is the capacity to transmit desirable values in the society. While positive values are promoted, the negative ones, adverse to the society and which tend to divide us, should be condemned in the process. For this purpose, Ganguli (1981) has provided the general scope of values worth cultivating in children through an enviable social studies programme. These are (i) material and physical; (ii) economic; (iii) moral; (iv) social; (v) political; (vi) aesthetic; (vii) religious or spiritual, (viii) intellectual and professional, and finally sentimental values. The subjects contributing to the positive cultivation of these values are therefore accorded adequate attention in the scheme of things.

As a result, the concept of health, comfort, productivity, honesty, courtesy, freedom, justice, beauty, piety, intelligence, professional competence and love should be given recognition in the social studies syllabus or progamme.

Self-Reliance

A fourth characteristic of a viable social studies programme is the emphasis that is placed on the suse of local resources, before dependence on foreign sources. This brings into focus the question of self-reliance where it is necessary, without sacrificing the need for mutual coexistence, trade and cooperation among neighbouring countries. For this purpose, the new social studies programme should create independence of thought in the child while removing the negative consequences of out-right reliance and dependence on other people's economy. The banana-republic syndrome must be eradicated from the Third World. The same thing applies to the realm of culture, an aspect of life where the Third World identity was terribly decimated through the colonial experience. If there is an area in which the educated person in the Third World has become at variance with his society, it is in cultural identity. Affected people are neither here not there, hence social studies must be addressed to this problem. To tackle this sucessfully, society must choose between enculturation and acculturation in the emergent social studies programme. A starting point, no doubt, is enculturation (instead of acculturation) through the assimilation of the tenets of the indigenous culture of these areas. This is the period of initiation and indoctrination in the modes and ways of life which constitute the traditional psyche of the people. Next to this stage is acculturation or exposure to the culture of other lands. In this regard, it should be stressed that, be it enculturation or acculturation, only the good aspects of both the local and foreign cultures should be introduced or exposed to children through social studies. The moment this is achieved through the new programme, then success in evolving a dynamic culture for posterity is attained in the process.

Implementation Phase

The provision of appropriate social studies programme is not complete without implementation and effective supervision. This is a major stage in the social studies programme. Under implementation, it is necessary to stress that pilot simulation is necesary to find out the expected level of effectiveness of any desired programme before it is finally adopted. Thus, pilot simulation of real life situations should span at least a period of three years. This should be among a selected group of people in order to find out whether the programme is adressing what it is expected to address. As a result, if a programme is expected to instill in pupils certain worthswhile values or ideology, then pilot simulation should reveal whether such values or ideology are apparent, after a period of test-run. This is why a fairly long period is required for pilot simulation. If this procedure reveals any inability to achieve the desirable goals for the model programme, then the factors responsible for such failure are identified, before arriving at an alternate and effective programme. After a programme is adopted through a successful test-run, it is finally subjected to continuous supervision to ensure effective implementation in the school system. Such supervision calls for the education and training of a high calibre or crop o f supervising officers who would be part of the implementation team, in addition to teachers and education officials. Through this approach, the implementation of a new social studies programme is subject to controlled surveillance and supervision, as applicable in physical development projects through the use of consultants. This is why the characteristic feature of pilot simulation is such a crucial stage in the implementation and supervision process of the social studies programme.

Comprehensive Skills

Of critical importance in the supply of suitable teachers, supervising staff and educational officials for the implementation stage, is the need to ensure that beneficiaries of training schemes are exposed to comprehensive skills to enable them function in various capacities in the rural environments. Such teams of social studies experts will inevitably be the apostles of rural development in the Third World, for they will be required to focus special attention on the rural areas for useful results. This is essential for the overwhelming majority of rural dwelleres. As Coverdale (1974) has revealed in his discussion of education for rural development, such teachers participating in the implementation of the new social studies programme need some competence in vocational education, in addition to functioning as adult education agents and extension workers in the field of social studies. Social studies cannot be taught in isolation, hence it should be blended with other functional subjects, which could help make the rural population active and productive members of the society. At this juncture, it is necessary to point out that the much coveted idea of national unity in the developing societies is meaningless if the vast majority of the population is unproductive. Ideology without production of economic muscle is nonsense.

In fact, if it is agreed as Chan (1971) revealed, that national unity is either political unity by consent/force in the face of external threat, or the ability of a nation to cope and absorb stresses and strains from internal conflicts; then social studies must be taught beyong the confines of the classroom. It would touch on the organized structure of society, the language, the productive forces and the social dynamics which are favourably disposed to national unity.

Problems

From the foreging it is apparent that various factors and characteristics of the planning process, put together, call attention to the need for the elimination of the major constraints in the implementation of an effective social studies programme. Thus, as vividly put by Ruscoe (1969), both the political and administrative constraints and bottlenecks have to be eliminated, especially in the evolvement of a good social studies programme. In this respect both the political cum-administrative roles and the technical-cum-professional roles are distinguished in the shceme of things. The latter is under the full control of social studies experts, while the former, to a considerable extent, is left to the state bureaucracy, especially in the study, evaluation, regeneration and recycling stages of the planning process. In other words, to achieve success, both facets need effective co-ordination all through the gamut of the planning process.

Evaluation

The question of evaluation brings into focus the form of examination that is suitable in the new framework before the programme is left to recycle or regenerate. This is why Hawes' (1922) position is essential, and this shows that the evaluation of programmes, such as the new social studies programme, is objective in nature. This is to say that answers should be full-proof correct, out of the lot available. This where the move towards continuous assessment is very essential in the programme. By this approach, pitfalls are identified early in the system, instead of waiting till the terminal year of the school system when it is impossible to rectify the odds. Once these odds are identified, the programmes are then subjected to recycoling and regeneration, through the cyclical process.

Implication

The relevance of the proposals presesnted in this chapter provides a challenge to the preparation of social studies experts. If current trends are anything to go by, it is found that most social studies teachers in the field were actually trained and brought up in the distinct disciplines and subjects from whihc social studies struck its identity. Such an arrangement is not good enough for the emergent field. As a result, institutions of higher learning whicy are still hesitant in offering degree programmes and integrated approach, should wake up to their responsibilities. This in addition to the conventional roles or faculty programmes in the social sciences. To succeed, issues must be addressed by devising suitable programmes at the undergraduate and graduate levels to prepare the distinct crop of experts and specialists in social studies, in order to actualize the goals and objectives which developing societies have for this field in their quest for development.

8

Radio in Support of Women's Empowerment

If the child has to be developed as a national resource and if improvements in the health of mothers and children are to be achieved, it is essential that individuals, the families and the community participate in affordable and low-cost health care interventions. This calls for some behavioural changes individuals. Pofessionals with their knowledge, Attitudes and Practices (KAP) studies in recent years have established that to bring about any change in behaviour, attitude change is often a prerequisite. Many other studies in the field of agriculture and market research corroborate these findings. People interested in tangible returns allocate large sums of money to sell their ideas. Radio, TV and motion pictures are used more and more in the service of marketing both products and ideas. The men behind these media can, and do, inform, educate, modify attitudes and also entertain simultaneously.

With the belief that education is an essential component of every human development eneavour, UNICEF in India has been trying to facilitate acquisition by media and other specialised groups of the knowledge and skills in support of development of children and women. Planning and providing motivational information, ensuring its dissemination and the resultant feedback, devising and demonstrating appropriate communication interventions, helping improve the communication abilities of various media, adapting and exploiting the traditional media resources and encouraging both government, as well as voluntary agencies, to become active partners in advocating and promoting the cause of women, children, youth, the destitute, the disabled and the downtrodden have been its basic objectives.

Beginning of an Experiment

Recognising the potential of radio in India, UNICEF decided to put it to good use in order to overcome the problem of motivating and educating large masses of widely dispersed rural people and to help improve their lives through some innovative programming on maternal and child health care. In cooperation with the Ministry of Information & Broadcasting, and the Ministry of Social and Women's Welfare,UNICEF initiated in 1982 an experiment in field-based softwere development for radio. As a result a radio workshop was held at Koraput. It helped learn many lessons. The next workshop at Trivandroum in December 1982 was more tightly organised and proved to be the second step in learning the use of radio for maternal and child care. Although each successive workshop had something to contibute to our learning experience, a clear strategy had started to emerge by the time the third workshop at Rohtak was over.

With the planning of the fifth workshop at Lucknow, the experiment had already majored into a project. The series of experiments in orientation has not only provided a workable formula for the improvement of radio programming for child development, but has also cemented as already promising partnership with the Ministry of Information and Broadcasting, and opened up new areas of coperation with State Governments and other non-governmental resource institutions at subnational and local levels. The approach has been flexible and responsive to local situations and therefore the formula always remained under evolution.

The Orientation Projects Strategy

The radio orientation project focuses thematically on 'The First Year of a chil's Lift', so that the content does not too ambitious and therefore ambiguous. This helps the organisers keep in sharp focus the critical subject-matter areas of information and education that are vital for ensuring the survival and proper growth of a child with better health prospects for the mother and, therefore, the family in the long run. The broad objectives the project aims at are :

1. *Educating and motruating people to act*
   Adoption of healthy lifestyle is a prerequisite for ensuring child survival and better development of rural families. The project aims to achieve this by effective dissemination of information through radio and improving listeners knowledge of health. It attempts to demonstrate that radio can be a positive force in bringing about changes in behaviour and action.
2. *Promoting serutces for maternal and child health care*
   The communities is rural and semi-urban areas are unaware of low-cost, yet highly effective, technologies and services, the time and places of their availability, and the circumstances under with they should be used. The project strives to use radio as a medium for transmitting information related to the existence of such technologies. It is also supposed to eradicate incorrect notions and misconceptions about certain health and nutritions practices in the community.

3. *Providing support to front-line workers*
The success of the Child Survival and Development (CSD)-related programmes depends largely on the capabilities of the grass-root level workers. Providing them a continuing education; keeping them up-to-date and giving them ongoing support in successfully undertaking their tasks is another objective of the radio orientation project. This also lends prestige to institutions of community workers and helps legitimise their role in the community.
4. *Fostering community participation*
The radio station participating in the project is expected to generate community discussion and aslo the feedback for media producers and programme adminstrators and programme administrators. The participatory use of radio (discussion based feedback and answering questions) gives rurual listeners a greater sense of confidence, self-respect and strength—the basic attributes of my community-oriented programme. This facilitates organisation of the unorganised into special-interest groups enabling them to participate in community welfare activities and work as watch-dogs of community services.
5. *Sensitising broadcasters and decision-makers to the problems of women and children.*
The project aims at providing information input in planning and production of need-based and community problem-oriented programmes. An interaction with the target audience and programme beneficiaries is expected to bring about a willingness on the part of radio programmers and service departments to constantly review and further improve their programming. The crucial element of "empathy" resulting from face-to-face interaction and feedback would enable communicators as well as decision makers to adjust their reactions and make the programmes relevant to the needs of the poeple.

6. *Orienting the broadcasters and decision-makers to the subject-matter of Maternal and Child Health-Care (MCH)*
   The radio project is epected to facilitarte a constant interaction between the subject-matter specilists, the broadcasters and the decision-markers in the govenment to bridge the communication gaps in areas of MCH.
7. *Demonstrating the value of 'action research' in planning and production of media*
   Systematic study, incorporated into an operational programme, the results of which are fed back directly and immediately to the operational staff to help them improve the effectiveness of their activities is a sound principle of media production. The project is to demonstrate the value and importance of team work in media production; to provide on a continuing basis a sound base for fruitful interaction between the media planners and producers, subject-matter specialists, the decision-makers and administrators, the field workers and the audience for the ultimate benefit the community.

The Project Planning

The hallmark of a successful media support project for MCH extension is adequate planning, full commitment of government departments, community involvement including political support. Cooperation for better communication in support of child survival and development services was first discussed with the Ministry of Information and Broadcasting in 1980-81. After continued deliberations for field-based experimentation in software development, the Ministry agreed to the proposal. With the success of the first few experiments, the Ministry concurred with the proposal of actual programming commitments on the priority themes identified during the workshop. This commitment forms the basis of project.

The partnership between UNICEF and the Ministry of Information & Broadcasting gets further impetus with the active involvement and support of State Governments through their departments' of Social Welfare, Health and Rural Development, other non-government organisations and media agencies. The project involves the management and coordination of many disparate activities and, therefore, at the outset an assessment of management needs and capabilities is made to determine the existence of requisite resources in men and material in particular area identified for the project.

UNICEF, the Air India Radio (AIR) and the nodal state department together work out the details of proposal. With the success of the first few experiments, the Ministry concurred with the proposal of actual programming commitments on the priority themes identified during the workshop. The commitment forms the basis of project.

Audience Profiling

Research is essential to exactly identify the audience, and its demographic composition problems related to a specificc subject-matter areas the prevailing knowledge, attitudes and practices in the areas of Child Survival and Development Revolution (CSDR). The resources and limitations, etc. and also the radio/media exposure patterns of the community. Presented as a backgrounder to profile helps in determinig the message content of radio programmes. A detailed guideline is provided to the identified resource institutions to conduct the study and prepare a profile report to be presented at the beginning of the radio workshop. Subsequently this also serves as reference material for the media to produce audience targeted programmes.

Media Orientation

This critical phase of the project aims at identifying the formulating vaild, credible and acceptable messages for the benefit of the target audience. The workshop is held for sensitising all concerned to the problems of women and children in the area, to orientate them in the use of radio as a supportive medium in the delivery of basic services and to enable them to interact with the listerners and identify basic communication needs so as to build up an area-specific and need-based broadcast series with a definite strategy for the widespread dissemination of identified messages with ensured audience feedback.

These workshops usually last for six days. The ensure full pparticipation of grass-root workers, the workshop is invariably conducted in the regional language and a participatory approach is used throughout. At the outset the workshop objectives and its methodology are deliberated upon. Following this, the audience profile is presented on the first day.

(a) *The participants :*

The workshop brings together those who prepare the broadcasts, who provide the technical subject-matter knowledge and those who could use them for better delivery of child-related services. A crossection of field functionaries and officials with a preponderance of frontline workers of the departments of Social Welfare. Health Services and Development, a group of programmers from radio stations of a common liguistic area, other media people and representatives of voluntary agencies working with the community in the area form the participants of the workshop. Their total number usually ranges from 50 to 90 depending on the expanse of the project area determined by the liguitic and cultural homogenity within the primary service area of the radio station selected for the project.

(b) *Field visit :*

With the presentation of audience profile the

participants, particularly the media people and the subject-matter specialists, gain some insight about the audience. These vague insights need to be given a more factual base before any masseges can be determined. The participants are divided into small groups of 8-10 persons each with at least one representative of each of the categories represented in it. During the next two days a systematic social investigation designed to discover the demographic characteristics of the target and listening audience, the specifics of pre-natal, natal and post-natal practices and an analysis of predipositional knowledge and attitudes to design genuniely persuasive programme series, is carried out. The participants are provided with a comprehansive guideline for this purpose. They visit the identified village on both the days and interact with the people to gather first hand information about them.

(C) *Field Testing of radio programmes :*

Most producers believe that they know what their audience likes, understands and accepts. To an extent they are right. But no producer is infallible particularly when producing a programme on subjects new or unfamiliar to the audience. The workshop gives an opportunity to radio programmers to field-test their programmes on a sample audience in order to avoid any programming failures. This only validates their programming approach as they try to establish if any aspect of the programme is not communicating effectively and why it is so. The radio station of the project area provides one or two sample programmes. On the second day of the field visit these programmes are played back to sample audience to discover how far they have understood the programme and can recall the essential elements of the message. The interviews for this purpose are conucted on the basis of guidelines provided but no structured schedule as such is produced before the audience. The instant feedback is the first step towards getting the massage dlivered and accepted. The producers get reoriented to the sound principles of media production.

(d) *Identifying information needs :*

The findings gathered by the participants during the field visit which, when analysed skillfully, bring out the communication needs of the audience. They must be translated into messages. The participants deliberate in groups on the observations they have made and try to analyses them systematically. The format circulated earlier enables the groups to define in unambiguous terms to problems observed, the present-day knowledge status of the audience, their perceptions and predispositions about the problems and their solutions. this exercise given an inventory of information needs which leads the participants to prepare widely acceptable messages.

(e) Preparation of messages :

Further continuing their work in groups the participants work out the topics based on the identified problems on which the programmes should be broadcast. While suggesting titles the groups also work out the scope of each broadcast. Subject specialist provide the technical information to be covered under the broadcasts. Each broadcasts topic divided into sub-topics has a well-defined scope giving points to be covered under each head. With each topic the groups also suggest a few leading questions. These serve the twin objectives. Apart from providing guidance to the subject specialists, the script writers and the programme producers to answer these questions, they serve as a lead to the group animators to initiate discussion at the end of the each broadcast. These group reports are integrated at the end of the workshop so that an all-agreed series of messages/ topics for broadcasts is given to the radio station.

(*f*) *Identification of support media :*
Radio has some limitations. If lacks visual dimensions; broadcasts cannot be used as reference material. its sgnal may be weak or distorted, resulting in poor reception or no reception at all. It was, therefore, considered appropriate the supplement the radio broadcasts with some other media channels. Hence, the workshop devotes one full session on identifying support media to be disseminated in synchronisation with the radio broadcasts. This has tended to make it multi-media project. At the workshop the photographs, posters and publications are displayed. The groups go through them and deliberate on the possibilities of involving one or more of these and other media. Low cost publications, posters and folk media are invariably recommended by the participants; particularly the print medium has now become more or less an integral part to the project.

(*g*) *The workshop outcome:*
The workshop in its final session spells out all the details for successful implementation of the project. Based on the audience feedback the days, timing and language of broadcasts, the procedure to ensure full utilisation of the media, the number of listening groups to be organised and other related details are spelt out. Also a local steering committe is set up to oversee the implementation of the project.

Ensuring Media Accessibility

Although aggregate figure for this country may show a high proportion of radio ownership yet much of the intended audience of CSD messages does not have an access to radio. This is particularly true of rual women who, despite the availability of a radio in the family, never get an opportunity to listen to it. To overcome this difficulty the mode of organised group listening has been incorporated in the project. The women, are organised in to small groups to meet regularly at the appointed hour, on the identified day each week and to listen, discuss and decide on action, if any, on the messages broadcast. Anganwadi Integrated Child Development Services (ICDS centres)—the newly emerging institution of women's and children's welfare at the village level, the adult education centres, women's Charcha Mandals, Balwadis, etc. wherever they exist organise the women into listening groups. Child survival and development is not the exclusive concern of women only and, therefore, men are also encouraged to form their own listening groups so that the process of decision-making at family/village level is facilitated. Listening groups work under the leadership of trained animators. Each of these groups is provided with a transistor radio set. The messages are repeat-broadcast for men, under the regular 'Farm and Home' programmes during evening hours. All other support media are diffused in the community through these listeners groups only.

Training of Group Animalors

The essence of group listening is organisation. The group members must be prepared to assemble, listen, discuss and learn. Organisation of large scale groups require a high degree of field-work, staff time and management skill for trained group leadership and the animators receive training in these skills. Their training curriculum covers topics on group organistion, the discussion process, its importance, the role or group animators and members in field communication, use of support material, discussion leadership and eliciting feedback etc. Core trainers from resource institutions in the project area are imparted this training in a participatory and role-playing manner. They in turn train the animators at block level and impart them the skills in group discussion.

Assimilation and Diffusion of Messages

The facts disseminated through mass media become part of people's behaviour only when these are deliberated upon with persons of confidence. Organised listening provides the listeners a form where they can receive the messages, exchange their views on them, get clarified the new information and record their reactions on it. This facilitates the process of decision-making, as rural communities are known to take decisions only collectively. People learn better as they pool their experiences, seek and offer clarifications on different perceptions and interpretations. At the end of discusion, the learning becomes part of one's thinking process which is more likely to get transformed into practice.

In most cases Anganwadi workers happen to be the group animators and they routinely visit different families each day. This helps in diffusion of information among the families. The broadcasts provide them enough subject-matter to talk about during the next six days of the week. Thus while the media update the knowledge of these front-line workers, their discussions and home visit facilitate diffusion of new knowledge in the community. Other community workers also derive a similar advantage out of these media exposures.

Organisation of Feedback

Discussion always result in emergence of some points requiring further information of clarification. Project takes care of this quest for knowledge of the listeners through written feedback to the radio stations. The groups are supplied with pre-addressed, pre-stamped letter-cards, with a very brief questionnaire and enough blank space. At the end of each discussion following the broadcast the animator record the reactions of the group on this card and uses the blank space for writing other details to be feed back to the radio programmers, the subject experts or the service departments. These letters are mailed to the radio station. This makes it a two-way communication which helps the producers produce need-oriented programmes, keeps the experts in touch with their clientele and helps the government departments streamline their services.

Monitoring and Evaluation

While monitoring helps keep track of project implementation and its reception by the people. Evaluation helps us gauge whether the programmed of broadcast could achieve the objectives it was designed to do. The responsibility is assigned to an independent institution, not responsible either for the production of media, or its diffusion or delivery of services for which the media may generate some demands at community level. While the feedback letters help in monitoring the broadcasts to a large extent, the field investigators visiting the groups and the villages monitor the group-working, animatior leadership, the people's reactions and their participation in follow-up. Invaluation is carried out at five different levels of organised listeners, unorganised listeners non-listeners, the group animators and the village families. It deals with listening, comprehension, and acceptability, of messages which influence action or behaviour. This invariably helps in assessing the success or failure of the project and the reasons for the same so the necessary corrective meassures are taken for future planning.

Follow-up

At the end of the broadcast series, the All India Radio, the coperating government departments and related organisations review the outcome in the presence of UNICEF representative. Monitoring and evaluation reports help them in taking appropriate decisions regarding the continuance of the programmed. So far 14 such projects have been initiated involving 52 radio stations covering 87 districts in 17 states. With almost all the radio stations where the broadcast series have concluded, the broadcasts on mother and child health care and development have become a regular programme. They are being broadcast at the time and days identified by the 10660 listeners groups from as many villages. This only speaks of the popularity of programmes initiated as experiments with active involvement and support of the Ministry of Information & Broadcasting, UNICEF and the State Governments.

Reading

The Importance of Reading--The ability to read is recognized generally as one of the most important skills that a person can have, Reading is a tool of the acquisitive mind; it is the vehicle for obtaining ideas that cannot be transmitted verbally. The individual who reads well has at his command a means for widening his mental horizons and for multiplying his opportunities for experience. Reading is a crucial factor affecting intellectual and motional growth.

The need exists for more and better reading by persons of all ages. Good reading by any individual requires a knowledge of word meanings and of concepts; the reader must bring something to the printed page in order to take anything from the printed page. Insofar as schooling is concerned, reading is the most important single study tool. Next to the teacher, the textbook is usually the principal educative agency contributing to pupils' academic success. The knowledge contained in textbooks is useless to pupils if they cannot read; the ability to read and to comprehend the printed English language is a prerequisite to academic success. Reading plays a significant part, also, in the citizenship, in the vocational success, and in the recreation of adults. Reading results from the immediate needs of the individual, whether the reading occurs in the process of mastering an assignment in school or in connection with doing one's job.

Reading is important not only to the individual; it posseses also great social significance. Man's cultural and social heritage is transmitted from generation to generation and is communicated readily from on individual to another by means of permanent printed records. Such records usually are easily accessible, and they may be read at any time by any person in accordance with his needs. As individuals mature and as their understanding of society expands, their experience is augmented to include an increasingly clear perception of the social environment in which they live. Contact with printed materials aids in raising standards of living in developing appreciations, and in broadening sympathies. Surveys have shown that adults read books that are related to their work and to their avocations. Individuals want to know how to write letters, how to care for children, how to make model airplanes, and the like. Adults read stories, biographies, and travelogues to escape from the "daily grind". People always are ready to read printed matter that is related to their experience by bonds of meaning and of need. The authorities agree that in only a few activities of modren society does reading fail to make some essential contribution to individuals and to the social group.

Reading a Fundamental Skill

Reading is not taught now as it was formerly taught. The subject matter of textbooks and the methodology of reading have undergone many charges. Years ago the ability to read was the possession of few people, but with the passage of centuries literacy increased. As early as the ninth century people read the Bible. The first printed books were religious in nature because religion furnished the only available material. This tendency persisted in early American education. Pamphlets were printed in 1643 in New England stating that well-trained ministers were more important than any others class of persons and the schools be set up in homes to teach reading and religion.

In 1600 the first attempt was made to secularize children's books in the publication of the *New England Primer,* which contained the alphabet, illustrated rhymes for the letters, tables of syllables, catechisms, and prayer. This volume, one of the most famous text books used in American schools, was popular for more than 100 years and was displaced in the latter part of the eighteenth century by Webster's *The American Spelling Book,* a combination speeler and reader. Textbook content underwent a gradual evoluation as an effort was made to interest the child. Material of a religious nature was replaced by stories on ethics, mythology, science, history, travel, literature, and childhood activities: but reading continued to be one of the leading school subjects.

Today, as in the schools of the past, reading is one of the most important tool subjects. The emphasis, however, is now placed on reading to learn, rather than on learning to read just to be able to read, as in the early American school. The need for reading ability by pupils mounted as the variety of the school activities in which they engaged increased. Children must read extensively in modern schools; therefore, pupils must be equipped with skills to enable them to read with proficiency. The statement has been made that "reading constitutes about 80 per cent of the study of the elementry-school pupils and about 75 per cent of the study of high-school pupils. If we are to do good academic work in our schools, our pupils must be good reders".

Increasd Interest in Reading

The social significance of reading has increased greatly during the last two decades owing to the growing complexity of human affairs. The growing mechanization of life, the increased interdependence of people in the social environment, the improved means of communication, and the added amount of printed material that is available have made imperative more effective reading. Citizens in a democaracy must gain a wide knowledge of various social, industrial, political and economic problems in order to form adequate attitudes and habits. Merely to gain information is not sufficient; knowledge must be applied if individuals and society are to progress. An attitude of critical-mindedness in solving problems arising in life situations must be developed. The increase in the vlaues of reading had been accompanied by many evils of indoctrination, as is evidenced by the work of the propagandist who holds the attention of the multitude and influences the beliefs of individuals.

Recreational reading has increased greatly owing to the growing amount of leisure time that is possessed now by workers generally. One index of receational reading is found in the number of newspapers that are published annually. Cross states that, according to Ayres's "Directory of Newspapers and Periodicals" for 1938, 2,084 daily newspaper were published in the United States during the preceding year, with a daily circultion of 41,300,000 copies. These were published also 10,629 weekly newspapers, each furnishing reading material to several hundred families. The evidence indicates that reading is playing an important role in the life of modren people.

Added interest in reading as a subject of instruction in the schools of the United States has paralleled the increasing prominence of reading in general society. Since 1870, when the first scientific reference to the reading problem was made, many research projects have been carried out and reported. Over 1,200 studies dealing with the psychological and physilogical aspects of reading have been published since 1925. These investigations have definitely established the place of reading in the curriculum as a fundamental tool subject. They have stressed the importance of methodology and of teacher training, analyzed reading difficulties, and provided for their prognosis, diagnosis, and remedy. Strikingdeficiencies in the reading abilities of pupils have been revealed. Suggestions have been made that these difficulties can be remedied by carefully planned instruction that is adapted to the capacities, needs, and interests of the pupil. Many local, state, and national conferences and clinics have been held during recent years to study problems arising in the field of reading and to evolve means of solving these problems.

A study of the comparative values of the oral and silent reading was an outgrowth of these investigations. Standardized tests were prepared and used extensively, revealing facts about pupils' achievements and lack of achievements in reading. The test findings stimulated studies seeking to provide better treaching methods and materials. More material realting to reading, including and materials. More material relating to reading, including professional books for teachers and textbooks for pupils, became available as interest in the subject increased. Much of the reading matter for children has now been organized in thought-provoking units and problems, as well as round child interests, as contrasted with the unrelated content in earlier books. Library facilities have been developed to provide interesting and attractive books by means of which an attempt is being made to develop a permanent and worth-while interest in reading.

Adult Reading

According to one report, "The volume of the general publications read by the average adult has increased 170 per cent since 1900." This expansion may be traced to vocational, recreational and cultural development during the last four decades. Adults realize the importance of publications relating backgrounds and new developments in their vocations. Reading makes it possible to extend one's experiences, to relaxe from the tension of the modern world, and to promote personal growth leading to greater enjoyment of life. One writer has noted that the average American is "hungry" for books because of his new national curiosity, which was "brought about by the dislocations of the thirties and forties, by the increasing mechanization in both industry and agriculture, by the turbulent world scene, by the war raging in Europe. The industrial worker finds difficulty in satisfying his curiosity because books on his level and of his interests are not for him.

Newspapers and magazines furnish the bulk of the reading material of the public. Gray and Monroe state that about 50 per cent of the people read books, 75 per cent read magazines, and 95 per cent daily newspapers.

A survey of 2, 131 householders in San Digo, Calif presents similar data on the popularity of newspapers. Almost 95 per cent of the San Diego families either subscribed to a daily San Diego newspaper or brought such a paper into the home each day. Approximately 90 per cent of the homes that were surveyed reported the regular receipt of magazines. *The saturday Evening Post* ranked first in popularity, with *Coliter's, Liberty,* and *Good Housekeeping* in second, third, and fourth places, respectively. Another investigator reported somewhat different preferences in a nationwide survey. Of the 688 magazines published in America, *The Reader's Digest* was read most frequently, followed in order by *Life, Time* and The *Saturday Evening Post.*

A report of a similar survey, made in two Washington high schools and in the Chevy Chase Junior College in an atempt to determine the interests of pupils in the field of contemporary nonfiction, contains a list of preferred magazines. Boys and girls both rated *Life, the Reader's Digest,* and *The Saturday evening* Post among the three leading periodicals. The findings show that magazines have a significant part in American life. Periodicals satisfy every type of reader, supplement the news in the daily papers, and furnish amusement and entertainment.

The public is not on the whole a book reading group. Liraries have assumed thier share of the responsibility for this lack of interest. Through numerous surveys libraries have attempted to discover the cause of and a solution for the problem. Approximately one-half the present patrons of libraries are individuals of school age. The general suse of libaries delines among persons over the age of thirty. This fact may be due to a lack of training in the use of the library on the part of older people. If this is true, the schools must assume responsibility for training pupils along these lines. Librarians in many communities of all sized realize their part in adult education and are organizing study groups, forums, and book clubs, Libraries also are providing advisers to cooperate with other adult education agencies.

Space does not permit a discussion of the many available library reports. One such report will be given as an example of types of reading by the public of one city, *viz.* St. Louis, Mo. During the year 1939, 22.94 per cent of the total circulation was adult nonfiction; 32.78 per cent, adult fiction; and 44.28 per cent, books for children. February 20 was selected as a typical day, and the withdrawals on that day were analyzed. Of the 2,161 books that were checked out, 148 were on the subject of biography, 238 came directly within the scope of the jobs of the readers, 225 dealt with the social sciences, 175 were on literature, 128 were on scienece, and 63 were on religion. Other book that were withdrawn dealt with hobbies, the fine arts, home making, history and travel. The data reported are local; the information, therefore, cannot be considered truly representative of library use, but is does represents a typical cross section of reading interests.

9

Transfer of Technologies of Communication

The lessons to be learned from the technico-economic difficulties inherent in advanced technology are beginning to be carefully examined: the difficulty of financing costly equipment in tropical countries, the reluctance of officials in developing countries to commit themselves to a heavy drain of hard currency, and an insufficient high local level of technological resources to ensure the smooth operation of the system. There are other, human, limitations inasmuch as setting up these systems that would make considerable demands on the country's supply of qualified technical personnel.

Economic difficulties are not the only ones. One of the most remarkable boomerang effects of sophisticated technological innovation is that priority is given to apportioning economic resources for installing equipment to the detriment of developing content organization and, often, of the technological research needed for effectively adapting the new techniques. Sophisticated technology of communication, when introduced, requires at least as much in the way of human and economic resources for the contents as for the equipment (software-hardware balance). Besides, it is through the effort made to work up original software carefully adapted to needs that it becomes possible for a new technique to effectively take root. Mass educational technology is only acceptable based when on industrial production of standardized teaching material of high quality. Only then it is possible to uniersalize it and justify the expense, as it may take a team of specialists one hundred hours to produce one hour of programmed instruction and up to two hundred hours to produce one hour of computerized instruction (figures are often higher for film-making or teaching packages).

Importing new apparatus and contents, as they are is only one step in the use of sophisticated technology. Up to now, attention has mainly been given to the imported technological apparatus whose development and universalization has been paid for in the developed countries. Sometimes the very appearance of this apparatus reflects the aggravating excesses of a consumer society. Neither bright chrome on cars nor luxurious cabinet for television sets contribute to their efficiency. Experience has shown that it is possible to strip down some sophisticated equipment for use in the developing countries by reducing the number of wavelengths a radio or television receiver can pick up replacing costly studios with light shooting equipment for outside work, and simplifying language laboratory booths, thus cutting cost, by half or more.

Moreover, there are many low-cost techniques which require neither elaborate equipment nor a large, highly qualified staff: this is the case, for instance, with slow-scan television, rarely used in the developed countries, by which series of successive still images can be instantaneously and widely broadcast. There has been little exploration of these possibilities because their use in the developed countries is blocked by other more complex techniques.

Unfortunately, research in the developed world is generally directed towards the most elaborate techniques and is illequipped for reorienting itself towards low-cost or stripped-down techniques. The latter are to be worked on in the developing countries which have acquired sufficient mastery of Western techniques (India or Brazil, for instance) to be able to develop new adapted communication models of technological organization. Some advances have already been made. There is the example of India producing antennas from chasken wire for group reception of satellite signals for thirty dollars. Their cost in the developed countries is about three thousand dollars. Unfortunately, very few such efforts are being made and then only sporadically. They should be coordinated through more systematic international cooperation.

The sociocultural problems, however, appear to lie deeper and be less easily measurable. The difficulties met up to the present involve primarily the ill-suitedness of some techniques to the type of society they have been grafted onto or arbitrarily introduced into. When grafted, they disfigure without transforming. When arbitrarily introduced, they tend to have a disruptive effect on the educational systems of these countries, rather than to further their development.

More than one government hesitates to redefine the roles of teaching staff which often constitutes an influential intelligentsia. But here is one definite danger which ought to be stressed: using sophisticated technology can lead to arresting educational development at a particular level if it is done in a way that subjects the system's evoluation to technical limitations. For instance, setting up an educational television network should not preclude its later transformation into another more elaborate or differently structured system of telecommunication. The objectives laid down for a system of educational techology must be modular and capable of being integrated into other or more general aims (as was the case with the Ivory Coast ITV project). What is especially original in educational technology is that which makes possible the gradual development of self-organizing and self-regulating units. Through more and more numerous informational and analytical apparatus, increased powers of memory, more and more sophisticated regulating mechanisms, educational technology can enable an educational system to guide itself according to the reactions it proves and thus to develop, adapt, and grow by keeping control of change. In addition, the sophisticated systems offered to the developing countries could be designed with a degree of openness and flexibility that allows adaptation of the requirements of development.

In another connection it has been seen that it is not enough for a country to reach the level of technological development which ensures that grafting sophisticated technology onto it will succeed. Provision must also be made for effectively integrating and controlling all the consequences of technological innovation. Whether with regard to the Aswan dam or DDT, we have seen that hasty technological development can have consequences difficult to keep under control, both because of their complex nature and because they often do not show up till a later date. The inference is that insufficient foresight, not so much the technique itself, is generally at fault. The large-scale introduction of sophisticated technology is not a strategy whereby structural changes can be avoided. On the contrary, it makes them inevitable; just as the "green revolution" requires agrarian reform to reach its aims, so the introduction of technology into education will only make sense if it serves more humane concepts.

Finally, other investigations concern the preservation of local cultures. In this respect it has been found that the greatest difficulties do not always exist as predicted. The "wildcat development" of certain advanced communication media, such as television, has been enough to reduce to their proper proportions the warnings abundantly proffered by specialists regarding the "perceptive incapacities" of some primitive milieux. Today, it appears that the errors made in interpreting visual messages should not be assigned a percepective origin. They appear to be of a cultural nature (unfamiliarity with the message's codes of reference) and consequently can through training be quickly reduced into appropriate recording.

But, on the other hand, some people feel that the incongruity between the essential nature of these techniques and the environment in which they are to be applied make the two incompatible and do disservice to the very concept of development. It is not easy to align mass communications transmitted by television with a functional literacy campaign, which is primarily centered on the occupational environment but at the same time strives for self-improvement among illiterates and express their desire to step up from the environment. Obviously television could help establish a system of reference for such an aspiration.

Recently, ecological seruples induced European experts in an African educational television project to promote an ecological approach in rural education programms, which resulted in justifying inertia among African peasants rather than encouraging the struggle for the development of agriculture. To the extent education is to serve development, technology of learning has a role to play in it. It is difficult, however, to decide today where the necessary circulation of educational knowledge as a basis of development ends and the danger of foreign cultural invasion and recolonization leading to cultural genocide begins.

It must be regretted that the required instrument to control such forms of communication, especially the indicators of cultural penetration, do not yet appear to have been developed. Only a greater number of studies, preparing for large-scale operational undertakings, like the surveys presently being conducted for the UNESCO/ UNDP educational satellite project in Latin America (SERLA), will make it possible to clear up these problems.

In actual fact, the concern shown by the developing countries in this respect is indicative of the difficulties they have had in defining education for development which does not simply satisfy material needs, but also answers individual and collective psychic needs. The importance of radio broadcasting, the only sophisticated innovation to have spread all over the Third World, should serve as a support to and also as an example of educational development. It became universal the day it reached an adequate technico-economic level : transistors and miniaturization make it possible to produce inexpensivc, reliable apparatus adapted to conditions in all countries. At the same time, radio has shown that it answers the cultural needs of societies with oral traditions and unwritten values. But for the moment it is an isolated case and it must be admitted today that all types of technological apparatuses do not appear neutral to developing countries. Some technologies are felt to be "cleaner" than others, but on the whole, least developed countries tend to consider that their presence may introduce a set of Western values and preexisting ideologies. Therefore, economic limitations in some instances and cultural reservations in others have encouraged the development of the concept of "intermediate technology."

The Concept of "Intermediate Technology"

The concept of "intermediate technology" has emerged in the economics of development objectives. Exportation of sophisticated technology from the developed countries to the developing countries has generally been limited to certain results of industrialization and confined to urban areas, which tends to create cultural conflicts and increase imbalances in development between town and country. Part of the purpose of developing intermediate technology would be to reduce such conflicts and imbalances. The main idea is to start with intensive work, as opposed to an abundance of capital, and seek ways to make better use of the cultural, economic, social, and technical resources available in the environment itself, especially in rural areas. Intermediate technology aims at mobilizing local, particularly human, resources and encouraging the inhabitants to participate in discovering the implements of their own development. In practice, this means that efforts are made to give priority to using locally raw materials, to further the development of small industries oriented towards the local environment (particularly as regards agriculture), and to systematically modify existing equipment in order to make it more efficeint, rather than seek to import foreign equipment and experts.

Undertaking based on these principles have so far covered a very wide range of activities, extending from the search for new energy sources (e.g., the setting up of methane lighting systems using gas produced from household refuse) to the transformation of public services (developing new hospital equipment, including that which is adapted to local condition—incubators for maternity hospitals, for instance). In any case, the aim of these efforts is to speed up progress at the local level, ensure participation of the existing labour force, and make the best possible use of available material resources. Specialists are of the opinion that it is probably China that has most actively pursued research of this nature and gone farthest in applying it.

It may be wondered whether education has given this endogenous approach to the development of new techniques all the attention it deserves. Educational technology experts tend to reject the concept of the individual teacher's work as that of a palliative industrialization of education based on mass production of materials and messages. The structure, organization, and the contents of education in the Third World countries are still conspicuously marked by colonial models; education has not yet developed to the point of reaching an adequate stage of critical awareness and technological inventiveness, and it tends to fall back on the "stopgap" use of educational technology. A further reason would be that the programme of intermediate technologies is usually presented in its strictly economic version as a simple attempt to provide work for a greater number of people, whereas the main problems of education today is to increase the efficiency and productivity of personnel already in service. But the employment approach of intermediate technology is only a technical factor, a means and not an end, as the ultimate objective of intermediate technological programmes is to encourage technological inventiveness and creativity in archaic cultures (which is in itself an important goal of concern to all educators.)

In another respect, the search for new technological schemes without heavy investments may open new possibilities for parallel integrated efforts in education. Might not the regrouping of handicraft workshops, as they begin to appear in the economic sector, provide useful models for reorganizing traditional classroom-type work units into more effective collective units, based on a better division of pedagogical labour and leading up to the school factory? It seems likely that if pedagogical thinking started from these analogies, fruitful results would be obtained by devising combined sets of methods and specific techniques answering the needs of a region, state, or even a tribe, subculture, or dialect. These methods and techniques will be intermediate between standardized national or international industrial production and craftsmanlike efforts left to the initiative of the individual teacher, alone in his classroom.

Of course, the authorities in the developing countries may not wish to encourage a too diversified technological development, which would necessarily be heterocultural and consequently liable to have a dispersive effect as regards national unity. This diversification will generally be tolerated in regard to primary education oriented towards rural life, but at all other educational levels it may appear to be opposed to the unifying function most developing countries assign to the educational system. Some countries, however, such as India, seem ready even now to adopt a diversified approach at all levels.

The purpose of trying to evolve intermediate technology of communication and organization is to bring educational development into line with preexisting structures. For these largely determine the ability to adopt and adapt an innovation. Japan will serve as an example in this respect. Owing to its preeixsting integrated handicraft structures, it was able to adapt television to its own ends, both with regard to production of hardware and creation of software. Far from conflicting with Japanese traditional culture, the media seem to help strengthen it. Thus a better knowledge of local sociocultural structures ought to be able to facilitate development of new techniques and make them assimilable or at least acceptable to existing cultures instead of destroying them.

So far, research in the use of adapted technology in education for developing countries has been scattered and piecemeal. It has been chiefly concerned with pedagogical accessories or aids without any attempt at developing methods and systems. In some research centres or teacher training institutes, simplified slide projectors have been introduced which are operated by solar energy—some even had a simplified optical system which could be made from the bottoms of beer bottles. Mainly owing to UNESCO, it has been possible to use locally available materials in the construction of elementary equipment for science teaching. In fact, without wishing to cast a slur on the creative merits of their individual work it may be said that almost all this equipment is a crude substitute for that produced and used in wealthy countries. These poor copies of Western models have generally been developed with a view to serving traditional, imported education. Consequently, it would be difficult for them to provide the basis for a forward thrust towards original and better adapted forms of teaching. This explains their limited expansion so far.

It seems more advisable to encourage, whenever possible, the development of simplified techniques within general learning strategies in order to provide the basis for new educational strategies in order to provide the basis for new educational configurations adapted to the country. Such strategies should include redefining the educational institutions which is to serve as the technical unit (neither a large factory nor a group of individual workshops, which waste teacher's time and talent); stressing group work and "teach-another" techniques; utilization of standardized messages and team teaching; appropriate material for group viewing; stepping up the circulation and exchange of teaching material produce by means of simplified techniques (a school press, for instance); development of educational "self-service" facilities comprising sets of simple teaching machines; making each student a producer as well as a consumer of educational materials; installation of uncomplicated educational radio and television systems that could be the basis for work sessions with travelling specialists, and so on.

When defining the elements of an intermediate technology development strategy, a distinction should be made between those countries where development will still require another ten years or more of saving of qualified manpower and those in which such manpower already exists (or will shortly) and where the aim is to provide work for it (as in many Asian countries). According to this strategy, the first efforts should be made with view to sectorial improvements in the educational system, particularly where costs per pupil justify them and where the optimum combination of investments and manpower would be easiest to achieve—vocational and teacher training, high level technical training, and higher education. It is only by beginning to work at the microlevel that it can be hoped to apply later these techniques on a larger scale to rural and primary education.

Such confrontations in a field where there has so far been little systematic exploration are likely to be fruitful. Let it suffice to mention the example of intermediate technology in which all the technical principles are applied but the corresponding equipment is not used. This is the case with the administration of a developing country which has tried to organize the processing of information in its offices according to data-principles, employing only the large available labour force. Here, the administration imitates the computer but does not use one. Some of the technological principles of the computer are thus turned to account, while many of its practical advantages, such as rapid calculations, are dispensed with. It may be asked if such an approach is not of particular relevance to education. To come back to the computer, we know that today's generation of computers respond much too rapidly to justify using them in a learning process requiring a machine-student relation. Computers responding much more slowly are quite adequate for such a dialogue. The fact is that in computer teaching it is the concept of the learning algorithm which is basic and not the sophisticated technology of the transistor. Probably other areas of education should be considered as activities that can be made more fruitful by technological research without being crushed under the weight of the latter's apparatus.

Is Post-mechanical Technology a Way Out?

We are thus let to wonder if the future of educational technology does not lie in applying principles before using machines and sometimes in dispensing with the latter altogether. In the sophisticated technologies, methodology up to now has appeared inseparable from a specific apparatus. Would it not be possible to deduce principles from these technologies which could help education in the developing countries without, however, employing complex equipment? Modern technology is indeed on the way to achieve what the mechanical advances of the nineteenth century could not, i.e., organize society on a rational basis. Mumford has shown that machines have often been used to "disguise man's inefficiency" and it will be readily admitted that technology is the subtle and discriminating use of machine principles.

It is not the teaching machine which is important but the programming principles which make its application possible, then we can imagine an educational technology which would be based on "mock machines," rebuilt according to the functions they are to fulfill. It is thus, for example, that when the mathematician Dienes wants to introduce small children to modern mathematics, he prefers to do it by using "little machines" which have no actual mechanical parts and simply offer new ways of thinking, in the guise of games. A similar approach is adopted in the diagrams commonly used for training in data processing: any allusion to actual operation and utilization of computers is scrupulously avoided.

Efforts along these lines should not be considered native dodges aiming at transferring the essence of sophisticated technology while avoiding the necessity of purchasing the apparatus, but as a guarantee that intermediate technology will servive. Unless these theoretical principles are developed and applied to education, intermediate technology runs the risk of becoming a blind alley for development rather than constituting a necessary stage. It is technological creativity which, as it outlines new methods, will ensure the indispensable standardization of intermediate technology and consequently its universalization. Such an effort would be justified on the grounds that it would improve educational productivity in a country (for instance, by bringing about quicker ways of making and keeping people literate). But it could also facilitate access of archaic cultures to a higher technological order, not through forced superimposition but by endogenous rediscovery. It could include development of techniques for organizing contents and duties, which should make it possible to universalize systems analysis and programming a type that future teachers would practice in their preparation. Cybernetic models and learning algorithms would be used as they deserve to be. Also included would be investigation of the contributions of communication techniques such as information compression (the procedures used to teach speed reading), which would radically alter the present uses of printed educational matter. One should stress here the importance of giving the young experience with the symbol systems divorced as far as possible from the complex technologies involved in their transmission.

Simulation techniques, stripped of their complex operational apparatus, should offer exercises in which events are speeded up and require decisions regarding complex alternatives, just as games, instead of simulating reality, should develop competition and group efforts in the planning of imaginary futures.

It will be noted that only contributions inspired by Western techniques have been mentioned here. Their development in the Third World may raise as many cultural problems as does the use of sophisticated equipment. For instacne, with regard to visual communication and programming procedures, experiments in progress tend to show that there is no possibility of their being effective here either, unless forms and contents are adapted to different cultural frames of reference. This is a new challenge, at once anthropological and psychological, to technological creativity. And technological invention is not necessarily tied to a given level of GNP.

Could a "Designed" Education be based on Technologies?

Technologies of communication can only play a decisive role if associated with technologies of organization in systematic patterns. It seems that we are presently moving away from thinking about technology in education (i.e., thinking chiefly concerned with equipment, elaboration of ad hoc symbolic codes, and then incorporation into traditional teacher-centered activities) to thinking about the technology of education (i.e., rationalizing and optimalizing the chain or processes that each individuals has to go through in order to acquire and use knowledge.) The aim behind such thinking should be to move away from dispersion of wasted effort or worse still, the overhasty adoption of techology as a means of patching up shaky educational systems to a full and integrated use of all the resources of the technological age. Hitherto, these areas in education to which technology has been applied have all to often resembled patches of ground strewn with machine parts that no one would attempt to assemble.

Instead of attempting merely to recruit and train an ever increasing number of teachers, the time may have come to try to analyze the various educational functions with a view to redistributing the human and material resources available to wherever in the educational system their potential can be most fully realized. This of course, implies the acceptance on our part that instead of continuing to let the machine do only what the teacher cannot do, we should ask ourselves what it is the teacher should do that the machine cannot do. This further implies the acceptance of far-reaching changes in the organization and hierarchical structures of the educational establishment and in the responsibilities and functions of pupils and teachers alike. There may be some hope that technology will cease to be a miscellaneous collection of new-equipment and methods designed to lighten some of the teacher's traditional tasks and will provide education with a coherent set of liberal methods and original concepts of learning and training.

Such are most of the means now at our disposal—new display devices and, more important still, image and sound-recording and reproduction devices, the storage and collective or individual retrieval of image and sound, self-scoring and self-assessment possibilities, the feedback facilities and flexibility offered by some techniques (ranging from the individual-response control system to the computer), and particular methods of presentation (programming)—that modern technology, with its methods of organization and measurement, its evaluation and experimentation techniques, can provide education with the guiding principles upon which to base a definition of the relationship *(a)* between various new techniques and methods, and *(b)* between them and the institutions' content and existing methods of education, which they could help transform from within. The transition from technology in education to the technology of education involves a thorough reappraisal of the existing educational system, of its objectives, and of the means used to attain them before any decision is reached to employ these new techniques for specific teaching purposes. The time has come to consider whether the teacher-turned-technologist could not gradually assume the function of an "education engineer" whose job it is to increase the output of the entire teaching machine.

The Comprehensive Approach

Over the past few years experience has shown that educational innovation, technological or otherwise, cannot simply be introduced in the form of a local transplant on to the existing educational anatomy. Such innovations are meaningful and effective only in relation to their effects upon the body as a whole. Wc have recently had the opportunity of seeing the futility of introducing school curricula involving, for example, the acquisition of new knowledge or of new methods of teaching without the involvement of instructors and teachers and the manufacturers of teaching materials. We have learned the absurdity of teaching a particular section of population to read and write and then not supplying them with satisfactory printed material (local press, occupational handbooks, and so on). The school today is an organic unit in which the teacher is only one teaching agent among others, just as the school itself is only one component of a larger overall educational activity. The need for technological change bids us today to turn the eye of the biologist to the mechanic on the educational system and see it as an organism.

The methods of organization which have developed over the past few years under such names as operational research or systems analysis appear to be suitable intellectual instruments for an overall critical study of existing systems and for suggesting new educational configuration based on scientific principles in which there would be a place for the resources of technology. Why not apply relevance trees or critical path analysis to the bottlenecks in the educational systems? Would it not be possible to apply the principles of feedback and self-correction to the active functioning of educational institutions? Again, more generally, how can there be hope for a rational improvement in educational activities without measuring and analyzing their functioning?

We know that by the term system, analysts mean the sum of separate parts acting both inadependently and on one another to achieve predetermined objectives; the system is, therefoe, defined by reference not only to its constituent parts, but to the organizations that allows it to function. In any analysis of a system the aim is therefore to measure exactly the objectives to be attained in terms of performance, to define the levels of application, to allow for the constraints under which it operates, and to derive rational operating models. Can this effort the aim of which is to define logical structures incorporating all the constituent parts and to marshal the various agents into a unified process in pursuit of maximum efficiency, be applied to educational process?

In human activities other than educational these coherent sets of methods have made it possible to detect the weak points and failings in a given oganization, to choose from a range of schemes for improvement, to rearrange the constituent parts of a body in various combinations, or to add new parts to it in order to secure new results. Systems analysis should make it possible to define for any given oganization an optimum structure which maintains equilibrium by means of successive readjustments to the environment. True, the experts are ready to admit that education is too complex an overall process to be analyzed otherwise than in terms of probability: education is an open system. However, the thing about systems analysis is that it makes it possible to incorporate uncertainty into action. Since the new technologies are constantly coming up with further sources of information and analysis, increasingly powerful memory units, and increasingly sophisticated control mechanisms, if becomes possible to envisage the development or further development of self organizing and self-regulating educational systems, both at the individual level and at the level of the educational institution. The educational system itself could thus steer a more accurate course than at present by means of the incoming reactions and hence be able to evolve, adapt, and grow by mastering change.

An Example of Analysis: A Learning Sequence

First, however, the educational system must be given the means of establishing correlations between the objectives, the learning processes, the means of instruction, and the teacher's functions. The analysis of the various components and various points in the act of learning will then make it possible to use on each separate occasion the situation and the means best adapted to the end in view. In one act of learning we are led to distinguish, for example, an information stage, characterized by research and the collecting of the data have to be acquired; an exploitation stage, which involves the marshalling, criticism, and processing of the data; an assimilation stage, in which knowledge is fixed; a transfer stage, in which the knowledge is applied; and, lastly, an assessment (or self-assessment) stage.

Only the new technologies of communication allow each of these stages to combine with maximum efficiency. At the first, or "information" stage, technology facilitates acquisition of individual information by means of visual or audio-visual data banks and documentation and information centres (record libraries, film-slide libraries). The acquisition of information may be collective in form and involve mass communication (e.g., the cinema and television). The second or "exploitation" stage is generally characterized by group work and involves the use of individual response control systems. The period of assimilation and fixation may be individual and involve the use of programmed instruction teaching machines, and learning laboratories and may also involve group work—for example, joint utilization of programmed material or group work on computer terminals. The "transfer" period lends itself to the employment of simulation techniques (closed-circuit television and teaching machines). Response analyzers and testing machines in general can be brought in during the "assessment" segment of the process. Lastly, recording machines and computers make it possible to keep an individual record of the pupil's progress throughout his school career.

Obviously, at each point in the learning process the teacher comes in for each application of a particular technique with a corresponding and different function. Befoe carrying out any educational operation, he will have to find the teaching strategy required to apply all the various procedures chosen. During the course of the infomation phase his role is that of the guide who prepares the stimulants and supplies the documentation which he has himself prepared or chosen. During the exploitation phase his role is that of a mediator or of a group leader who motivates the interactions (and who must gradually train the members of the group in group leadership). He sees that the ideas which have been acquired are properly understood and help to discover and correct misunderstandings. During the assimilation and fixation stage his role is diagnostic—he prescribes the treatment best suited to the capabilities of the learner. During the transfer phase, his role becomes that of an adviser-cum-guide. During the last phase of the learning process his role becomes one of checking, ensuring that the system of marking is uniform, and seeing to it that continuity is maintained in the assessment process.

The teacher's use of technology will have made him more receptive and will have placed him in a more central position so that pupils more easily approach him with their individual problem. In this connection, it cannot be stressed too strongly that the use of educational technology—far from implying any qualitative decline in the role of the teacher—frees him from certain purely mechanical tasks of exposition and repetition, thus enabling him to devote himself to the noble and irreplaceable functions of stimulation of interest, diagnosis, motivation, and advice.

This, of course, implies a fairly radical overhaul of the existing educational and administrative arrangements, which are based generally on the individual unit or class—reorganization of timetable, the splitting up of groups of classes, full-time use of schools, continuous assessment, the preparation of educational activities in interdisciplinary teams, dividing and distributing work among teachers according to their aptitude and experience, adaption of buildings to give greater flexibility, responsibility of the pupils themselves for discipline, and the production of a considerable amount of teaching materials. Educational technology can help to reintroduce a certain amount of flexibility of the functioning of the school system, which has been in a rut for decades.

However, it should not be thought that there is any single strategy for scientific reorganization of this kind. The point about systems analysis is rather that it helps to define strategies differentiated according to the degree of economic development, resoruces, and type of educational system. For example, as far as the distribution of educational information is concerned, it is possible to think of the dissemination of information in the form of audio-visual broadcasts, either through a user-controlled system involving the use of telephone lines and computer networks, Systems for the distribution of recordings supplied direct, either to educational institutions or to individual students at home, are another possibility. These systems of distribution, which are more complex and slower than the broadcasting systems but which are also more selective and better differentiated, can either be centralized, e.g., in the form of film-loan libraries and correspondence tuition centres, or decentralized in the form of commercial distribution direct to customers (e.g., institutional tape library or personal record library).

In countries where there are fewer industrial and professional resources these new systems could be based upon simpler or more cost-effective equipment, taking into account the needs and objectives of the educational system. In a developing country, therefore, if a system of inertia-free instantaneous broadcasting such as radio or television is chosen, a particular technique must be employed so as to get the best out of it. Where television is available it will be employed both for school and out-of-school educational purposes. If it is used to transmit programmes for group use, it can also be used to show programmed learning exercises, which would be transmitted by other means (teaching machines) in a country that was better equipped. Television is also used to give instructions to the teacher or instructor as to how he should conduct his teaching and how television can be incorporated in it, and provide in-service training. Here a multipurpose one-medium system may prove more effective than a multimedia single-purpose system.

With a systems approach, it is not only possible to coordinate uses and techniques and to organize them rationally on a continuous basis for the individual fact is that in computer teaching it is the concept of the learning algorithm which is basic and not the sophisticated technology of the transistor. Probably other areas of education should be considered as activities that can be made more fruitful by technological research without being crushed under the weight of the latter's apparatus.

Is Post-mechanical Technology a Way Out?

We are thus let to wonder if the future of educational technology does not lie in applying principles before using machines and sometimes in dispensing with the latter altogether. In the sophisticated technologies, methodology up to now has appeared inseparable from a specific apparatus. Would it not be possible to deduce principles from these technologies which could help education in the developing countries without, however, employing complex equipment? Modern technology is indeed on the way to achieve what the mechanical advances of the nineteenth century could not, i.e., organize society on a rational basis. Mumford has shown that machines have often been used to "disguise man's inefficiency" and it will be readily admitted that technology is the subtle and discriminating use of machine principles.

It is not the teaching machine which is important but the programming principles which make its application possible, then we can imagine an educational technology which would be based on "mock machines," rebuilt according to the functions they are to fulfill. It is thus, for example, that when the mathematician Dienes wants to introduce small children to modern mathematics, he prefers to do it by using "little machines" which have no actual mechanical parts and simply offer new ways of thinking, in the guise of games. A similar approach is adopted in the diagrams commonly used for training in data processing: any allusion to actual operation and utilization of computers is scrupulously avoided.

Efforts along these lines should not be considered native dodges aiming at transferring the essence of sophisticated technology while avoiding the necessity of purchasing the apparatus, but as a guarantee that intermediate technology will servive. Unless these theoretical principles are developed and applied to education, intermediate technology runs the risk of becoming a blind alley for development rather than constituting a necessary stage. It is technological creativity which, as it outlines new methods, will ensure the indispensable standardization of intermediate technology and consequently its universalization. Such an effort would be justified on the grounds that it would improve educational productivity in a country (for instance, by bringing about quicker ways of making and keeping people literate). But it could also facilitate access of archaic cultures to a higher technological order, not through forced superimposition but by endogenous rediscovery. It could include development of techniques for organizing contents and duties, which should make it possible to universalize systems analysis and programming a type that future teachers would practice in their preparation. Cybernetic models and learning algorithms would be used as they deserve to be. Also included would be investigation of the contributions of communication techniques such as information compression (the procedures used to teach speed reading), which would radically alter the present uses of printed educational matter. One should stress here the importance of giving the young experience with the symbol systems divorced as far as possible from the complex technologies involved in their transmission.

Simulation techniques, stripped of their complex operational apparatus, should offer exercises in which events are speeded up and require decisions regarding complex alternatives, just as games, instead of simulating reality, should develop competition and group efforts in the planning of imaginary futures.

It will be noted that only contributions inspired by Western techniques have been mentioned here. Their development in the Third World may raise as many cultural problems as does the use of sophisticated equipment. For instacne, with regard to visual communication and programming procedures, experiments in progress tend to show that there is no possibility of their being effective here either, unless forms and contents are adapted to different cultural frames of reference. This is a new challenge, at once anthropological and psychological, to technological creativity. And technological invention is not necessarily tied to a given level of GNP.

Could a "Designed" Education be based on Technologies?

Technologies of communication can only play a decisive role if associated with technologies of organization in systematic patterns. It seems that we are presently moving away from thinking about technology in education (i.e., thinking chiefly concerned with equipment, elaboration of ad hoc symbolic codes, and then incorporation into traditional teacher-centered activities) to thinking about the technology of education (i.e., rationalizing and optimalizing the chain or processes that each individuals has to go through in order to acquire and use knowledge.) The aim behind such thinking should be to move away from dispersion of wasted effort or worse still, the overhasty adoption of techology as a means of patching up shaky educational systems to a full and integrated use of all the resources of the technological age. Hitherto, these areas in education to which technology has been applied have all to often resembled patches of ground strewn with machine parts that no one would attempt to assemble.

Instead of attempting merely to recruit and train an ever increasing number of teachers, the time may have come to try to analyze the various educational functions with a view to redistributing the human and material resources available to wherever in the educational system their potential can be most fully realized. This of course, implies the acceptance on our part that instead of continuing to let the machine do only what the teacher cannot do, we should ask ourselves what it is the teacher should do that the machine cannot do. This further implies the acceptance of far-reaching changes in the organization and hierarchical structures of the educational establishment and in the responsibilities and functions of pupils and teachers alike. There may be some hope that technology will cease to be a miscellaneous collection of new-equipment and methods designed to lighten some of the teacher's traditional tasks and will provide education with a coherent set of liberal methods and original concepts of learning and training.

Such are most of the means now at our disposal—new display devices and, more important still, image and sound-recording and reproduction devices, the storage and collective or individual retrieval of image and sound, self-scoring and self-assessment possibilities, the feedback facilities and flexibility offered by some techniques (ranging from the individual-response control system to the computer), and particular methods of presentation (programming)—that modern technology, with its methods of organization and measurement, its evaluation and experimentation techniques, can provide education with the guiding principles upon which to base a definition of the relationship *(a)* between various new techniques and methods, and *(b)* between them and the institutions' content and existing methods of education, which they could help transform from within. The transition from technology in education to the technology of education involves a thorough reappraisal of the existing educational system, of its objectives, and of the means used to attain them before any decision is reached to employ these new techniques for specific teaching purposes. The time has come to consider whether the teacher-turned-technologist could not gradually assume the function of an "education engineer" whose job it is to increase the output of the entire teaching machine.

The Comprehensive Approach

Over the past few years experience has shown that educational innovation, technological or otherwise, cannot simply be introduced in the form of a local transplant on to the existing educational anatomy. Such innovations are meaningful and effective only in relation to their effects upon the body as a whole. We have recently had the opportunity of seeing the futility of introducing school curricula involving, for example, the acquisition of new knowledge or of new methods of teaching without the involvement of instructors and teachers and the manufacturers of teaching materials. We have learned the absurdity of teaching a particular section of population to read and write and then not supplying them with satisfactory printed material (local press, occupational handbooks, and so on). The school today is an organic unit in which the teacher is only one teaching agent among others, just as the school itself is only one component of a larger overall educational activity. The need for technological change bids us today to turn the eye of the biologist to the mechanic on the educational system and see it as an organism.

The methods of organization which have developed over the past few years under such names as operational research or systems analysis appear to be suitable intellectual instruments for an overall critical study of existing systems and for suggesting new educational configuration based on scientific principles in which there would be a place for the resources of technology. Why not apply relevance trees or critical path analysis to the bottlenecks in the educational systems? Would it not be possible to apply the principles of feedback and self-correction to the active functioning of educational institutions? Again, more generally, how can there be hope for a rational improvement in educational activities without measuring and analyzing their functioning?

We know that by the term system, analysts mean the sum of separate parts acting both inadependently and on one another to achieve predetermined objectives; the system is, therefoe, defined by reference not only to its constituent parts, but to the organizations that allows it to function. In any analysis of a system the aim is therefore to measure exactly the objectives to be attained in terms of performance, to define the levels of application, to allow for the constraints under which it operates, and to derive rational operating models. Can this effort the aim of which is to define logical structures incorporating all the constituent parts and to marshal the various agents into a unified process in pursuit of maximum efficiency, be applied to educational process?

In human activities other than educational these coherent sets of methods have made it possible to detect the weak points and failings in a given oganization, to choose from a range of schemes for improvement, to rearrange the constituent parts of a body in various combinations, or to add new parts to it in order to secure new results. Systems analysis should make it possible to define for any given oganization an optimum structure which maintains equilibrium by means of successive readjustments to the environment. True, the experts are ready to admit that education is too complex an overall process to be analyzed otherwise than in terms of probability: education is an open system. However, the thing about systems analysis is that it makes it possible to incorporate uncertainty into action. Since the new technologies are constantly coming up with further sources of information and analysis, increasingly powerful memory units, and increasingly sophisticated control mechanisms, if becomes possible to envisage the development or further development of self organizing and self-regulating educational systems, both at the individual level and at the level of the educational institution. The educational system itself could thus steer a more accurate course than at present by means of the incoming reactions and hence be able to evolve, adapt, and grow by mastering change.

An Example of Analysis: A Learning Sequence

First, however, the educational system must be given the means of establishing correlations between the objectives, the learning processes, the means of instruction, and the teacher's functions. The analysis of the various components and various points in the act of learning will then make it possible to use on each separate occasion the situation and the means best adapted to the end in view. In one act of learning we are led to distinguish, for example, an information stage, characterized by research and the collecting of the data have to be acquired; an exploitation stage, which involves the marshalling, criticism, and processing of the data; an assimilation stage, in which knowledge is fixed; a transfer stage, in which the knowledge is applied; and, lastly, an assessment (or self-assessment) stage.

Only the new technologies of communication allow each of these stages to combine with maximum efficiency. At the first, or "information" stage, technology facilitates acquisition of individual information by means of visual or audio-visual data banks and documentation and information centres (record libraries, film-slide libraries). The acquisition of information may be collective in form and involve mass communication (e.g., the cinema and television). The second or "exploitation" stage is generally characterized by group work and involves the use of individual response control systems. The period of assimilation and fixation may be individual and involve the use of programmed instruction teaching machines, and learning laboratories and may also involve group work—for example, joint utilization of programmed material or group work on computer terminals. The "transfer" period lends itself to the employment of simulation techniques (closed-circuit television and teaching machines). Response analyzers and testing machines in general can be brought in during the "assessment" segment of the process. Lastly, recording machines and computers make it possible to keep an individual record of the pupil's progress throughout his school career.

Obviously, at each point in the learning process the teacher comes in for each application of a particular technique with a corresponding and different function. Befoe carrying out any educational operation, he will have to find the teaching strategy required to apply all the various procedures chosen. During the course of the infomation phase his role is that of the guide who prepares the stimulants and supplies the documentation which he has himself prepared or chosen. During the exploitation phase his role is that of a mediator or of a group leader who motivates the interactions (and who must gradually train the members of the group in group leadership). He sees that the ideas which have been acquired are properly understood and help to discover and correct misunderstandings. During the assimilation and fixation stage his role is diagnostic—he prescribes the treatment best suited to the capabilities of the learner. During the transfer phase, his role becomes that of an adviser-cum-guide. During the last phase of the learning process his role becomes one of checking, ensuring that the system of marking is uniform, and seeing to it that continuity is maintained in the assessment process.

The teacher's use of technology will have made him more receptive and will have placed him in a more central position so that pupils more easily approach him with their individual problem. In this connection, it cannot be stressed too strongly that the use of educational technology—far from implying any qualitative decline in the role of the teacher—frees him from certain purely mechanical tasks of exposition and repetition, thus enabling him to devote himself to the noble and irreplaceable functions of stimulation of interest, diagnosis, motivation, and advice.

This, of course, implies a fairly radical overhaul of the existing educational and administrative arrangements, which are based generally on the individual unit or class—reorganization of timetable, the splitting up of groups of classes, full-time use of schools, continuous assessment, the preparation of educational activities in interdisciplinary teams, dividing and distributing work among teachers according to their aptitude and experience, adaption of buildings to give greater flexibility, responsibility of the pupils themselves for discipline, and the production of a considerable amount of teaching materials. Educational technology can help to reintroduce a certain amount of flexibility of the functioning of the school system, which has been in a rut for decades.

However, it should not be thought that there is any single strategy for scientific reorganization of this kind. The point about systems analysis is rather that it helps to define strategies differentiated according to the degree of economic development, resoruces, and type of educational system. For example, as far as the distribution of educational information is concerned, it is possible to think of the dissemination of information in the form of audio-visual broadcasts, either through a user-controlled system involving the use of telephone lines and computer networks, Systems for the distribution of recordings supplied direct, either to educational institutions or to individual students at home, are another possibility. These systems of distribution, which are more complex and slower than the broadcasting systems but which are also more selective and better differentiated, can either be centralized, e.g., in the form of film-loan libraries and correspondence tuition centres, or decentralized in the form of commercial distribution direct to customers (e.g., institutional tape library or personal record library).

In countries where there are fewer industrial and professional resources these new systems could be based upon simpler or more cost-effective equipment, taking into account the needs and objectives of the educational system. In a developing country, therefore, if a system of inertia-free instantaneous broadcasting such as radio or television is chosen, a particular technique must be employed so as to get the best out of it. Where television is available it will be employed both for school and out-of-school educational purposes. If it is used to transmit programmes for group use, it can also be used to show programmed learning exercises, which would be transmitted by other means (teaching machines) in a country that was better equipped. Television is also used to give instructions to the teacher or instructor as to how he should conduct his teaching and how television can be incorporated in it, and provide in-service training. Here a multipurpose one-medium system may prove more effective than a multimedia single-purpose system.

With a systems approach, it is not only possible to coordinate uses and techniques and to organize them rationally on a continuous basis for the individual learner, but also for the group (class or school grade) and the institution, at the regional level. It is therefoe possible, proceeding by analyses, to design a complex set of harmonized functions, ranging from the microsystem of the individual learner to the national macrosystem Although it is generally accepted that the degree of complexity of systems should increase in poportion to the resources available and the difficulties of the learning process (thus the establishment of a complex technological system will generally be more justified in the case of higher education), in practice there is no reason why such a complex system could not be applied to functional litracy.

A Factory or Self-Service Establishment

By making it possible to redistribute human and material resources and by lending support to the attempt to find ways and means of increasing the internal output of the educational institution, the development of educational technology opens up the prospect in the years ahead of developing new types of educational institutions radically different inform from the elitist and selective establishments of yesterday. The establishment in which educational technology (audiovisual communication, learning laboratories, data banks) has been incorporated would, according to one model, tend to resemble an enterprise in which educational technology would be used to reduce wastage to minimum and to optimize the act of learning by establishing precise mechanisms to produce effective individuals by dint of intellectual constraints, fear and the spectre of failure having first been banished from their training.

In contrast to this deterministic model based on efficiency, there would be another model, no doubt using similar means but arranged in different configurations. It would offer a community service of individualized self-instruction for safe guarding individual freedom of action—a complete self service system adaptable to individual needs, to which the pupils would feel an allegiance based on individual involvement.

The first of these formulas would prove particularly useful in immediate vocational training. However, since the society of tomorrow is to be founded on lifelong education and since the spirit of one's initial training determines the practical interest he shows in his subsequent training, the self-teaching centre will, more so than the learning enterprise, be bound up with lifelong education. Teaching is less and less a matter of forcing infomation upon pupils or exposing them to knowledge, but rather is one of instructing the young by the practice of self-teaching—a method calculated to ensure social mobility—how to shape their education by mastering a system and progressing beyond it. Thus, educational technology will not be confined to increasing the internal efficiency of the school center; it also will increase its involvement with social reality.

Assistance to Strategies of Technological Innovations

In the past, reforming education meant converting from one relatively stable system to another equally stable. Now the time has come for leaps to be made under conditions of permanent instability—from autocratic, fixed, closed, and ponderous systems to planned, open, flexible and self-adjusting ones that will admit of the possibility of forecasting and integration.

It seems that there are three different strategies for technological innovations. The first is to change everything at the same time, but so far there has been little instance of this having been undertaken successfully. The second one involves modifying the existing state of affairs by introducing innovation at the lowest level in the system and carrying on from there, the new system pushing the old one in front of it; such is the case with the gradual introduction of television year by year, involving, in the case of the Ivory Coast, the transformation of primary education and, in the case of El Salvador, of secondary education. The third strategy involves setting up and developing a new system parallel to the old one and capable of influencing it and eventually substituting for it; such as in the case, for example, of educational television for elementary schools in Niger or, another level, of the Open University in the United Kingdom.

In the long term, this latter strategy is no doubt the most effective, although, this is not to say that we should not optimize right away the use of technology in education, such as it is, and undertake localized projects without waiting until all the conditions are right. It is not inconsistent with an attempt to rationalize the use of educational technology on the basis of models that combine all the data into an integral system. Planning by segment and long-term planning are only two aspects strategical and tactical—of the same productive effort.

Criteria for Applicability

It must be remembered, especially regarding developing countries, that a comprehensive body of experience is lacking and it is still dificult to suggest definite, universally applicable strategies. Sophisticated technologies do not yet offer more than a few really large-scale projects and intermediate technology is still considerably dispersed. It appears difficult at present to give one form of technology precedence over another. For instance, deciding for intermediate technologies probably means renouncing for a long time the possibility offered by the sophisticated technology to keep back the corrosive effects of traditional environment upon innovative projects. It means also replacing a strategy of shock and abrupt change with one of gradual change and abandoning the hope of accelerating evoluation by taking shortcuts and reintroducing the time factor as one of the inevitable trammels of development. Might it not be considered, therefore, that each of these technical choices corresponds to a specific development effort within the framework of a general strategy and in connection with a definite objective? It may appear necessary to give priority to a shock effect and therefore make sacrifices for sophisticated technology (Ivory Coast). Elsewhere, on the contrary, when all available local resources must be mobilized, intermediate technologies will be applied (China).

Decisions can only be reached after establishing the economic alternatives of the various technologies (by means of what configuration can be best instruction be given to the most individuals in the shortest time?), their organizational limitations (training, maintenance, evaluation), and, finally, the learning criteria for selecting a technology—relevant to the general objectives of the system, sufficient power for effecting changes in structures and contents, orientation towards helping the learner than the teacher, capcity to remain open and to be developed and adapted.

International Strategies

Such criteria help in drawing up complex strategies combining the various resources for instance, radio broadcasting as low-cost, wide-ranging medium for mass instruction (primary and rural education), sophisticated multimedia techniques for fields capable of both financing and integrating them (e.g., higher technical instruction and intermediate technologies where priority is given to developing technological creativeness and devising schemes adapted to the environment).

Such systems which can be developed first will probably be in areas less burdened by antiquated structures and therefore present less risk of an abrupt rejection—the out-of-school and informal sectors, "remote-controlled" education, part-time education, or sectors under review because of strong external pressures, such as higher education or technical education. Even at the microsystem level, care will have to be taken to define an operational critical mass that is sufficient to bring about a chain reaction leading to renewal. Properly conducted, technical innovation should be a focal point for energies around which could be grouped, efforts at reorganization which could not be undertaken otherwise. There have already been frequent instances of the catalytic effect of school television or programmed instruction in hastening the reform of the school curricula and teacher training. The more limited the resources of the country, the more urgent it will be to identify existing technological resources that could be more fully utilized: broadcasting agencies, printing facilities, data-processing centres, and so on. It will be essential to coordinate the use of such resources in the framework of an overall plan.

An attempt will also be made to improve cooperation between the various occupational groups concerned with the development of education. In order to achieve progress in this direction it is essential that the manufacturers of teaching equipment and programme producers rally around explicit educational objectives. In some countries electronics engineers and visual-aid manufacturers, textbook publishers, and the developers of programmed instruction methods are already trying to combine their efforts. Elsewhere, national agencies for the production and distribution of new teaching materials have already been set up (Sweden, Netherlands); and in some countries (e.g., Japan and the United Kingdom) various authorities or ministries have worked together to coordinate their use of the existing communication networks.

Particular care is being taken at present to develop centres for the promotion of innovation, whose task it is to produce or get those concerned to produce—new school curricula, new systems of evaluation and control, and new teaching material, as well as to form centres of excellence and truly experimental establishments based on new organizational principles, with the aim of bringing them together, of linking them, and, if possible, of coordinating them in a flexible manner calculated to ensure mutual benefit and to increase their impact and their capacity for innovation.

Consequently, it is applied research conducted by multidisciplinary teams that should be encouraged. Its results will not be in the form of reports but of products, which may be new teaching materials, and also methodological systems or new institutional forms. Research done as a pretext and research of the academic kind with a bias towards theoretical generalization should be avoided. Industry and medicine are a standing proof that effective methods can be generally introduced without being given a formal basis in theory.

Lastly, there is need to inform more and train better. We must inform the public since it is the customer of the educational system, and especially pupils' families, whose attitude is often wary. We must train the teachers and change the old patterns they have been used to, in order to prepare them for the new roles that educational technology entails for them, especially their roles as in school and out of school leaders. Such training should be given to in service teachers as well as to student teachers, and this will be possible through the transformation of the professional training institutes into lifelong training institutes having at their command all the resources of modern educational technology. Further, special attention will have to be given to the training of a crops of educational technologists, may in twenty years time account for anything up to 10 per cent of the total of all those employed in education: specialists in the revision of objectives and curricula, testing and measurement specialists, administrators of new systems, communications specialists, production and maintenance technicians and the like.

International assistance programmes are also being rethought with a view to the systematic development of innovation, taking due care not to spread resources too thinly or to disperse efforts too widely. New avenues have been opened up way of tentative start on integrated educational planning that has been made in Algeria and in Indonesia and is presently being developed in many countries under the guidance of UNDP and UNESCO. Aid should stimulate, not paralyze, communications between the motive elements of innovation within the country concerned (research centres and production centres). For most of the creative efforts will fall to research and development institutes, probably in association with local universities, with local personnel predominating, and with the assistance of experts from the developed countries being reduced to a minimum. The institutes' activities should be oriented toward working up materials, developing critical methods (feedback, evaluation) and elaborating team production techniques (systems analysis and programming).

It seems, therefore, that more serious considera-tion should be given to the idea of international networks of liaison between these elements throughout the world, involving (wherever possible) the use of the most up-to-date means of communication and exchange (computers and space communication in particular) and making it possible to achieve a better division of assistance work. Some national centres could be formed into support centers to develop educational technology at the regional level, as in the case of Institute for Educational Communication in Latin America (ILCE) in Mexico, or of the Asian Centre of Educational Innovation for Development (ACEID) in

Bangkok. Both are information centres using the most up-to-date communications technology and centres for training and research geared to technological innovations. Such regional networks and centres should be backed by task forces made up to specialists who, at the request of the governments, may be called in to help fit new educational strategies based on systems analysis and technology to the country's special needs. These agencies should have a strong anthropological component in order to advise educational authorities on how to assimilate new developments without disrupting the traditional cultural balance.

Guidelines for Economic Decisions

Since the final purpose of educational technology is not to provide each individual teacher with his own personal audio-visual outfit but to reform the functioning of the educational system, and since its introduction provides the opportunity for analyzing—and perhaps for reorganizing—the existing institutions, it is within the available for foreseeable budgetary provisions of a country that educational technology must be introduced, by adjustment of educational practices to resources and vice versa. In a number or European countries, the establishment of experimental institutions has been rendered possible by an all-out effort to reorganize teaching spaces and to rethink fittings and equipment. Within the given context this involves a comparison of the effectiveness of the old system with that of the new educational pattern. It is a question of finding out which teaches more subjects best in terms of quantity and quality in more places and in equal or less time.

Conversely, the costs of integration of educational technology could be calculated not in terms of additional expenditure per capita, but in terms of overall expenditure of the redeployed system. This is the case, for instance, of the programme that has been undertaken in the Ivory Coast for the incorporation of television into primary education. It is based on a planned reduction by half over a period of ten years in the present dropout rate and on an increase in operating costs of primary education of approximately 8 per cent, which would be covered by the estimated increase in national revenue. In assessing unsophisticated versus advanced technologies, economists should be on their guard against concluding too hastily that the utilization of advanced educational technology will a priori weigh too heavily on the economics of the developing countries. Modern communications apparatus particularly those involving electronics are among the rare manufactured products whose cost continues to decline rapidly. For instance, a transistor which cost ten dollars a decade ago has today been replaced by an integrated circuit which costs one dollar and does the work that fifty transistors did ten years ago. The cost diminishes as the extensiveness and reliability of the service increases. The cost of the same series of computer operations has become about six hundred times less than it was twenty years ago. Moreover, it has to be admitted that innovation today is a costly affair and that we can hardly choose between whether to innovate or not to innovate. It is a matter of knowing how to innovate at greater or lesser cost and over a longer or shorter period of time. It is then possible to look beyond the individual cost-benefit ratio and to compare costs and performance in global terms. Recent studies by economists would seem to indicate that there is a level for the distribution of resources within an educational system beyond which there is no longer any improvement in the results. It is this state of equilibrium which must be sought and attained and the place of educational technology at last defined.

It has been established that in most countries, whether developing or developed, educational expenditure is tending to mount regularly year in and year out by anywhere from 5 to 8 per cent. Most of this increase is accounted for by rising salaries of teachers. The question today is whether priority should not be given to investment that seems likely to have a positive long-term effect on the efficiency of the education. The time may have come for educationists to ask—and governments to decide—that some of the increase in national educational expenditure already scheduled for the coming decade (say, half) be devoted exclusively to refining the ways and means best calculated to ensure a rapid increase in the efficiency of educational system and, more especially, to the rational development of technologies of organization and communication of knowledge.

It may well happen that the developing countries will not be the only ones to benefit from this industrialization. On the whole, international assistance is helping to develop new techniques according to a "shared risk" assistance scheme. The contribution of the highly developed countries to projects of this type is intended to encourage a universal movement towards innovation, but they themselves may benefit from the pedagogical or technological fallout from these projects. This is particularly the case with regard to the Spanish project of computer utilization, which could lead soon to a counterflow of Spanish technical assistance to the donor countries.

Novissima Verba

Education may indeed be regarded as an economically depressed sphere of activity in all countries. Consisting of activities based more on work than on capital (as can be seen from the size of the staff budget in relation to the whole operational budget of education) and entrenched in its traditions, education resists progress. If it is established that educational systems throughout the world (in the developed as well as in the developing countries) are and will remain an area of general economic and intellectual underdevelopment for a long time, perhaps they should all be subjected to the same thorough and cooperative examination in terms of the respective roles to be played by sophisticated, intermediate, and rational technologies in their development.

True, education, which is concerned with values, cannot be entirely rationalized, if only because the demand for education is in itself an irrational phenomenon. Education has a great many other functions than transmitting acquired knowledge and turning out lucid and effective future citizens. Educational institutions, according to their various level, function as places for child-minding and protection, as centres in which national unity may be forged and in which a civic education or a premilitary training may be given, and also as places where the individual learns to find his place in society and as a ritual instrument by means of which the individual is initiated into adult life.

The crisis of education is not going to be completely overcome by the introduction of technological principles and communication machinery. But by inducing each educational system to reexamine its functions of production and control, to create for itself, a new and more flexible structure, and to generate whithin itself new roles and new human relations by making it adaptable and flexible, is not technology enabling education to fulfill its other functions better and to reconsider its ultimate purpose with the requisite lucidity?

❑❑❑

Index

T

U

V

●●●